AF247512

The
Mystery of
Contemporary
Iran

The Mystery of Contemporary Iran

Mahnaz Shirali

Translated by Bernice Dubois

Transaction Publishers
New Brunswick (U.S.A.) and London (U.K.)

Library of Congress Catalog Number: 2014006095
ISBN: 978-1-4128-5462-7
Printed in the United States of America

Library of Congress Cataloging-in-Publication Data

Shirali, Mahnaz.
    [Malidiction du religieux. English]
    The mystery of contemporary Iran / Mahnaz Shirali; translated from the French by Bernice Dubois.
        pages cm
    Includes bibliographical references and index.
    ISBN 978-1-4128-5462-7 (acid-free paper) 1. Iran--Politics and government--20th century. 2. Iran--Religion--History--20th century. 3. Iran--Social conditions--20th century. 4. Islam and politics--Iran--History--20th century. 5. Social change--Iran--History--20th century. 6. Democracy--Iran--History--20th century. 7. Conservatism--Iran--History--20th century. 8. Clergy--Political activity--Iran--History--20th century. 9. Shi'ah--Iran--History--20th century. 10. Islam--Iran--Functionaries--History--20th century. I. Title.
    DS316.6.S55613 2015
    955.05--dc23
                                                    2014006095

I want to express my gratitude to Dominique Schnapper without whom this book would not exist and its author's life would have been very different.

Contents

Preface

In her last book, Mahnaz Shirali analyzed the return of young Muslims to an extremist Islam; they found there a compensation for the failure of their democratic hopes.[1] Victims of collective choices made by French society, they felt frustrated and humiliated by their partial and ambiguous "democratization." To this frustration and humiliation, the radical discourse of Muslim preachers—simplistic but thereby immediately understandable—brought an answer. Precisely because of their formalism, radicalism, and simplicity, so completely contrary to democratic values, these preachers fulfilled the needs and hopes of those who felt they had always been despised and insulted. To the democratic "all is permitted," the preachers opposed an "all is forbidden" that conferred order and meaning on the world. Democracy allows each person the freedom to define the meaning he wants to give his existence, but not all have the social means to discover or invent this meaning alone. Mahnaz Shirali showed that the preachers' words brought to these marginalized and unhappy youths, filled with resentment toward society, a moral security, enabling them to recover their dignity.

In that work, Mahnaz Shirali had already posed the problem of relations between Islam and democracy. She questioned the "dogmatic closing" that, since the thirteenth century, has frozen Islam in a literalism contrary to democratic modernity with its critical thought and individualist values, on which are founded a citizens' community. Can this "dogmatically closed" Islam, which forbids free exercise of thought, particularly with regard to sacred texts, be opened to democracy founded on critical thinking and the value of criticism? She has often previously invoked the efforts of Muslim intellectuals to apply the scientific spirit to Islamic tradition and to change literalist conception of its texts.

---

[1] Mahnaz Shirali, *Entre Islam et démocratie, Parcours de jeunes Français d' aujourd' hui*, Paris, Armand Colin, 2007.

She pursues this research in all its breadth in this new work where, probing deeply, she proposes a historic sociology of Iranian destiny in the twentieth century, torn between Shiite Islam and aspirations for modernity. She undoubtedly benefits from her past experience but, trained to rigor by the sociologists and philosophers of the Ecole des Hautes Etudes of Social Sciences, she develops an objective analysis of the great intellectual and political stages of a difficult and, at times, paradoxical road toward political modernity.

It is not Islam per se that opposes this advance, but the century-old overlapping between the Shiite religion—and the clergy as a religious body—and politics. The separation of politics from religion or the Great Separation, according to the formula proposed by Mark Lilla, echoing that of Karl Polanyi's Great Transformation, founded political modernity.[2] This idea is exceptional in history. In most civilizations, people called upon God's authority to solve the problems of their lives together. Regimes organized by a political theology are normal, if we give this adjective its statistical meaning. Democracy constitutes a radical break. The proclamation of citizenship as the source of political legitimacy makes the separation of politics from religion a founding principle of democracy. Democratic society is not linked to the destiny of any clerical affiliation or belief system; it refuses to dictate to individuals the meaning they must give to their destiny by dictating a particular conception of this world or of what may lie beyond it. Henceforth, the social link is ensured by politics rather than by religion. Democratic society is autonomous, exclusively human; it no longer accepts any principle of heteronymous legitimacy.

Before this project attained consistency in European countries or those stemming from Europe, who invented modern democracy in action, centuries of rivalry and conflict had to be lived through. The need to reinterpret the relationship between the government, churches and religious groups, in the process of establishing an autonomous power in Europe, has imposed itself over time. How long will it take in Iran?

The imbrication, deep and close, of religion and politics in all structures of Iranian society is not the only obstacle to achieving political modernity. For Iranians, the democratic idea was brought into disrepute by their country's contacts with the West. Democracy for them

---

[2] Mark Lilla, *Le Dieu mort-né. La religion, la politique et l'Occident moderne*, Paris, Seuil, "La couleur des idées", 2010 (2007).

is linked to British and American imperialism. The national reaction of a country with a high and just idea of its own great culture linked the revolt against foreign powers to a rejection of democracy. If Iranians call themselves democrats, they harbor a strong mistrust toward democratic principles and societies.

What this exciting book shows, through the Iranian case study, are the obstacles encountered by any democratic project. Democracy is fragile. To establish it, it is not sufficient merely to respect elections and the way in which these take place—even if this is essential because honest elections guarantee the legitimacy of those elected. One must first reflect clearly on the intellectual conditions of a new political legitimacy, accept the reinterpretation of traditions that, in all countries of the premodern world, closely associated religion and power. To prepare democracy supposes that this concept has been thoroughly thought through. Such efforts by Iranian thinkers, whose theories Mahnaz Shirali analyzes, never went all the way in critically reflecting on the heteronomy principle.[3] They either did not know how to, or could not, radically question the meaning of religion. Hence their often pathetic efforts to conciliate values taken from various, sometimes contradictory, traditions. Their voices remained weak compared to the intellectual and political power of the clergy.

Finally, citizens must really interiorize the idea that Others must be respected both as to their rights and their religious practices—whatever the religion. To grant equal rights to all, Muslims and non-Muslims, Shiites and Sunnites, to reinterpret the meaning of the principle and of the limits of religion, to respect the rule of law and the dignity of all citizens, can one dream of this for the future?

Mahnaz Shirali's book makes us think about Iran's destiny, its progress toward modernity, the obstacles encountered by a democracy, never truly achieved, always fragile. We are grateful to her.

Dominique Schnapper

---

[3] Heteronomy is the condition of being under the dominance of a transcendent authority, as opposed to autonomy.

Introduction

More than thirty years after the advent of the Islamic Republic, the mystery remains unsolved. Not a day goes by without Iranian leaders surprising the world, and doubt hovers over the precise nature of a regime that claims to be both a republic and Islamic but that is neither one nor the other. After three decades of this Islamic Republic, the unpopularity of the Shiite clergy has reached an unprecedented level, while radically changing the place of religion in society.

The enigma of the present situation can only be explained by examining the historic conditions in which the relationship between religion and politics unfolded. It is the complexity of the part played by religion and the religious ideologies that makes the Iranian political scene so difficult to unravel since the start of the twentieth century.

The course of Iranian history was always noted for the complicity between politics and religion, so that the latter became an instrument for manipulating the population. Religion is regularly involved in a usually tacit compromise with politics. Politics puts its means of coercion at the disposal of religion to enable the latter to maintain its position of strength. In exchange, religion guarantees recognition of politics' legitimacy and the obedience of its subjects.[1]

Thus the relationship between religion and power will serve as our analysis grid for interpreting the transformation of Iranian society historically and politically. Ideological Islam, as it began to act from the middle of the 1960s, plays a central role. It so invested the Iranian revolution of 1979 as to give birth to that strange regime, the "Islamic Republic," an oxymoron.

The Historical Framework

From the start of the constitutional revolution (1905–1907), the classical scheme of the relationship between religion and politics stepped

---

[1] One therefore finds a minimal religious element, regularly involved in every legitimate power, whatever its structure." Max Weber, *Sociologie des Religions*, Paris, Gallimard, 1996, p. 247.

out of its traditional framework. The clergy then saw a new kind of enemy: the liberals. The process began with the birth of a new balance of power between three protagonists: the clergy, the royalists, and the liberals. Contrary to the ancient monarchic principle ensuring the monarch's rule over the people—thanks to the blessing of religion—the newly arrived liberals called for participation of the people in political life. Their aim was to install political modernity in society. They reaped only the contempt of the royalists and filled the clergy with feelings of abomination and desolation.

This triangular conflict, marginalizing the clergy during the shah's reign, lasted until the 1979 revolution. The economic and social policies of the Pahlavi regime (in the 1960s) enabled the country to enter the twentieth century and endowed it with modern infrastructures. But this rapid modernization paradoxically strengthened the clergy; heretofore marginalized, the clergy became more popular with the majority of the population that feared the shah's modernizing intentions.

Aside from rehabilitating the clergy, if the 1979 national revolution found no other language than that of religion, if it was finally obliged to think of itself in terms of Shiism, it was because no other ideology spoke to the masses. Marxism, present at the beginning of the revolutionary process, as the ideology of reference of the Iranian activists, was revealed as a total failure when faced with the ideological discourse of religious intellectuals. Ali Shariati and the other revolutionary intellectuals, filtering Marxism through a religious analysis grid, found the ideological framework that could move the masses. The new Islam of these religious thinkers gave rise to a massive mobilization: the 1979 revolution. This mobilization, however, was swiftly recuperated by the religious orthodox. What twenty years earlier might have been a Marxist revolution became a religious revolution, giving birth to an extremely ambiguous regime, proclaiming itself a republic based essentially on the secular interpretation of religion that constitutes ideological Islam.

Today, more than a century after the constitutional revolution, democratic thought in Iran has great difficulty in asserting itself. Whether from fear or from conviction, free thinkers do not dare to challenge "divine law." None of them invoke the fundamental right of human beings to elaborate their own laws and lead their lives according to their own rules. They all feel obliged to remain within the ideological framework imposed by the Islam of the regime—what further on we shall call "khomeinism." In the writings of even the most advanced, democracy is limited to its outward signs. They refer to freedom and equality, but within the limits defined by Islamic norms and values, the rules imposed by the men of the regime.

Nonetheless, the regime's ideological Islam spectacularly and paradoxically accelerated the escape from religion. Excessive politicizing of the Muslim religion and its manipulation for immanent purposes emptied it of its spiritual meaning and pushed it toward an extreme secularism. This secularized religion has become, more than ever, a repressive tool in the hands of the clergy, today's "statesmen." This uniting of religion and politics represents, both symbolically and politically, a major event. It made it possible, in the first place, to consolidate the power of the clergy, but it also resulted in the demystification of religion. Today nothing remains of those believing masses of the start of the twentieth century, masses both ignorant and amorphous, always subject to the will and caprices of the clergy.

Uniting religion and politics completely transformed the nature of each. On the one side, the power of the clergy dominates society so obviously that no external legitimacy seems any longer necessary to justify it. On the other side, religious justifications, worn to a shred by thirty years' use, have lost their effectiveness. Steeped in their own power and drunk with the strength of petrodollars, the rulers of the Islamic Republic call on Islam less and less to validate their choices. Henceforth they see themselves able to rule with no need for religious justification.

This political paradox is of the highest importance. By exercising political power, the clergy are gradually freeing themselves from their hold on religion, and they henceforth affirm themselves as an autonomous entity. Why justify politics by referring to religious principles, when those who control politics believe themselves to be the direct representatives of "heaven" or, yet more, believe they personify it? When political power is held by those who are even beyond religion, why should they bother to justify themselves religiously?

Indeed, the men in power are convinced they are superior to other members of society. The principle of *walayat-e faqih* (the absolute power of the doctor of Islamic law), as presented in the Iranian constitution, separates people into two distinct categories: the clergy and the others. The latter are credited with no capacity for thought. They must obey the former in private as well as in public life. The leaders of the Islamic Republic believe they are the voice of God. Whether a simple guardian of the revolution (*pasdar*), who pretends to communicate with the Twelfth Imam; or his Supreme Leader, called *waly-e faqih* (doctor of Islamic law);

or President Ahmadinejad, who claims to receive his instructions directly from the Twelfth Imam[2] in person—most of the men of the regime claim privileged relations with the divine.

Despite the tremendous hypocrisy and the lies contained in their speech, these metaphysical self-interpretations designate a voluntary process by which those who seek power convince themselves that they are above all other beings. In accordance with the logic of *walayat-e faqih,* men are divided into two categories: on the one hand, the weak and impious; on the other, the strong and devout, men humanly superior. This belief of political leaders in their substantial superiority renders all justification, including a religious one, unnecessary. It engenders a particularly repressive atmosphere where submission becomes the *sine qua non* condition of living together.

The Process

This book proposes to examine the timid awakening of modernity in Iran, through a slow and progressive struggle against religious conservatism. These phenomena are among those that are conceived in movement and whose development continues for centuries, making them difficult to seize. On the one hand, we face the slow process of reforms aimed at introducing political freedoms into the Iranian social organization by founding a system based on the rule of law. On the other, we have the insistence of religious structures that want to maintain society in submission to the will of the clergy, those so-called representatives of God on earth.

If the essence of this reform movement is, in its principles, to break the mechanisms of religious conservatism, we must not imagine their immediate replacement by new ones, nor a radical break with religious forms. On the contrary, what is startling is the continuity of relations—now compromising, now conflicting—between reformers and conservatives. The difficulty in analyzing the Iranian political scene stems from this constant mixture of continuity and breaking off. The perseverance and incredible vitality shown by the Shiite clergy when faced with the country's social and political changes are, to say the least, remarkable. On the one hand, they attack and disrupt their opponents and, on the other, they empty religion of its spiritual essence and expose it to an unprecedented secularization.

Such is the dual phenomenon of integration and repulsion that we shall attempt to clarify. We must see it in a historical perspective of

---

[2] Regarding the Twelfth Imam, see chapter 7 of the present book, "An Evolving Thought," p. xvi.

successive religious dominations at work in the development of the Muslim world, since the "dogmatic closure" of the end of the thirteenth century. Preceded by a phase of forced modernization, between 1940 and 1970, after the highly politicized safavide Shiisme (*tashayo-e safavi*) ideological Islam comes to enclose Iranian Islam in a theology of resignation.

Why and how could this ideological Islam dominate Iranian society in the 1970s, at the expense of the reform movement, until it acquired a remarkable audience in the entire Muslim world? What we shall see in this book is the global historical movement within which this new configuration is inscribed. We are faced with a religious conservatism that opposes political modernity and, by constant metamorphoses,[3] repels the slightest attempt by Iranians to install democracy.

To simplify, we can distinguish three major periods:

- The first, which we shall call the "incubation" phase, goes from the constitutional revolution of 1905 to the modernization of the Pahlavi era (1925–1979).
- The second is characterized by two very closely linked movements. First, a phase of "suppression" when the modernizing policies of the Pahlavi marginalize the clergy with regard to national affairs. Then, the return of the "suppressed," that sees the clergy's triumphant return to the Iranian social and political scene and the downfall of the Pahlavi regime.
- The third, Khomeinism or the phase of "domination of ideological Islam," goes from the founding of the Islamic Republic to the present day. Khomeinism takes control on several levels: ideological, political, economic, financial and military.

To understand this situation, we must adopt a broader, longer-term view of the modernity movement as a whole. From this historical orientation, we can see the emergence of ideologies and a movement toward the future that in itself is but a part of a much broader phenomenon that began with the constitutional revolution: the process of leaving religion (i.e., the religious organization of the world).[4] This passage from the

---

[3] This does not only concern the history of ideas. Not that I have any doubt as to the usefulness of that history. At the proper time, it is indispensable. But ideas take on their full meaning in the global context in which they function. The purpose of this book is to provide that context.

[4] "Leaving religion does not mean leaving religious belief, but leaving a world structured by religion, one where religion orders the politics of societies and where it defines the economy of the social link. In traditional (heteronymous) societies, religion is an integral part of social functioning. Leaving religion means entering a world where religions continue to exist but within a political form and a collective order that they no longer determine. I add, and this is the decisive point, that in this change, there is a metabolizing and a transformation in the very heart of the social link and of the political organization of what, in ancient societies, was provided by religion." Marcel Gauchet, *La Religion dans la démocratie*, Paris, Gallimard, 2000, p 13.

heteronymous structuring of the human and social world to *autonomous structuring* is indeed the process generating modernity in its various dimensions, what can be called the modern revolution. We must understand the *march toward modernity in Iran as a slow and continuous movement,* that is in no way a spontaneous and categorical upheaval.

The 1979 revolution is particularly important in that it saw simultaneously a spectacular break with the past and an in-depth transformation, whose surface consequences are known but whose underlying organization is hidden. The change that began with the 1979 revolution caused Iranian social organization to enter a new configuration. As we shall see further on, religious political power, exercised for the first time in Shiite history, is a major factor that transforms the nature of both religion and politics. Three decades later, profound changes appear on the political scene and cause the radicalization of the Islamic regime. This radicalization leads the relationship between politics and religion to new horizons, ending in the destruction of religion. The phenomenon is all the more disconcerting in that everything happens in subterranean fashion.

1

Constitutionalism (1905–1909)

The logic of political modernity is based on the right granted to each sovereign citizen to see himself assured of economic and social conditions that respect his dignity and enable him to fully exercise his political rights.
Dominique Schnapper[1]

If there was, in the twentieth century in Iran, a single political event whose consequences have not been determined, it was the bombing of the first parliament (*Majles*) in June 1908, by the order of Mohammad Ali Shah. This major event can be considered as the first failure for proponents of political liberty in Iran.

For more than a century, foreign countries have been continuously blamed for conspiracy, without taking into account the role and position of national elements in the failure of the constitutional movement, impeding Iranian progress toward political modernity. These conspiracy theories, which dominate the Iranian intellectual landscape, prevent one from seeing the originality of the constitutional movement and lead to grave misunderstandings of both its contributions and the causes for its failure. On the contrary, one must consider the decisive role of national actors to understand the strength and the novelty of a change that tried to redefine the mode of living together in Iranian society.

The radical difference of the first Iranian parliament was that it gave the country a constitution almost entirely free from religious laws. This was the result of a vast social mobilization that had grouped together, several years earlier, intellectuals, clergy, merchants, and ordinary people against the authoritarianism of monarchic power. All called

---

[1] Dominique Schnapper, *La Démocratie providentielle. Essai sur l'égalité contemporaine*, Paris, Gallimard, 2002, p. 40.

for a constitution and for a judicial system so as to implement the rule of law in the entire country. Of course, at this start of the twentieth century, there was as yet no idea that Iranians could create their own laws,[2] for nothing could take precedence over "divine law." Nonetheless it was the first time in the history of Iran that the general population, until then submissive and obedient, claimed its right to participate in power and to decide its own fate.

The collapse of parliament clearly brought out the conflict between conservatives and reformers, thrusting into the background former rivalries between clergy and royalists. A huge change took place on the Iranian political scene: the clergy's priority was no longer to increase their control over political power as such, but to maintain their power over the people in an open war against reforms. The participation of Iranians in the power structure, their will to act in the political destiny of their country, these cherished ideas of the reformers, were unthinkable to many of the clergy. Such novel ideas would endanger the power of those who had dominated the devout population for more than ten centuries.

The constitutional revolution opened a new page in Iran's history. The genesis of the reform movement, despite its weaknesses and its timidity, despite the obstacles placed in its way, led the country to combat religious conservatism. This fight is part of a more general process, the conflict between the autonomy of the social world and the heteronomy or submission of this world to transcendence. The reforms offered the possibility of redefining the collective condition in line with a new orientation, that of leaving religion. This meant leaving a world where men had to submit to religion as the foundation of the collective order and entering a world in which they could organize social and political life in accordance with their own laws. This did not mean burying all religious belief but leaving a universe structured by religion, where it ordered the political shape of society and defined the economy of the social bond.

In light of the conflict between autonomy and heteronomy of the social order, we can reread the constitutional episode that then orients us toward unexplored perspectives. This presents important reappraisals, and questions those received ideas on which a good part of Iranian collective memory is based. It also supplies the first elements with which to reexamine a political episode that inaugurated in Iran the passage from religious structuring to free and autonomous structuring.

---

[2] And this is still not the case today.

The Awakening

The roots of the upheavals that occurred are in the past. They were linked to Iranian discontent with the interference of foreign powers—in particular, Russia and Great Britain—that marked the Qajar period.[3] These rival countries each demanded from Iran additional concessions that ran counter to Iran's national interests.[4] The strange mixture, on the part of the Qajar kings, of incompetence and curiosity with regard to the West, doomed the country to economic and political decline. At the same time, their curiosity concerning the west aroused an interest in many current novelties and in modern Western technology.

At the start of the twentieth century, two distinct powers ruled Iran: the shah and his government, and the high-ranking clergy who commanded in the name of the *shariat*.[5] At times, the ayatollah fought among themselves. At other times, they compromised with the politicians, leading the country into delicate situations. The more they extended their influence, the more they pretended to contribute to the advance of the *shariat*, the more delighted were the people. The people asked no more than that. They did not yet think of fighting poverty, resisting foreign powers, or installing justice and peace. Iranians of that time knew nothing of the political affairs of their country and were interested in nothing that occurred beyond the four walls of their private lives. Docilely, they obeyed the *mollah* and followed their precepts religiously.[6]

Under the reign of Nasseredin Shah (1848–1896), Iran drew closer to foreign countries. Impressed by the period of modernization of the Ottoman Empire,[7] the sovereign dreamed of transforming Iran's administrative system and modernizing the country.

---

[3] The Qajar dynasty ruled Iran from 1786 to 1925. The Qajar, of Turkmen origin, came from the Qezelbash tribes that served the Safavides dynasty.

[4] From the start of the nineteenth century, Iran began to feel pressure from Russia and Great Britain. The British wanted primarily to protect their trade routes toward India, while the Russians wanted to expand toward the Persian Gulf. After 1850, Russia forced the Qajar to surrender to them all the Iranian territory of Central Asia. At the same time, Great Britain sent troops to Iran to prevent the Russians from taking over Herat and the other Afghan territories that had been lost under the Safavides. *Cf.* Elton L. Daniel, *The History of Iran*, New York, Greenwood Press, 2001. See also *Encyclopædia Iranica*, http//:www.iranicaonline./

[5] In this book I use the Persian terminology.

[6] Ahmad Kasravi, *Tarikh mashrouteh Iran* (*Constitutional History of Iran*), Tehran, Amir Kabir, 1940, p. 179.

[7] This period began in 1808. It continued with the Tanzimat edict in 1839 by which the central administration announced legislative measures to modernize the empire. It culminated with the first royal constitution on November 23, 1876. *Cf.* Dimitri Kitsikis, *L'Empire ottoman*, Paris, Presses Universitaires de France, 1994.

To carry out these aims, the shah's prime minister, Amir Kabir, instituted a number of reforms: central administrative tools were renovated, and the first attempts were made to adapt the Iranian state apparatus to the new world. Amir Kabir intervened in all areas. He modernized the fiscal system, strengthened central control over administration, created the police, encouraged trade and industry. One of the most important initiatives of this exceptional prime minister was to found the *Dar-ol Fonoun* (the center of Arts and Crafts), the first establishment of higher education in Iran. But his attempt to limit the influence of the Shiite clergy was in vain. Those around him were jealous, the clergy detested him, and he was assassinated in 1852 by order of Nasseredin Shah.

After the death of Amir Kabir, nothing any longer protected the country from the incompetence of its leaders. This signaled the opening of one of the most chaotic pages of Iranian history.

Toward the 1890s, the government was faced with many financial problems: property taxes declined and inflation rose. The decline of the value of silver lowered the value of Iranian currency (the silver *Qerân*). The State's economic policy, in conformity with *shariat,* did not correspond to international market mechanisms, and tradesmen suffered colossal losses. In addition, the country had to finance the expensive foreign travels of the shah and his family. The government was therefore obliged to borrow heavily: £2 million from Russia in 1900 and another £1 million from Great Britain in 1902.

Under the reign of Nasseredin Shah, many privileges were granted to foreign countries, and political affairs practically fell into the hands of the ambassadors of Russia and Great Britain, who ended up sharing control of the country several decades later.[8]

The clergy disapproved of all this, not because they wanted to protect the country against foreign threats but because they were hostile to any

---

[8] Agriculture represented 80 to 90 percent of the national revenue. Exports consisted mainly of dried fruits, raw cotton, rice, opium, and rugs, while imports were primarily textiles, oil, sugar, and tea. Russia was Iran's principal trade partner, far beyond Britain, France, and Turkey. The national budget (only 2 percent of the national product) was in line with the central government's weakness; its resources came from taxes raised by provincial governors on land, crafts, crown property, customs, and, above all, the sale of concessions or rights for new services. These mediocre resources were scarcely sufficient to maintain a semblance of an army or central administration nor to pay for the expensive court life, especially since Iranian rulers had conceived a taste for traveling to Europe. Confiscations, extortion of funds, and the sale of public positions were the surest means to fill the treasury of a state without any pre-established budget or economic policy. *Cf.* Abdolhossein Zarinkhoub, *Ruzgaran tarikh-I Iran as Aghz ta sakut saltnat Pahlvi*, Tehran, Sokhan, 1999.

4

idea of change. They believed things should remain as they were, and that nothing should change from what had been known and established in the past. For them, the gravest danger was to lose their control over the social order, essentially based on Islamic laws.

Nasseredin Shah's fascination with the West, his desire to transform the traditional organization of the country, and his political incompetence shocked the clergy. Wherever they went, they preached fear and opposition to reform; whether the building of schools[9] or the opening of taverns, they criticized everything. In the mosques, during religious ceremonies, on holidays, or at funerals, they cautioned the people against politicians: "They want to westernize Iran. They want to give our country away to foreigners," protested the angry *mollah*. Although at that time nobody was interested in politics, far less knew what the westernization of a country like Iran meant. But the idea of giving oneself up to foreigners frightened them.

When Nasseredin Shah, in 1890, assigned the control of tobacco to a British company, the people's anger exploded. Iranians found it unfair to sell tobacco leaves at low prices to foreigners while they themselves were obliged to pay top prices for the same leaves. A clergyman, Mirza Reza Shirazi, declared a *fatwa* (religious decree) forbidding cultivation, trade, and consumption of tobacco. This *fatwa* was strongly followed. It even had repercussions on the shah, whose wives forbade him to use tobacco.

Under popular and religious pressure, Nasseredin Shah had to renege on his decision. The "tobacco rebellion" (*Qyâm-e tanbakou*) is still spoken of. For the first time in Iranian history, the people had meddled in politics. Despite its somewhat limited impact, this event revealed politics in a new light. From then on, the division between the leaders and the people was evident, and Iranians became aware of their capacity to alter their country's destiny.

The fifty-year reign of Nasseredin Shah placed the country before an unknown future, and revealed the hostility of the clergy to reforms. In 1896, the sovereign was assassinated by a *mollah*. This unheard-of event preceded the constitutional revolution, the first in any Muslim country.

---

[9] Toward the end of the nineteenth century, Mirza Hassan Roshdieh, son of a clergyman, built the first secular schools (*madreseh Roshdieh*). They were open to all, and pupils learned only to read and write. Nonetheless, under the pretext that the teaching methods were too innovativw, the clergy succeeded in closing them. *Cf.* A Kasravi, *Tarikh Mashrouteh Iran, op. cit.*, pp. 55–61.

The Coalition

The shah's contacts with foreign countries and his fascination with Western culture resulted in opening the cultured Iranian elite to European democratic thought. While the Qajar were especially attracted to the luxury, opulence, and outward aspects of life in the West, the erudite, the learned, and the literary were powerfully attracted by liberty and democracy. They called themselves "liberals" (*Azadi-khahan*) and ardently desired to install social justice and political freedom at the center of collective life.

The elite of Iranian society rapidly realized the historic backwardness of their country as compared with European societies, not only technologically, but especially in intellectual and philosophical areas. These men were convinced of the need to reform the Iranian political system in line with the principal European democracies. They fought against the shah's absolute power and in favor of social justice by demanding the creation of courts of justice (*'edâlat khaneh*) throughout the country. Their purpose was to protect the people against abuses of power, particularly those of political leaders. This idea found a favorable echo with the *Bazaar*[10] merchants and with some of the clergy who joined the liberals.

If the religious dignitaries (the *olama*[11]) rarely took part in politics, and if the conservative wing of the clergy tended rather to maintain compromises with monarchic power, the "popular clergy" were distinguished by their desire for change. Like the liberals, they preached the need for social justice. This idea corresponded to the Shiite belief in the messianic coming of the Twelfth Imam, the *Mahdi,* who is to return to earth to establish justice and peace throughout the world. By reviving this belief, these clergymen awoke the people and made them conscious of the misery of their condition.

---

[10] A bazaar is a "network of merchants, bankers, and craftsmen who work in a permanent enclosed merchandising area, marketplace...." This network was, and remains, a powerful actor in Iranian society.

[11] Arabic word, *olama* or *'ulamâ*, plural of *'alim,* "wise." It refers to senior clerics, both in Shiite and Sunni Islam. Already present in the Koran in its first meaning, the term gradually received a technical sense in Islam. Undoubtedly, very early, it designated the man who had acquired fundamental "knowledge" in the community, i.e., the knowledge of the Koran and of the prophetic traditions. By *olama,* we understand more broadly all those who are wise in religious science and who polarize themselves on the *fiqh* in the narrow sense of that word—Muslim law. *Cf. Encyclopaedia universalis;* Claude Gilliot (ed.), *Dictionnaire de l'Islam,* Paris, Albin Michel, 1997, pp. 669–672.

The liberals—inspired by the ideas of the French revolution, of freemasonry, and of other currents of free thought—found a new resonance in this Shiite conception of justice. They thought themselves able to conciliate this with the revolutionary ideals of social justice and of equal rights of citizens. However, they never realized the paradoxes of this undertaking, or the finesse it would require to accomplish it. To say the least, its success was improbable.

The major *Bazaar* merchants also found their advantage in this very ambiguous vision of social justice worked out by the intellectuals and supported by the popular clergy. In direct commercial contact with the international market, the merchants suffered from the insufficiency of the country's judicial apparatus and traditional administrative system, both of which proved incapable of facing new problems. Demanding a market economy in order to avoid capricious State interventions, as well as ruinous monetary and budget policies, the merchants supported reforms and financed antigovernment protests.

Since the dawn of the twentieth century, the need for social justice had therefore become the central point around which gravitated the claims of society, but nobody knew precisely to what social justice corresponded. The term, whose exact meaning remained ambiguous, had been used for the first time by Mirza Malkom Khan in the 1870s. Formerly one of the prime ministers of Nassaredin Shah, Sépah Sâlâr admired the reforms of the Ottoman Empire (*Tanzimat*) and had already attempted to set up provincial courts under state control for the purpose of receiving complaints and rendering justice to the people. But it was not until 1890, when Mirza Malkom Khan compared the advances of the Ottoman Empire's legislative system with Iran's archaic system that the reformists made the establishment of *'edâlat khaneh* their principal demand.

The merchants, the intellectuals, and the popular clergy were united in their common desire to reform the country, but their alliance was based on confusion and misunderstanding. They created a coalition that enthused the people. But, despite its national dimension, it remained intrinsically fragile.

The Merchants

The important merchants, who had suffered from the government's brutal interventions in the market for several decades, also demanded social justice. They too wanted courts of justice and law courts to arbitrate their lawsuits on legal bases.

Their objectives were at first rather limited, but, more precisely than the others, they knew what they wanted. Faced with the government's incapacity to protect Iranian trade against foreign competition—and as victims of discriminatory practices—they wanted fairer trade rules and stronger government protections against Russian and British penetration into the national market.

This all began in 1898, when Mozaffaredin Shah[12] gave the general directorship of customs to a Belgian, Joseph Naus; the merchants' situation became thornier than ever. The new Director quickly raised custom rates—custom revenues flew from £200,000 to £600,000 per year. But it was Iranian merchants who bore the full brunt of this, while Russians and British were exempt. Naus's action caused deep discontent among the merchants as well as serious price inflation for essential products on the market.

In 1904, Russia, Iran's principal trading partner, went to war against Japan. This conflict weighed heavily on the merchants, and their situation grew still worse. Iran's foreign commercial debt grew particularly worrying, and the negative balance of the state budget automatically drew the country down. The war was not the only cause. Added to it were the serious shortages of essential products, the absence of any price controls, the economic fluctuations of the international market, the insecurity of trade routes, and, finally, the financial exclusivity granted to the British Imperial Bank of Persia and to the Russian Loan Bank.

The creation of a national bank, Bânk melli Iran, then became one of the merchants' first demands. On the eve of the constitutional revolution, many merchants, land owners and city notables—and even some members of the royal family—were heavily indebted to foreign banks. Economic independence seemed to them the only solution to their financial problems.

As a sign of protest, the merchants backed the constitutionalists and financed their antigovernmental activities. Demonstrations were organized in all the large cities. The reformers gained in strength.

Several ayatollah defended the merchants and intervened in their favor. They invented religious arguments to show that the *shariat* was compatible with the country's new economic situation, and that this made it possible to protect the merchants. By so doing, they also

---

[12] Mozaffaredin Shah (1853–1907), son of Nasseredin Shah, was king of Iran from 1896–1907.

wanted to "save the clergy." However, it was clear that—faced with the problems of modern economy and of international trade—the *shariat* had no adequate solutions.

If throughout the constitutional period the merchants were relatively lucid concerning their difficulties, none of them recognized that the archaic religious laws—in particular, the prohibition of usury—were one of Iran's major handicaps in trade agreements with foreign countries. Instead of facing these problems squarely, the merchants judged foreigners to be responsible for their difficulties. They continued to support clerical initiatives in economy and trade and, henceforth, tended to believe that the country's evils and misfortunes all came from outside—from the Russians and the British who plotted to rob the historical patrimony and the national wealth of Iranians.

The Intelligentsia

The merchants' financial support of the reform movement bore rapid fruit, inaugurating an unprecedented period of debate. The emergence of the press, of pamphlets, and of books, impressed the public. At the end of the nineteenth century, the tiny state-controlled Iranian press reported, albeit haphazardly, on Western political events. Iranian readers followed not only the tales of colonial expansionism and imperial rivalries but also the constitutional crises in France, the shake-ups of the British parliamentary system, the heroic Japanese resistance to the Russian army, the struggle for independence of the United States at the end of the eighteenth century, and then the first American presidential elections.

During the reign of Mozaffaredin Shah (1896–1907), newspapers in several Iranian cities played a decisive role in propagating constitutional ideas for a public desirous for information on outside world events. *Sur-Esrafil,* one of the most famous daily papers at the time, had a large popular readership. Its editorials, in a greatly appreciated satirical form, exposed revolutionary ideas, defended radical changes, called for patriotism, and issued a wake-up call to the people.

Translations, adaptations, and publications of European texts on political philosophy and history also helped the reformers to work out a revolutionary rhetoric. Similarly, translations of literary works were very successful. They contributed to opening new intellectual horizons by providing a clearer view of European social and political life. Reading Fenelon's *The Adventures of Telemaque* and Adam Smith's *The Wealth of Nations,* Iranians discovered new ideas.

Under the reign of Mozaffaredin Shah, a new intelligentsia thus emerged who used the press and modern education to gain the support of clergy, merchants, and the people to oppose tyranny and to reform the political system. One of the notable figures of this intelligentsia was Mirza Malkom Khan (1833–1908). He was the first Persian writer with an excellent knowledge of both French and English, which enabled him to distinguish the different schools of liberal thought. He was thus able to introduce modern concepts such as law (*qânoun*), Constitution (*qanoun assassi*), reform (*eslâhât*), nation (*melat*), and peoples' rights (*haq â-nas*)[13] into the political vocabulary of his time. In his writings, we find an unrelenting criticism of tyranny and of the political corruption of the Qajar.

A decade before the constitutional revolution, while the ideas of a parliamentary system or a constitution were still very vague for most Iranian thinkers, Malkom Khan's presentation of modern political thought contributed decisively to the dawning revolutionary ferment. His books propounded the separation of powers, a rational political system, and the need to govern a country according to a constitution. He described how this would guarantee the rights and freedoms of the national community.

Some of his ideas were taken up by other activists and thinkers, among whom one finds the names, famous in Iran, of Akhundzadeh (anti-clerical), Mirza Aqa Khan-e Kermani (agnostic), Mostashar-al Dawleh (Muslim intellectual), Seyed Jamal al-Din-e Afghâni (clergyman), and two important ayatollah, Tabatabai and Naiini.

With but a few exceptions, the main preoccupation of reformers was to "Islamize" European democratic ideas so as to introduce them in Iran. Some went so far as to quote the Koran and the hadith to prove that democratic ideas were an integral part of Islamic thought.

However, they quickly discovered the divergences between the democratic view of power and the religious conception of order as issuing from God. Democratic power is the expression of society representing itself and defining its own laws. European legislation is, above all, the result of a consensus between the state and the people, it is universal in its applications and deals only with temporal affairs.

---

[13] *Cf.* Mirza Malkom Khan, *Daftar-e tanzimat* (The Book of Reforms), 1858–1859, pp. 1–52; quoted in Mohammad Mohit-Tabatabai (ed.), *Majmu-e Asar Mirza Malkom Khan* (*Complete Works of Mirza Malkom Khan*), Tehran, Foruk, 1948.

Such ideas, according to the reformers, would not do for a Muslim country like Iran where the subjection of society to transcendence is dogma: any deviation would be labeled heresy.

While the reformers dared to criticize the monarchy and the king's authority, it was difficult for them to question the role of religion in directing collective life. They knew that religions were not merely beliefs and institutions. Throughout human history, they were something more: a way of global structuring that conferred clearly defined forms on social organization. It was difficult for Iranian thinkers of that time to conceive of an autonomous society functioning without religion: a society where religions continue to exist but within a political form and a collective order that they no longer determine; a society where religions are held as marginal and relegated to private life.

Gradually, they realized that democratizing Iran was far more than simply translating democratic ideas into Persian. It meant going from a world structured by religion to one where religion was a bond linking man to his God. At that time, this seemed impossible to them.

The search for compatibility between Islam and democracy, which always concerned Iranian thinkers, shows the difficulty of questioning the religious principle of a heteronymous social order. Seeing religion as an integral part of social functioning was so deeply rooted in Iranian minds that the idea of an autonomous society was seen as the death of religion itself. To leave a world where religion orders the political shape of society seemed then—and in Iran still seems today—an abandonment of faith and religious beliefs. With no tradition of critical thought about religion, and in a country deeply rooted in its religious heritage, the nearly thousand-year-old block of what is deemed unthinkable in Islam stifles the idea of abandoning religion. Since that time, Iranian intellectuals have been torn between two tendencies. Devout thinkers forbid themselves the slightest questioning of religious social order and cast no critical eye on Islamic practice, for fear of prejudicing Islam itself. The other intellectual tendency is to reject religion completely and view it as an obstacle blocking the road to modernity and democracy.

Akhundzadeh (1812–1878) was an early proponent of antireligious thought. A fervent admirer of Russia, where he spent a good part of his life, he considered himself both anti-Islamic and atheistic. His writings advocate a cultural awakening, by breaking away from the Muslim religion. According to him, religion was not only the source of the peoples' ignorance but also the main cause of the country's historical backwardness. Hostile to religious superstition and to the mentality characteristic of that kind of belief, he championed education. In his famous book *Maktubât* (1863), he showed his contempt for the crass ignorance of Nasseredin Shah and his rudimentary religiosity. He criticized the sovereign's legendary incompetence in ruling as well as his strong taste for luxury. At the end of the book, he advised the shah to adopt modern laws so as to lift the country out of the morass into which he had dragged it. The author invited the Iranian people to get rid of the yoke of submission, to join Masonic lodges, so as to free themselves from the despotism of the Qajar by espousing free thought and rationalism.

Mirza Aqa Khan-e Kermani and Mirza Habib Esfahani were two other thinkers and political activists who, like Akhundzadeh, imputed the political, economic, and cultural stagnation of the country to its religious heritage. This contrasted with thinkers for whom recognizing religious tradition as a central aspect of Persian culture was both a devout and a patriotic act. Religious intellectuals, who feared losing their faith and their religious belonging, felt paralyzed by the prospect of reform. Antireligious intellectuals meanwhile relentlessly combated religion as the sworn enemy of modernity and democracy.

The Clergy

The dominance of the clergy in Iran has ancient roots. Its course, its stakes, its forms, only become clear when placed in their historical origins. In this country, understanding contemporary history is closely linked to analyzing the role and the position of the clergy.

The highest ambition of the clergy—in Iran as elsewhere—has always been to influence secular power and to turn the balance of power in their favor. In turn, political leaders counted on the manipulative power of the clergy to subjugate the people and guarantee an untrammeled reign. However, because of the ambiguous position of religious authority in Islam, and without the functional legitimacy that other religions confer on the "professionals of faith," the clergy were never able to assert themselves independently of the politicians. Throughout the history of the Muslim world, this dependence systematically made relations between clergy and politicians problematical.

At the end of the nineteenth century, the arrival of the reformers—a new political force in the country—deeply modified these relationships, bringing important changes. No constitutional reforms were yet definitively acquired. For ordinary people, a constitution was only a word without the least concrete meaning. In a country with numerous ethnic and religious minorities, the population was more divided than ever. Most Iranians were absorbed by interreligious disputes—between Shiite and Sunnite, Babi and Baha'i, Sheykhi and Karimkhani—so that they were scarcely interested in politics. True, there were no more bloody outbursts, as during the Safavides period, but segregation still existed. Each congregation had its religious leader, its mosque, its faithful, its ceremonies. Each lived among its own; there was no intermingling with other congregations, and slander was widespread.

The majority of Iranians were Shiite and spent more than a third of their time in religious rites: praying to God, mourning the death of saints, repenting, or celebrating religious events. They collected funds to go on pilgrimages and spent their lives listening to sermons by clergy, who blamed all the ills and misfortunes of the people on the ancient enemies of Islam's prophet.

Shiite clergy have a hierarchy whose roots go back to the Zoroastrian tradition. But the resemblance is purely formal and, unlike the powerful Zoroastrian clergy, Shiite clergy never acquired real religious legitimacy[14]—no more than the Sunni who have no clerical hierarchy at all. The crucial point of Islamic thought is the dependence of religious power on the economic and political power structures. Islam's internal structure, based on the individual autonomy of the believer in his relationship to God, required no hierarchy comparable to that of the Catholic Church for transmitting divine grace to the community of believers.[15]

Theoretically, the Shiite clergy should remain in the *incognito* of an *Ecclesia spiritualis.* The esoteric hierarchy cannot enter the profane sphere because the spiritual world and this earthly one are radically incompatible. The clergy are those who have spiritual charisma, and their role is to initiate the faithful into the true meaning of God's message. Their task is to gradually introduce Muslims into the inner knowledge of divine revelation.

The complexity of this situation is linked essentially to the original ambiguous relationship between the clergy and the politicians. On the

---

[14] The presence of clergy is unnecessary for any of the basic acts of life—birth, marriage, burial, etc.

[15] In Sunni Islam, the situation is simple: in the absence of such a hierarchy throughout the centuries, the *olama* were unable to prolong their spiritual authority by an efficient economic and political power. They could not even work out a coherent and critical theory of relations between political power and the spiritual authority that they were supposed to exercise. They were soon transformed into an auxiliary of the political arm. See: Henry Corbin, *En Islam iranien: aspects spirituals et philosophiques*, vol. l, *Le shi'isme duodécimain*, Paris, Gallimard, 1971, pp. 34–35.

one hand, politicians need the clergy's support to legitimate their power over the people. On the other hand, the tremendous ability of the clergy to tame the faithful masses has given birth—in Iran as elsewhere—to a real symbiosis between the political and the religious elite.

At the highest rank of the clerical hierarchy, we find the *mojtahed* or the great ayatollah, known as *olama*.[16] They are considered as *marja'e taqlid*[17] (sources of imitation) for the faithful. According to certain Shiite dogma, each Muslim must obey a *mojtahed* and follow his orders implicitly in his private and public life, failing which he will be rejected from the community of believers. These sources of imitation therefore exercise real authority over the lives of a large part of the population. Furthermore, the *mojtahed* were not materially dependent on the political power, since they levied religious taxes (*khoms* and *zakât*) on their devout followers and received voluntary gifts (including legal alms). To this is added the management of mortmain bequeathed to clergymen for religious works, all of which provided them with great financial security. In exchange, they were supposed to spend this money to develop the *shariat*.

This economic independence, the public fame of the *mojtahed,* and the support shown by the devout provide them with unlimited power. Politicians, who fear them, have always been very careful to do nothing to incur the *mojtahed*'s indignation. If the latter were perfectly capable—when the occasion arose—of efficiently opposing measures they deemed unjust, they rarely communicated with politicians and were satisfied with exercising symbolic power over them. To the *mojtahed*, religious affairs were far more important than those of the state. They were, in fact, deeply convinced that "God protects the country, but that it is up to them to protect Islam."[18] And if, by chance, they took a stand in a political or social matter, they expected to be followed by the faithful with the same devotion as for religious affairs, and that is what happened.

At the second rank of the clerical hierarchy are the ayatollah and the *hojajol-eslam*. Since they do not enjoy the same degree of religious authority as the *olama,* they have managed to maintain privileged relationships with the secular power throughout the years. Past masters

---

[16] See note 19.

[17] The title of *marja'e taqlid* designates the highest function in the Shiite clergy traditional hierarchy. It is moreover a highly contested function by Muslim intellectuals in Iran, whose faithful do not have to imitate anyone but must follow their own ideas in any matter concerning their own lives.

[18] Kasravi, *Tàrikh mashrouteh Iran, op. cit.,* p. 43.

14

in the art of eloquence, they know how to seduce the people and to direct them toward their chosen aims. Politicians have, therefore, always considered them an instrument for manipulating the masses. This aptitude enabled them to establish their own "kingdom" side by side with that of the monarchy and to live in opulence. This level of the clergy was always part of high society (*a'yân*).

On the lowest level of the clerical hierarchy are the *mollah* and the *talabeh* (the seminarians) whose only winning card is their popularity. Of modest social origins, the mediocrity of their religious status—as compared to the aforementioned—makes them conscious of life's realities and gives them a certain objectivity that the others do not have. Sharing the same misery as most of the people, they were, at the end of the nineteenth century, the first to adopt—only temporarily indeed, but with some sincerity—the constitutional cause, rebelling against social injustice.

Nonetheless, the borders are not quite as clearly defined as this succinct classification might lead one to believe. It sometimes suffices to be more charismatic than others or to preach a brilliant sermon that pleases everybody to climb higher in the clerical hierarchy. All in all, conservatism is the common denominator of all levels of the clergy. Their activity consists mainly in inviting the masses to beg God. For them, interest in the affairs of state is apostasy, since it distracts the believer from his religion and disperses his attention. Muslims must therefore pray for the king to be generous with them.

Indeed the main ayatollah took firm positions on political change under Nasseredin Shah and virulently criticized his government. But far from any concern with the interests of the people, the clergy feared change. The primary reason for their discontent was their lack of understanding of the needs of the times. They were hostile to the shah's initiatives because they could not admit any need to reform a country living under a several-thousand-years-old tradition. Their conservatism prevented them from comprehending that political, economic, and social changes were essential for a people who wanted to be in touch with the modern world.

The Shiite clergy were not more backward leaning than others. Their concern was to restore the established order and to reject *a priori* any innovation. The difficulty of Shiism, as of religious thought in general, is that it does not face reality; it ignores it. The clergy's mistrust of change comes above all from its voluntary blindness to real contingencies. "In general, the clergy do not see reality as something to be known. They seek to triumph over reality, to conquer it. There is not the danger of a meeting that might force a reexamination of one's own way of thinking and a reconstruction of oneself. And this is not due to a 'lack of development' but to a rigorous disposition and a determined decision as to how they must behave in human society."[19]

Most of the clergy could not even seize the deep aspirations of the constitutionalists to reform the country. In fact, the support that some of the clergy gave to the constitutional movement, far from being inspired by any recognition of the constitutionalists' aims, was essentially a rebellion against injustices committed by political leaders.

The clergy's fears of the country's new orientations gradually modified their attitudes toward politics. These attitudes, which had always been those of compromise—at times tacit, at others explicit—gradually became oppositional and showed themselves in various ways. For example, when the high Shiite dignitaries disapproved some political reforms of the king, the popular clergy denounced the government's policies and incited the people to do the same. Their criticism was not induced by hidden compromises with political power nor by fear for their privileges, for they had nothing to lose. Perhaps without any privileged relationship with politicians, it was in their interest to gain popular support and to oppose unfair policies, but it is equally possible that they were impelled by a desire to defend social justice and felt a natural disgust for the deplorable state of the country. Whatever their real motivation, for the first time, a part of the clergy openly criticized the government and encouraged the people to do the same.

At the end of the nineteenth century, the popular clergy no longer preached submission. Loud and clear, they proclaimed: "the duty of each Muslim, worthy of the name, is to rebel against the injustices of the country's leaders."[20] Joining the camp of the constitutionalists, they not only caused the politicians to tremble, but they deeply divided the clergy. Some of the great religious dignitaries brought their prestigious support to the reformists in their turn, provoking indignation from the conservative wing of the clergy.

At the start of the twentieth century, the two great ayatollah, Behbahani and Tabatabai both supported the reformers, and that contributed to the success of the constitutional movement. Although both

---

[19] Gauchet, *La condition historique*, Paris, Gallimard, 2005, p. 165.
[20] Kasravi, *Târikh mashrouteh Iran, op. cit.*, p. 45.

were more motivated by the desire to combat social injustices than by real democratic convictions, their joining the movement was a great advantage. It shielded the reformers from the accusation of apostasy, enabling them to raise their voices and to express more virulent criticism than ever against the shah and his government.

Their ability to combine the reformist message with their religious charisma soon placed these two influential ayatollah at the forefront of the constitutional movement. Religious legitimacy gave credibility to constitutionalist aims and gained the confidence of the believing masses, accustomed to blindly follow the clergy. They certainly did not understand many of the new political ideas, even less the difference between democracy and religious thought. Nonetheless, galvanized by awareness of the historical backwardness and reassured by the leadership of important religious dignitaries, they brought the constitutional movement uncompromising support in line with their religious piety. They rapidly transformed the movement into a true national rebellion against the monarchic regime.

Very high in the Shiite clerical hierarchy, the Ayatollah Behbahani and Tabatabai both came from two ancient *mojtahed* families whose authority was strongly rooted for several generations. Nothing, however, prevented the orthodox clergy (the *olama*), strongly mistrustful of the reform movement, from criticizing them, or even from trying to sabotage their political action. The frank adherence of the two high Shiite dignitaries to the revolutionary movement destabilized the *olama* who had for long relied on their legendary conservatism.

Indeed, as we have seen, the former automatic complicity between the clergy and the royalist politicians had weakened, and some ayatollah were quite critical of the regime. Still, to criticize the governmental policy is one thing; to accept the leadership of a revolutionary movement is another. Until then, only the popular clergy had dared to reprove the Shah's policy; none of the high rank clergy had gone so far as to lead a rebellion.

However strong the reformist convictions of the Ayatollah Behbahani and Tabatabaï, they did not affect the other Shiite dignitaries. The latter wanted no constitution, unless it brought them some additional privileges. Later on, some of them entered the revolutionary arena, either in their own interest or for fear of losing control of events.

Most of the clergy did not, at that time, understand the importance of the constitutional movement. They thought of it as a simple episode that might strengthen the balance of power in their favor.

Underestimating the scope of change that was to overthrow the country's political and social framework, some conservative clergy at first supported the reformers, without however openly opposing the Qajar. Thus they sided with the constitutionalists, without knowing what was at stake.

Awareness of Historical Backwardness

Beyond all ideological differences, awareness of the country's historical backwardness united intellectuals of all tendencies. Heirs of a civilization several thousand years old, they felt responsible toward future generations and spoke of their national duty. Their writings reflect their will to act and to shape things differently. All were exalted by patriotic feelings, and none doubted the need to move toward the future to take the country out of its deplorable situation. "Iran does not deserve this" was a sentence often found in the writings of reformist thinkers. Some spoke of their "national shame" and encouraged the people not to remain silent.

This awareness of historical backwardness aroused the people and made it necessary to orient collective activity toward the future. It imposed the future, a time of progress and of projects, as the new horizon of common experience. It obliged society to progress and to change its political condition. The basic identity of human beings and their way of living together had to be defined in a concrete and practical manner in order to free people from their former dependence on royalty and religious constraints. Once a society is stirred by the desire to progress, it is clearly on the way to freeing itself from the despotism of the past and from the tyranny of power.

Aroused by the discovery of their historical backwardness, the intellectuals and the reformers turned against the absolute monarchy in a desire to install constitutional law over the entire country. Diametrically opposed to the past, ruled by tradition and the inheritance of religious thought, the reformers called for a constitution—intrinsically autonomous and independent of any religious reference. All those who did not dare openly approach the issue of the religious order found that, despite themselves, they were in opposition with regard to the heteronomy of the social order. It was indeed impossible to conciliate thought both according to heteronomy and to history.

The awakening of the population was not limited to the discovery of the creative ability of human action. It also opened the perspective of reflection on human and social status. From then on, the Iranian advance toward political reforms, freedom, and democracy did not only act, it thought while acting, whence the beginning of true political reflection in the writings of the reformers of that time.

All raised questions on the historical role of intellectuals in Iran's destiny, and the search for the proper political forms suiting the Iranian situation occupied all free spirits. Most thinkers wanted to create a constitutional order to guarantee social justice and national progress. Maintaining the country's independence toward European imperialism was their first wish, but this did not prevent them from learning about Western political philosophy and wanting to bring its fruits—democratic freedoms—to Iran. To this end, they sought how to limit the shah's power and to define the precise functions of governmental structures.

One can find many deficiencies in the reformers' ideas. There was no reflection on what divided democratic power from the religious concept of authority. Their writings limited democracy to freedom and equality. Nobody raised the question of the social order's autonomy. The relationship with the past remained at best ambiguous, and the reformers did not manage to explain the present in terms of the past.

Still, self-awareness, knowledge of what one was and of what one could do, appeared in their writings. Their desire to change the country's future enabled them to understand more and more clearly their role in history. The effect was to exalt the people, to enthuse them, and to launch them toward collective action for political and social change.

A historical awareness united the different groups of reformers and the people. This union quickly gave rise to a broad social mobilization. From there, the reform movement took the direction of a national rebellion, what historians later called the "constitutional revolution." By a very significant error in translation, this became in Persian the "conditional revolution." In fact, the revolution wanted only for the collectivity to go from an anarchic and unconscious state to an organized and conscious one.

True, the atmosphere of contradiction, confusion and amalgamation still persisted, and each social group had a different perception of the reforms; but the collective awareness of the country's historical backwardness aroused the people and made the demands of the reformers both audible and credible to them.

This awakening of the Iranians occurred when the neighboring countries, Russia and Turkey, were in full political effervescence. The eyes of all were concentrated on what was happening outside and followed with great curiosity the Russian Revolution of 1905.[21] The hope was for great political change, and that it would bring Nicolas II's czarist Russia to democracy. This gave the reformers an example for a popular revolt against a despotic regime. It seemed all the more important because Russia had long been the bastion of an absolute and military power.

At this dawn of the new century, nationalism emerged in both European countries and in Turkey and other Iranian neighbors. Most reformers of Tabriz (a large city in northwestern Iran) were fervent readers of the Young Turk magazines and very closely interested in what was happening on the other side of their borders. Local newspapers carried numerous articles on Turkish and Syrian nationalist ideas.[22]

The Revolution

At the start of the twentieth century, Iranians were aware of their collective capacity to take their destiny into their own hands. True, this was still a diffuse feeling, but it bore hope for the possibility of going beyond the present. From then on, the distance between the *state center of political will and the concerns of the population* became clearer. This distance was no longer limited by the authoritarianism of the state.

The government was more in debt than ever. Prices were soaring, and the stockpiling of flour for speculative purposes made it impossible to find bread in the large cities. Rumor accused the government of incompetence, and the people doubted the shah's good intentions. The Qajars' megalomania, their eccentric expenses, their costly trips abroad, their entrusting the country's affairs to the hands of foreign ambassadors, all this aroused public indignation. The popular clergy protested these excesses and supported the people. Collective action generalized the desire for change, and a major upheaval was in the wind. Discontent with foreign interference, concessions granted to Europeans, and the economic decline of the country was expressed openly. Iranians wanted to limit the shah's power and unanimously demanded the creation of a judicial system.

As of 1900, the merchants organized demonstrations in Tehran, Tabriz, Shiraz, and Ispahan. As soon as the Ayatollah Behbahani and Tabatabaï, who wanted the rule of law, began to negotiate with the

---

[21] This revolution began in January, 1905, and ended ten months later with the granting of a constitution: the October Manifesto.

[22] See, among others, Hassan Taqizadeh, "An Inquiry into the Current Situation in Persia," in *Historical Trials*-1905, vol. 3, New York, 1970.

government in favor of the people in 1905, the movement took on a revolutionary character. In this extremely tense atmosphere, one incident would provoke a huge mobilization of the population.

Following many risky innovations by Joseph Naus—the Belgian General Director of Iran's customs since 1898—to the detriment of Iranian merchants, the price of sugar went up suddenly. The people were furious. The merchants, obliged to buy sugar at the highest price, refused to sell it at the price demanded by the government. In 1906, in an attempt to calm opposition, two sugar merchants were arrested and publicly whipped by order of Alâ-o-Dawleh, governor of Tehran. This provoked the indignation of the merchants; they went on strike, and the Bazaar remained closed. The following day, a huge social demonstration took place in Tehran. With the Ayatollah Tabatabaï and Behbahani at their head, thousands of the city's inhabitants demonstrated in the streets and demanded the resignation of Alâ-o-Dawleh and of Joseph Naus.

Sheikh Fazlollah Nuri, a clergyman close to the government, concerned for his own interests, could not abide the great popularity of the Ayatollah Tabatabaï and Behbahani. This orthodox clergyman, who had never hesitated to use the most dubious means to achieve his aims, paid some of the city's notorious thugs to disperse the demonstrators and to beat up the two clergymen so as to intimidate them and ridicule them in front of all.

The two ayatollah barely escaped the trap set for them by taking refuge with more than two thousand faithful followers in the Mausoleum of Shah-Abdol-Azim, a Shiite sanctuary situated in Rey, a few kilometers south of Tehran.

The government violently refused the concrete demands of the demonstrators. It accepted, however, the old demand—the one closest to the hearts of the reformers but also the vaguest in their minds—to create the judicial system. But this did not calm the people's fury. The protests spread to all the large Iranian cities. The two ayatollah tried to calm the situation and warned the people against any attempt at radicalization:

> We hear on different sides that the *olama* are going to declare holy war (*jihad*) against the Shah. This is defamation. Our king is a Muslim. There is no question of war against a Muslim king.

But when the forces of order, in an attempt to frighten their opponents, killed some ten people, the Ayatollah Tabatabaï, in a historic speech, invited the people to rebel:

> You are responsible before God and before history. Awake. Recognize the cause of the evil that devours you and remedy

21

your misfortune. There is only one remedy against despotism, the Parliament of the people. Whether it lasts one year or ten, we shall not turn back. We want a Parliament (*Dâr-o Shawrâ*) where *the justice of Islam* will reign, where the Shah and the beggar will be equal before the law.[23]

Everywhere, the clergy preached the constitution and denounced despotism, capturing the enthusiasm of the people. In the large cities the *Bazaar* remained closed;[24] the demonstrations continued. Loud and strong, people demanded a constitution and did not yield to police intimidation.

At last, under popular pressure, Mozaffaredin Shah granted the people's wish on August 4, 1906. He died five months later. After the adoption of the first constitution by Parliament in 1907, Iran became the first country in the Middle East with a fundamental public charter that organized public powers, defined their roles, and created the basis of a judicial system independent of religious laws. The Qajar absolute monarchy was thereby transformed into a constitutional monarchy, and the shah's power was circumscribed by the limits set by the constitution. This event drew the attention of all European observers of that time, far beyond only that of the Orientalists.

Despite these successes, the conflict between the old regime and the new did not die out. The courtiers, like most of the religious dignitaries, scarcely tolerated the people's participation in the affairs of state. They constantly harassed the intellectuals and the merchants. They were wary of any direct confrontation. Slyly but persistently, the struggle between conservatives—politicians and clergymen—and liberals continued, opening the way to compromises between autonomy and heteronomy. From the start of the twentieth century to the present day, this struggle would be the great Iranian fight to install civil liberties in the heart of their collective existence.

The Reversal

Despite all the ideological ambiguities, the constitutional revolution gave concrete shape to the hope for deep change. Its principal political and social results marked a flourishing period (1905–1911). For

---

[23] From that time, this kind of behavior has become so embedded in the mores of religious conservatives that today the most peaceful demonstrations in Iran are still not safe from thuggish violence.
[24] *Ibid.* Following a *fatwa*, decreed by the *mojtahed* of Qom and of Nadjaf (two important Shiite bastions) women sold their jewelry in order to provide economic help for strikers' families.

the first time, Iranians tried to replace authoritarian power by law, a representative government, and social justice. However, at this start of the twentieth century, a constitution independent of religious laws was considered an insult to the *shariat.* The clergy opposed it openly.

The difficulties began the day after parliament adopted the constitution. The religious deputies who, until then, had ignored its content, debated endlessly about the priority of the *shariat.* Their hostility against an autonomous social order created tension among the *Majles.* At that time, just like today, few clergy were able to admit that the law could be founded on the will and the choice of citizens.

In the traditional clergy camp, the *sheikh* Fazlollah Nuri was undoubtedly the fiercest opponent of the constitution ever known in Iranian history. Despite the absence of popular support—particularly that of the merchants who did not want the reformers to be stifled by the *olama*—he played the principal role in the failure of the constitutional revolution. Soon after the reformers' success, he did everything possible to politically isolate the Ayatollah Tabatabaï and Behbahani, as well as the renowned clergy of Nadjaf, close to the constitutionalist leaders. He declared two of them guilty of apostasy—the Ayatollah Khorasani and Lahiji—for having supported the reform movement.

Nuri was the first cleric to understand that European liberal ideas endangered the traditional privileges of the clergy. In the early days of the movement, a number of clergy seemed to confuse the idea of setting up a powerful judicial system with promulgating the *shariat* on a national scale. Thus, their support for the reformers was based on a misconception. Nuri, too clever to overlook such an important point, managed to clear up this misunderstanding. Alone, he succeeded in changing the minds of a majority of popular clergy who, until then, had sincerely supported the constitutional revolution.

Denouncing the constitutional elite's admiration of the West, Nuri felt that borrowing the means of achieving modernity, technology, and scientific knowledge from the West compromised national honor. An open opponent of all economic and political progress, this orthodox cleric found it useless to reform state institutions and, even less, to create a judiciary system like democratic countries. According to him, those who tried to adopt foreign laws forgot that Muslims had no need to copy Europeans, since they had a religious law, the *shariat.* In his sermons, he went so far as to accuse the elite of allowing the enemies of the faith to violate Islam's territory. However, save for such religious circles, this violation did not move the rest of the population and certainly not the constitutionalist elite. The latter, convinced of the need to launch Iran on the road to progress, did not fully measure the danger that Nuri and his accusations represented for their movement.

Ardent defender of the heteronymous social order, the *shariat, Nuri* saw this as the only source of legitimacy. For him, none but laws of divine origin had the least credibility; no other law could be applied. He denounced the danger of adopting texts incompatible with *shariat* and declared it forbidden to respect a law made by men. Hostile to the assembly of those elected by the people, he judged that the responsibility for making laws belonged only to the *olama* and to the *foqaha*.[25] He particularly opposed the second article of the constitution, which recognized all Iranian citizens, regardless of their religion, as equal before the law. Fearing that the constitution granted citizens the right to hold opinions different from those of the clergy, he asserted: "Islam is incompatible with liberty and equality."

In fact, his real fear was that religious courts would be eliminated in favor of a state judicial system; in his eyes, this was only a preliminary measure before eliminating a large part of clerical power. He was bitterly opposed to building schools, especially for girls, since he was convinced that learning foreign languages and science made pupils disobedient.

During the entire summer of 1907, by use of the press and the telegraph and with the financial aid of Mohammad Ali Shah, Nuri and his followers conducted a media campaign against the constitutionalists. As much as the constitutionalists wanted a regime of parliamentary law (*mashruté*), Nuri saw the absolute monarchy as the incarnation of divine will. His alliance with the monarchists against the constitutionalists and his ceaseless criticism of the constitution—which he called the "book of shame" (*Zelâlat-nameh*)—aroused the fury of the liberals.

Unlike his father, Mohammad Ali Shah was authoritarian and hostile to the constitution. Parliamentary initiatives attempting to put the state's finances in order[26] displeased him, and the new king found a

---

[25] *Foqaha, plural of faqih, doctor of Islamic law.*

[26] Parliament calls on an American technical adviser, Morgan Shuster, who comes to Tehran in 1911 with sixteen coworkers. His mission lasts only a few months. He meets the ferocious opposition of the Russians, on one side, and the courteous hostility of the British of the Imperial Bank, on the other; all are "strangling Persia" with the help of numerous corrupt important persons and courtiers, whose pensions represent 20 percent of the state budget, while the court (10 percent), the administration and especially the army (50 percent) share the rest. See also: Janet Afary, *The Iranian Constitutional Revolution: Grass Roots, Democracy, Social Democracy and the Origins of Feminism*, New York, Columbia University Press, 1996.

powerful ally in the battle against the constitutionalists in this fundamentalist cleric. With Nuri's blessing, the shah insisted that the deputies replace the phrase "constitutional monarchy" (*saltant-e mashrouteh*) in the constitution with "religious monarchy" (*saltant-e mashrou'eh*). The constitutionalists never accepted this.

Gradually, Nuri's efforts bore fruit. Most of the clerics began to understand the true meaning of the constitutionalists' ideas and claims; they distanced themselves from the constitutional movement and changed sides. The Ayatollah Tabatabaï and Behbahani, the two prestigious leaders of the constitutional movement, hesitated to carry any further their support for the democratic claims of the liberals and the intellectuals. In their heart of hearts, they would have liked to conciliate political reforms, constitutionalism, and nationalism with the *shariat*. They were quite aware of the need to act and wanted to change the deplorable situation of their country. But they remained attached to a heteronymous social order and so did not defend the constitution with courage and determination.

The constitutionalists gladly exploited the rivalries between the important ayatollah and managed to divide the clerical community, but they weakened more than ever the fragile alliance spun between both camps. Their virulent criticisms of clerical obscurantism, complicity with politicians, and their massive corruption put the *olama* on the defensive. Moreover, the latter could not pardon the constitutionalists for their success in swinging the *Bazaar* to their side. The broad support of the merchants for the reform movement cost the clergy dearly, since they had always considered the *Bazaar* their traditional bastion.

Gradually, the *olama* realized what these new reforms represented for their power and finally saw the threat against their thousand-year-old domination over the people. From then on, they opposed them ferociously. The break between the clergy and the constitutionalists grew more serious, and the liberal deputies perceived clerical reaction as a danger for the Parliament.

The popular clergy, who had played an important part in transmitting the reformers' message to the people, turned their backs on the constitution and took advantage of every opportunity to publicly denounce parliamentarian action. They particularly reproached their lack of interest in the *shariat* and in religious requirements. As easily as they had formerly gained the people's support for change, did they turn them from the reformers. They spoke only of the danger that a constitution independent of the *shariat* posed to the people, to the country, and above all to Islam. By exciting public opinion against the reforms and by joining the conservative camp, these clergy tried to legitimate the government's repression of the reformers.

The clergy's turnabout comforted Mohammad Ali Shah in his absolutist positions and enabled him to attack parliament. It weakened the constitutionalists and, shortly thereafter, led to disastrous results.

Collapse of the Parliament

The constitutional coalition was beset by many confusions and misunderstandings. Rare were those deputies with a precise idea of their role in Parliament, and the Ayatollah Tabatabaï and Behbahani were unable to stand up to the threats of the politicians and the manipulations of their religious colleagues.

The first Parliament's ambitions toward independence seriously annoyed Russia and Great Britain. The deputies wanted to create a national army and reduce the privileges of the Qajar family. The same went for economy and finance. Parliament's first official decision was to so control governmental expenses that, without authorization of the deputies, neither the shah nor his ministers had the right to request financial aid from foreign countries. In 1907, Parliament posed a first symbolic act by refusing the government's request to borrow £1 million to finance Mohammad Ali Shah's trip to Europe. The king was furious, as were the British, who had expected juicy concessions in exchange for this sum.

The great powers would have preferred to deal with the king alone, rather than with parliament and its deputies. They therefore became more and more favorable to the maintenance of an absolutist regime in Tehran. On August 31, 1907, to ensure the borders of their respective empires, the British, worried about northern India, concluded an agreement with the Russians to divide Persia into two distinct zones of influence: czarist Russia in the north and Great Britain in the south, with a "neutral" or "buffer" zone in the center. The agreement was signed without the participation—or even the knowledge—of the Iranian government. Iran was only officially informed later, and parliament then expressed its bitterness. From then on, the Iranians no longer saw the English as defenders of liberty and democracy, but as accomplices of absolutism.

In December 1907, with the implicit support of the British and the Russians, the government organized a demonstration against Parliament. The most traditionalist of the clergy, like Nuri, were at the head. But the deputies resisted, the crowd dispersed and the coup d'état was foiled. Following the intervention of the English and Russian diplomats, the shah again swore allegiance to the constitution, and the deputies promised not to attempt to remove him from office. It was nonetheless clear that a lasting reconciliation between the two sides was impossible, and that the foreign intervention had only delayed a final accounting. The shah waited for a new opportunity to destroy Parliament.

The *Majles* was weaker than ever. On the one hand, countless plots were directed against it by the clergy, the government, and the Russian and British diplomats. On the other, the hesitations, inexperience, naïveté and even ignorance of the deputies augured no good. Save only a few experienced intellectuals, the vast majority of the deputies, like the two religious leaders, Tabatabaï and Behbahani, did not realize with what subtlety the government plotted against Parliament. They spent their time debating relations between the constitution and the *shariat*. Thus, ideological and political quarrels on creating a state judicial system to replace religious justice controlled by the clergy raged on. By blocking the application of judicial reforms, the *olama* were ever more hostile to people's rights.

Clearly, nobody saw the danger threatening the constitution nor took seriously the shah's Machiavellian maneuvers against Parliament. The government no longer respected the decrees voted by the deputies, and ministers did not feel obliged to report to the *Majles* who, deprived of all power, played only an apparent role.

Parliament was more and more divided, the constitutionalists ripped at each other, and some deputies received money to side with the court. Mohammad Ali Shah, for his part, knew he was supported by Moscow and had the implicit consent of the British. In June 1908, with the effective support of the Russians, he openly opposed the constitution. The *Majles* collapsed under the canon shots of a Russian army colonel, Liakhov,[27] whose name has remained infamous in Iranian history. Many deputies were arrested, and some succumbed to torture or were summarily executed. Numerous demonstrators took refuge in the British embassy. Tehran fell into the hands of Persian Cossacks, under the

---

[27] Vladimir Platonovitch Liakhov was a Russian army colonel, commanding the Persian Cossack brigade under the reign of Mohammed Ali Shah. As a sign of gratitude, after the downfall of Parliament and the execution of several constitutionalist leaders on June 24, 1908, the shah named him military governor of Tehran. *Cf.* Kasravi, *Tarikh mashrouteh Iran, op. cit.*

command of Liakhov and Russian officers who received their orders directly from their legation. The country returned to despotism for a period that lasted nearly a year.

Nevertheless, constitutionalism was not yet dead. If Tehran's clergy discovered new monarchist leanings to "defend Islam," the Nadjaf *olama* supported the partisans who sought a return to constitutionalism. They called the shah an enemy of Islam and proclaimed *jihad* (holy war) against the Qajar. In July 1909, after bloody battles that left many dead, constitutional forces arriving from Rasht and Tabriz conquered Tehran. Mohammad Ali Shah took refuge in the Russian embassy. The most ill-intentioned of the anti-parliamentarian clergy, the *sheikh* Fazlollah Nuri, was summarily judged by a revolutionary tribunal and publicly hanged in July 1909.

Elections were organized quickly, and the new Parliament removed Mohammad Ali Shah from office, putting his son, Ahmad Shah, aged eleven, on the throne. The constitutional regime was reestablished, but it was paralyzed by many difficulties ranging from the corruption of national politicians to foreign intervention, as well as by the downfall of the traditional monarchic order and the obstacles that arose in putting a new regime in place.

A new period of trouble began. During World War I, Iran was occupied by Russian, British and Ottoman forces. The king, who was idealistic and democratic but too young and weak, could not guarantee the integrity of the country or maintain order. The Qajar dynasty was denounced by Parliament in 1925 during the absence of Ahmad Shah, on a visit to Europe. Reza Khan (1878–1944), the powerful Minister of War, named prime minister, acceded to the Peacock Throne, on the request of Parliament. Ahmad Shah died in October 1930 in Neuilly-sur-Seine in France.

The tribulations of the end of the Qajar reign distanced the clergy from politics and paralyzed the reformers. The alliance of the crown and the turban was less and less popular, and plausible relations between the three political antagonists—royalists, clergy, and reformers—dependent on maintaining the country's sovereignty, greatly threatened.

Autopsy of a Failure

What proved fatal to the constitutionalists was their failure to understand the consequences of their movement. They did not measure its full implications in both its dimensions: the autonomy of society with regard to politics and the priority of society with regard to power; this explains their blindness in not seeing what opposed them to conservative clergy and politicians.

For their part, the conservative clergy had seen the consequences of the reform movement. However, they thought wrongly that it could be controlled and would not involve a real danger for the old religious and monarchic order. When they became fully aware of the threat, the clergy effected an abrupt reversal against the constitutionalists, whose terrible consequences were to impede the country's advance toward modernity and democracy throughout the entire twentieth century.

The constitutionalists had attempted to find a compromise between the heritage of the religious past and the drive of new ideas. However, by relying too much on the clergy and according great importance to their leaning for social justice, they committed an irreparable error. They thought naïvely that it would be possible to carry out basic political reforms in the framework of the old religious, monarchic, aristocratic, traditional, and corporative order. They also thought it would be possible to manage a synthesis between this traditional order and their wish for democracy.

Nothing happened as the reformers expected. They had no idea to what extent their ideas, once they became firmer and broader, would imply the overthrow of the old domination—political and religious—in favor of society's independence and priority. They failed to see that society could no longer be represented by a power that remained essentially religious. When political reforms come to fruition, society becomes the source of legitimate power with all that that implies. This power no longer incarnates a divine legitimacy; it does not fall from heaven; it is not inherited from the past; rather, it is a response to the concrete needs of the community of citizens. Iranian reformers of the beginning of the twentieth century were very far from measuring all the consequences of the constitutional movement.

One might have expected a sort of compromise to preserve the outer trappings of monarchy and religion, while yet reducing them to a symbolic form, so as to make room for the effective power by representation—that is, universal suffrage as existed in many European countries. The real power would then have been in the hands of Parliament, while traditional power remained in place. However, given the Iranian context at the start of the twentieth century, the resistance to change of traditional structures was so strong, and the complicity of monarchy and clergy still so staunch that royalty refused to grant the least leeway for emancipating society and freeing its actors and even less leeway to a representative government. Unable to accept an autonomous political organization, the too-powerful traditional order ruined the attempt of an emerging society. The failure of the constitutional movement was then inevitable.

This failure was caused first by the reformers' inability to realize the intensity of the resistance of traditional or heteronymous structures faced with the upsurge of novelty, and second by their inability to realize the breadth of their own action or the depth of the chasm separating them from the old monarchic and religious order.

2

Nationalism (1920–1953)

The collapse of the first Parliament left a bitter taste in the Iranian collective memory. Among the many factors fatal to the constitutional movement, only Colonel Liakhov's intervention captured popular attention. Of everything that contributed to the failure of the constitutional movement—the malevolence of Mohammad Ali Shah and his ministers toward Parliament, the clergy's treason, the deputies' naïveté in political affairs—only the open hostility of the Russians toward the democratic and national hopes of the Iranians is remembered.

Without the necessary distance to understand the reasons for the failure of the constitutional movement, foreign interference became the sole explanation for the situation. On the honors list of imperialist countries, certainly Russia was at the head, but Great Britain was not far behind. Despite the limited support of the English for the movement, nothing allowed them to remain above suspicion. Very quickly, they found themselves a target for criticism and became the object of more and more violent complaints. Russian arrogance and English scorn toward Iran only sharpened the people's hatred; they considered these two powers as their sworn enemies.

In fact, this animosity is ancient. Since the treaties of Golestan (1813) and of Torkamantchai (1828), both of which entailed the loss of a large part of Iranian territory,[1] colonial powers have been dreaded in Iran. The country's weakness under the last three Qajar kings and the 1907 Convention (signed between the British and the Russians unbeknownst to the Iranian government) accentuated resentment against Great

---

[1] After its defeat by Russia in the war of 1826–1828, Iran was forced to sign the Treaty of Torkamantchai, by which it yielded its northern territories (mostly populated by Armenians and Azeris) to Imperial Russia. As for the Golestan Treaty, conquered Iran had to sign the treaty drawn up by the Russians to avoid their seizing Tehran. *Cf. Encyclopædia Iranica, op. cit.*

Britain and Imperial Russia.[2] Toward the end of the Qajar period, both these countries often exercised great influence, intervening in internal affairs. By manipulating tribal chiefs, the important merchants, and a part of the *olama,*[3] they had their way at the expense of Iranian interests. Finally, fear of them made it more difficult to understand the situation. The most fantastic rumors were believed. In an atmosphere of despair and national indignation, a "conspiracy theory" gained credence, blaming all Iran's historical errors on foreign countries.[4] Russian and English influences were read into the smallest details of political, social, religious, even private affairs. All social, economic, and political problems were blamed on foreign imperialism. This collective illusion gave rise to complex beliefs attributing Iranian political history to the doings of foreign powers and their secret organization. Conspiracy theories abounded, comforting those who would not admit defeat. Such interpretations became the primary mode for understanding Iranian social and political history from the start of the twentieth century. They still wreak havoc among young people today.

Such were the ideas that triumphed at the start of the twentieth century. Nonetheless, they were deeply discrediting for Iranians themselves. It implied that national inferiority was to blame for Iranian inability to manage their relations with foreigners. It gave rise to a collective self-disparagement, a sort of national shame that influences history, affects the practical orientation of society toward the future, and troubles people's views toward the past, the present, and the future.

The Influence of World War I

The international crisis at the start of the twentieth century and, after that, World War I, multiplied internal Iranian crises. During the conflict, Iran declared its neutrality. From the start, the Russians in the north and the British in the south violated its territory, under pretext of protecting the oil fields against any German-Turkish attack. The English, interested by

---

[2] This convention was not unrelated to the treaty signed in 1919. The Iranian Parliament never ratified that treaty. *Cf.* "Anglo-Russian Convention of 1907," *Encyclopædia Iranica, op. cit.* See also: Rogers Platt Churchill, *The Anglo-Russian Convention of 1907*, The Torch Press, Cedar Rapids, Iowa, 1939.

[3] The English gave money to the *olama* of Nadjaf and of Karbala in Iraq—the majority of whom were Iranian—so that they would not interfere in politics. *Cf.* Saeed Nafisi, *Tarikh ejtémaï va siasi Iran dar doreye mo' aser (Histoire politique et sociale de l'Iran contemporain)*, vol. 2, Tehran, Ahoura, 1965.

[4] This theory gained its full scope during the critical period of the end of the Qajars and the start of the Pahlavis (1908–1930).

the discovery of oil in the Khuzestan[5] in 1908, wanted all of Iran in its sphere of influence to create a territorial continuity from Cairo to Calcutta.

During the war, the Qajar dynasty rapidly disintegrated. Increasingly brutal foreign intervention, the radicalism of patriotic reactions, and the confusion of corrupt politicians caused the central government to lose all organizing capacity and to become well-nigh inexistent. This weak political power, deprived of any army or other tool of coercion, made the elite aware of the need to constitute a strong central government. While both north and south borders were violated, and it was a real question whether Iran still maintained any autonomy, real or theoretical, Iranian patriots felt that a central unifying power would be able to ensure national unity and put an end to foreign intervention and attacks against the country's sovereignty. Aware of their country's decadence, some dreamed of abolishing provincialism and were persuaded that only an enlightened dictatorship could reestablish order and security, thereby concentrating Iranian energy on an entry into the modern world.

The country was ruined after a war in which it had officially refused to engage.[6] Weighed down by the disorder created by World War I, the conspiracy theories that had previously flourished broke down. The war played an important part in changing mentalities. In the absence of a strong state, the war accentuated the evils destroying the country. It revealed more than ever Iran's weakness on the international scene. It forced Iranians to see the danger that threatened them and to become aware of the integrating and mobilizing force of the nation.

The war caused the various elements of society to evolve and dissipated the fatalistic ideas that had prevailed before 1914. It renewed patriotic feeling and showed the need for collective action against foreign invasion. It discredited conspiracy theories in favor of a nationalist perspective to bring the country out of the chaos that was destroying it. It strengthened the factors contributing to the plausibility of nationalist arguments. The need to avoid the horrors of war made the population understand the nationalist message: never again!

In 1918, the program was to break with the past. After World War I, the entire nation seemed to agree that a powerful state was needed to

---

[5] Khuzestan is one of Iran's thirty provinces. It is situated in the southwest of the country, neighboring Iraq and the Persian Gulf.

[6] In 1917–1918, famine, influenza, and typhus epidemics ravaged the land, killing ten thousand of Shiraz's fifty thousand inhabitants. Commerce was disorganized and the price of wheat rose constantly in Tehran. Roads were broken, bridges destroyed, highwaymen made travel dangerous. *Cf.* Firuz Kazemzadeh, *Russia and Britain in Persia, 1864–1914*, New Haven, Yale University Press, 1968.

put an end to the hardships endured under foreign armies of occupation. Yesterday's constitutionalists now preached the need for a strong central government, and the idea of democracy upheld by universal suffrage receded into the background.

Foreign Intervention

After the war, Iran depended more than ever on foreigners. The national debt and the corruption of the political elite reached a high point. The Qajar monarchy had never been so weak and unpopular. The country was torn by local rebellions, and its key institutions—the army, economy, finances, banks, postal services, and higher education—were all in the hands of Russians or English.

The failure of constitutionalism had left a fictional constitutional monarchy in place, without organized political parties or charismatic political leaders. Some were still respected but only remained in place under foreign protection. The British embassy strongly influenced politicians. For more than a century, the English had succeeded in building a broad network of mercenaries among corrupt Iranians. Similarly, the Russians had their own network before the Bolshevik revolution of 1917, but after the revolution, these paid collaborators changed sides and joined the British.[7]

The Russians occupied northern Iran militarily, and their repression was particularly severe in Tabriz. The most respected clergyman of that city, Seqat ol-Eslam, was publicly hanged for having supported the return of the constitutionalists. In Mashad, the sanctuary of Imam Reza was bombarded, and many pilgrims were killed. Despite ethnic cleavages between northern regions and the center, the repressive acts of the Russians revolted the local populations to such an extent that patriotic feelings rose above ethnic differences. Defending national sovereignty became Iranians' primary concern, regardless of their origins.

The northern rebellions were directed against foreign colonial intervention. In the south, the situation was different. Good relations between the English and tribal chiefs, and the bribes offered by the former, aroused separatist tendencies. With the state's weakness and the absence of an organized national army, many tribes claimed their independence and received financial and political help from the English, whose main interest was the oil fields of the south. Masters of the art of dividing those who resisted them and of profiting by conflicts

---

[7] Cyrus Ghani, *Iran and the rise of Reza Shah*, London, I. B. Tauris Publishers, 2000.

between the central power and the various ethnic groups—Kurds, Lors, Bakhtyaris, Qashqa'ïs, Arabs, and others—the English thus used the military capacities of all these to regain control in the south.

Since the threat of czarist Russia had now disappeared, England became the most threatening imperialist country for Iran. The massive presence of the British army ensured its complete control over that whole territory. Their systematic interventions in politics, and the dependence of Iranian leaders on them sharpened more than ever the anti-British feelings of the people.

In those postwar years, a time of reconstruction and hope in the future, there were many reasons for Iran to be seen as a highly important strategic zone. Since 1912, Iranian oil production represented a source of immense wealth, particularly for the English who had just abandoned coal. At the same time, Iran was a *"cordon sanitaire"* permitting the defense of the British Empire in India against an eventual Turkish or German attack. Furthermore, London was convinced that Iran could play an essential role against communist expansion and Soviet intervention in the Orient. The "Red" presence in Iran worried the English, who feared a general contagion in the region. Tehran could not then be abandoned at any price.

Despite these fears, the communist leaders—Lenin, Tchitcherin, Trotsky—judged "Persia too backwards for a socialist revolution."[8] To counter English imperialism and break with the policy of the old regime, the new Bolshevik power forgave all Iran's debts to czarist Russia. They further put an end to its capitulary rights,[9] which had been humiliating to Iran. They promised never again to weaken or violate national sovereignty. The Soviets hoped thereby that Tehran would no longer be a springboard for the English, who might want to invade Soviet Central Asia. But things did not work out that way. The Iranians were worried by the extreme weakness of their country and of their successive governments, incapable of ensuring their national defense against imperialist powers.

The British were present more than ever. After World War I, in 1919, London prepared a treaty according to which Iran had to cede control of its military, economic, and financial affairs to Great Britain. Iran was so destabilized that it was easy for the English to take control over the

---

[8] Jean-Pierre Digard (ed.), *Iran in the twentieth century. Between nationalism, Islam and globalization*, Paris, Fayard, 1996, p. 68.
[9] The capitulary rights dispensed foreign citizens from being judged according to the laws of the country in which they lived.

entire country. To this end, they decided to isolate it internationally. In 1919, by order of the British embassy, all foreigners—except the British—were expelled from the country and forbidden to return.

That same year, the English refused Iran access to the Versailles Conference to prevent it from claiming damages, although it was one of the countries most affected during World War I.[10] Only American diplomats heard Iranian claims, and they alone upheld Tehran's presence at the Peace Conference. During that first part of the twentieth century, American politicians often contested British interests. The American minister of foreign affairs, Robert Lansing, declared: "So long as the Iranian government and its people are not unanimous in accepting this treaty, the United States will formally oppose it."[11]

Despite Great Britain's insistence, the Iranian Parliament rejected the treaty. The deputies knew how to use the divergent interests of the Americans and the English to block the "1919 Agreement" that they felt was degrading for their country. Indeed the agreement, had it taken effect, would have benefited only the British. By blocking the Iranian political system, they would have been the only foreigners to rule over Iran, giving them exclusive control of oil-production profits. In contempt of Iranian national sovereignty, the agreement would have prevented Tehran from calling in any non-British advisers.

The violation of Iran's neutrality during the war, the rejection of its claims at the Versailles Conference, and the shameful 1919 Agreement exposed Iran's deep dependence. These events only enhanced the need to defend national sovereignty. After that, nationalist ideas gained immense credibility with the vast majority of Iranians.

Nationalist Dominance

The appearance of nationalism was a worldwide phenomenon at the start of the twentieth century. In Iran, the presence of an exceptionally rich and living historical memory—that of ancient Persia—favored the rapid development of political nationalism. It followed the fall of the constitutional movement and was greatly strengthened after World War I.

---

[10] In a Green Book, Tehran proclaimed its rights to reparations because of the prolonged occupation of part of its territory by the Ottomans, by the Russians in the north since 1911, and even for the annexation by czarist Russia of Iranian possessions in the Caucasus in the nineteenth century. *Cf.* Digard, *op. cit.*, 1996.

[11] Ghani, *op. cit.*, 2000, p. 73.

By definition, nationalism is patriotism rooted in specific national experiences of which it claims to be the guardian and the strongest expression. There is a great difference between this and the universalism claimed by communism, founded on world revolution, an international proletariat, and the materialistic science of history and society.

Despite some resemblances, reactionary Iranian nationalism differed in several respects from European nationalism. The European version was more a radical remaking of conservatism, under the sign of the nation, at a time when the old monarchic, hierarchical, religious image was falling into disrepute. Iranian nationalism was founded on the somber background of a collective failure and reflected above all a deeply wounded patriotic feeling. At this time, its major objective was defensive. The purpose was to ensure the country's independence from English and Russian imperialism. It was based on the right of peoples to dispose of themselves. It quickly gained general sympathy and took a major place in the intellectual scene. Nationalism became the doctrine that crystallized the spirit of the age.

The triumph of nationalism in the Iranian context is due to two main factors. It offered the most plausible explanation of past and coming events. It was particularly able to supply a convincing demonstration of what had to be done to avoid future catastrophe. The second factor derived from its internal capacity. Stemming from a concrete event, it became a patriotic reaction against an immediate and real danger: European imperialism. Therein lay its great strength.

Both factors played an important role in the triumph of nationalism, a part of whose legitimacy was based on enabling Iran to reconnect with its glorious past of imperial power. Thus defending collective sovereignty seemed of the greatest importance. The situation seemed so problematical that the cause was rapidly espoused, not only by reformists and former constitutionalists but by all political leaders.

This change was amazing. It was the political reply to a specific situation that prioritized defense of collective sovereignty. The nation was clearly the tool for preserving a country whose survival was in grave peril.

By switching to nationalism, political conservatives also converted to the modern world, first to the idea of progress, then to the need for practical orientation of political action toward the future. Where they thought to find the secret of a return to the historical past of ancient Persia, they were launched into political and social modernity.

This conversion, squarely in the present, faced with very real enemies, accredited nationalist ideas. Far from the theoretical debates of the constitutional period that had confused a good portion of the population, the concrete nature of nationalist language and its specific aims appealed to many.[12]

Amid this collective infatuation for triumphant nationalism, the clergy remained aloof. National feelings, love for the country, and any other attachment to the nation were foreign to them. To counter the success of a patriotic movement that inflamed Iranian love of country, they proclaimed above all Islam's universality and the kingdom of God with no national borders. But the strength of nationalist speech and the powerful will of the people to regain their sovereignty dimmed the aura of the clergy. For the first time, despite their amazing manipulative powers, they failed to make the people hear them.

The clergy's hostility to nationalism cost them dearly; it reconfigured the balance of power. Just when the politicians, intellectuals, and the people were defending their national interests side by side, the clergy's determination to return to the past distanced them from power and enclosed them in a political conservatism for several decades.

The Two Pillars of Iranian Nationalism

From that essential period—marking the end of the Qajars and the beginning of the Pahlavis—nationalism became the principal inspiration of political leaders. Its repercussions and its impact on political reality began to be felt under the reign of Reza Shah (1926–1941). He seemed able to muster the required energy for restoring order within Iran's borders. By modernizing the political machine and the administrative system, carrying out important structural works, he made possible the birth of a modern economy, founded on state intervention and oil revenues. He concentrated his political action on national feeling and managed to lead the country—in an authoritarian but efficient way—toward twentieth century perspectives.

The second eminent figure of Iranian nationalism was Mohammad Mossadeq (1882–1967). He succeeded in mobilizing the people's national feeling and in transforming it into a true political force. Mossadeq was then able to go on to socialize the economy in a democratic framework. His major concern was to prevent the English from profiting from Iranian oil, and nationalizing this vital sector of the economy became the keyword of Iranian democratic nationalism.

Reza Shah's reign marked the beginning of the end of British influence in Iran. In 1951, Mossadeq put a period to this influence,

---

[12] *Cf.* Cyrus Ghani, *Iran and the West*, London, Routledge & Kegan, 1987.

concluding the movement begun by Reza Shah three decades earlier. Ten years after the humiliating elimination of Reza Shah by the Allies, because he had refused to enter the war on their side, how did Iran finally succeed in freeing itself from English imperialism? In a country paralyzed by the fatalism of conspiracy theories, how could nationalist ideas so mobilize Iranians?

Reza Shah: Defense of National Sovereignty

After World War I, Reza Shah took power by a coup d'état, with the blessings of the English.[13] A Cossack officer descended from a long line of army officers, he became successively Supreme Commander of the Armed Forces and head of the Persian Empire's government under the reign of Ahmad Shah, the last Qajar ruler. Parliament having voted to oust the young monarch in 1925, Reza Shah was immediately elected. He was enthroned Shah of Iran in 1926, thus founding the Pahlavi dynasty.

Although the English supported his accession to power, Reza Shah made the fifteen years of his reign a permanent fight against their influence on Iranian politics and succeeded in reducing it substantially. This led to his forced abdication in 1941, when the British put his son on the throne.[14]

Reza Shah's patriotism supported the nationalist movement. Immediately following his coronation, he hoped to place Iran firmly in the twentieth century. An admirer of Ataturk, he followed his example. He gave the country a modern education system where science and technology had a predominant position. He reformed the judiciary, until then controlled by the clergy, and promulgated a civil code that removed the exercise of justice from the clergy, for which the latter never forgave him. He thereby managed an in-depth change of state structures. Supported by a strong centralized government, Reza Shah modernized the country. The national railroad, built between 1927 and 1938 and linking the Caspian Sea to the Persian Gulf may be considered his masterpiece, even if this prestigious enterprise turned out to be very costly.

As soon as he became king, Reza Shah abolished the rule of capitulary rights—those rights granted to foreigners during the

---

[13] Ghani, *op. cit.*, 2000, p. 51.

[14] Reza Shah was forced by the British to abdicate on September 16, 1941, and exiled first to Mauritius and then to Johannesburg, where he died in 1944.

Qazar period—so as to limit Iran's dependence on Great Britain and Russia. In 1935, he officially requested the international community to no longer use the term "Persia" (which is the name of an ethnic group of central Iran), but that of Iran (the official name of the Persian Empire, from the Sassanides to the fifth century).[15] That same year, he decreed a ban on women wearing the veil and the obligation for men to wear "Western" dress. The most outstanding element in all these innovations was his will to rehabilitate the pre-Islamic Iranian past. This involved founding an academy to rid the Persian language of its borrowings from Arabic.

Despite these progressive measures, Reza Shah was not popular. He was not a charismatic leader adored by his people. Contrary to the clergy, who spoke eloquently and knew how to arouse the masses, he spoke little and in a forthright manner. His ideas were indeed admired and his efforts appreciated, but his dictatorial style of governing and his fight to modernize Iran, which ran counter to clerical positions, inspired mistrust in a part of the population.

He was first of all a soldier, with no intellectual pretensions. From a modest family, he entered the army at age sixteen as a groom and, thanks to his personal abilities, rose from rank to rank. His natural elegance, and his above-average height, aroused the admiration of those who came into contact with him and gave him the air of a leader. Very quickly, he joined those who mastered the art of giving orders by seeming to obey. His glacial look inspired respect and fear. He was an impassive and not very sociable man but determined and faithful to his objectives. The English who helped him gain power may have hoped to make him a monarch totally submissive to their will. But Reza Shah proved himself a good strategist, such as was rarely known in Iran. As soon as he was enthroned, he spoke clearly: "Iran will continue its road toward the future. Russia and Great Britain can only accept that reality."[16]

Having mastered the various tribes seeking independence, Reza Shah sought at all costs to limit Iranian political and economic dependence on England. Taking advantage of the diverging interests between the Soviets and the British—with great skill—he began politically manipulating both protagonists in turn. In 1924, he treated with the Soviets

---

[15] The Sassanides ruled Iran from 224 to 651 (date of the Muslim Arab invasion of the country). This period was a golden age for Iran architecturally as well as in politics and religion.
[16] Ghani, *op cit.*, 2000, p. 51.

for peace on his northern borders and to resist the British, far more threatening in the south and the east.

Nonetheless, despite his negotiating talent, Reza Shah did not succeed in benefiting from the divergent interests between the Americans and the English, nor in making allies of the former in his struggle against British influence in Iran. London quickly made it clear that Iran came under the Monroe Doctrine,[17] which forbade any country to encroach on British zones of influence. The United States, for their part, had no wish to contest British supremacy in Iran and ceased their favorable acceptance of Iranian demands. Reza Shah, who wanted to introduce a third power between the English and the Russians, finally appealed to the Germans for their expertise in the financial and administrative affairs of the country.

This proximity with Nazi Germany, who became Iran's first commercial partner in 1939, worried the British. When World War II broke out, the United Kingdom insisted that Reza Shah expel the German experts, but he refused categorically. And under his leadership, Iran refused to enter the war on the Allied side. But this affirmation of national sovereignty cost him dearly. In August 1941, The United Kingdom and the Soviet Union invaded Iran, took control of communication and transportation networks, and forced Reza Shah to abdicate in favor of his son, Mohammad-Reza Pahlavi (1919–1980). He was exiled by the British, first to Mauritius, then to Johannesburg, where he died in 1944.[18]

Reza Shah was not free from reproach. His avarice in taking over immense domains by confiscating private property remains unequalled in the history of Iranian monarchs. His desire to keep this real estate

---

[17] In 1823, for his seventh annual message to Congress, the American president, James Monroe made a speech directed toward Europeans; it set the directives that American diplomacy would adopt during the nineteenth and early twentieth centuries. As of 1854, this was called the Monroe Doctrine, in which three principles were defined. The first affirmed that the American continent would henceforth be closed to any attempt at European colonization. The second, stemming from this, stipulated that any intervention by a European power on the American continent would be considered an unfriendly act toward the United States. And the third, as a counterpart, guaranteed that there would be no American intervention in European affairs. The principles expressed by Monroe and his predecessors only became a doctrine in the mid nineteenth century when conflicts opposed the United States and European powers on the American continent. *Cf. Encyclopædia Iranica, op. cit.*

[18] Ghani, *op. cit.*, 2000, p. 201. In 1943, Iran drew closer to Western powers. That same year saw the Tehran Conference where Churchill, Roosevelt, and Stalin reaffirmed their commitment to Iran's independence, and the latter then became a member of the League of Nations.

prevented him from carrying out agrarian reforms, so much so that the rural structure of the country remained identical to that of the Qajar era.[19] This immobility was partly due to the presence of many landed proprietors in Parliament, among whom were numerous high-ranking clergymen who opposed all reforms in the rural areas from which they drew tremendous profits. Furthermore, Reza Shah carried out violent and unprecedented repression against nomadic tribes and, by settling them, reduced them to beggary and misery. This was a black stain on his record.

As time passed, he showed a paranoiac mistrust of his collaborators, whom he eliminated one after the other. The man who dreamed of international recognition for his country became deeply mistrustful toward foreign diplomats, to the extent that he ended by rendering his relations with their countries completely chaotic. His excessive authoritarianism made him so detested that his humiliating destitution in 1941[20] aroused no emotion among Iranians.

He remains nonetheless one of the most remarkable politicians in Iranian history. By glorifying Iranian past history as the foundation of his political action toward the future, he launched anew a country torn by internal strife and restored the self-respect of a people paralyzed by political fatalism. He left a nation proud of its wealth and capabilities, motivated by the will to enter into a new world. At a time when foreign threats were the central problem, Reza Shah's nationalism was clearly the only political path able to defend territorial sovereignty and to reshape the national community.

The Flowering of Patriotic Tales

The expansion of nationalist ideology during the reign of Reza Shah encouraged the flowering of a vast historical literature. Many books and articles were published about Iran's glorious past, its territorial integrity, and great civilization. Nationalist authors studied pre-Islamic history to define what they called "Iranian national identity," independent of Islam. By these narratives, and often at the expense of scientific objectivity, most authors invented an idealized image of ancient Iran (*Iran-e Bâstân*), able to overcome foreign and religious invasions—such as that

---

[19] Before Reza Shah, Iran was in the hands of landed proprietors. Agriculture was the only source of revenue of the country and its inhabitants. Iranian industry was but little developed at the start of the twentieth century and scarcely a quarter of the population was urbanized. *Ibid.*
[20] See note 48.

of the Arabs in the seventh century—thanks to the glory of Persian civilization and culture.

Such praise was used only for the distant past. Relations in the recent past were clearly more complicated, even ambiguous. Most authors blackened things even more and described that period as the age of national decline and moral decadence. This dramatization aimed, in part, at presenting the Pahlavis as the incarnation of stability, progress, and a return to past greatness. For nationalist authors, history became the best instrument for legitimizing the new dynasty and its modernizing policies. These ideas so influenced opinion that even those who criticized the regime shared them.

The tremendous interest in history shown by the new, resolutely nationalistic political leaders paradoxically harmed the credibility of historical work. State control was imposed on publishing during the reign of the first Pahlavi. To this was added the absence of any archives founded on reliable sources. These factors did not facilitate serious research with a true historical methodology. The dry, monotonous tone of historical writings made them particularly tedious. Gradually, the promotion of history as propaganda for the regime contributed to the appearance of a nostalgic pride that impeded any objective and comprehensive approach to the past.

Aware of these weaknesses, constitutionalist intellectuals and a part of the former Qajar elite met to define the bases for historical studies in accordance with critical principles. Several attempts to set up a methodology for reading ancient texts—verifying sources, comparing specialist opinions, refusal of fallacious reasoning—appeared. During World War II, this in-depth work bore fruit. Tehran University researchers and historians produced original and influential publications on the Qajar, constitutional and post-constitutional periods. Yet, at a time of such political unrest, it was difficult to remain objective when faced with current events. Without the necessary distancing, such work was halfway between journalism and academic research. With some exceptions, Iranian historical work was hardly recognized internationally. Four decades of historical research constituted an impressive literary work, but one that often lacked a solid and coherent theoretical framework based on a systematic analysis of original sources.

Nor was the work of Western authors on Iranian history exempt from methodological deficiencies. Most of these were caused by the colonial mentality of their authors, who shamefully neglected the symbolic dimensions that shaped Iranian history, as they did all historical traditions worldwide. Their scornful treatment of the democratic ambitions of Iranian intellectuals or political leaders—based on their conviction that democracy belonged only to the West—prevented them from realizing the strength of the ideas that so completely overturned Iranian social organization throughout the twentieth century. Furthermore, the writings of former foreign diplomats in Tehran were so imbued with personal sympathy or antipathy toward certain Iranian elites that they were difficult to comprehend.

This situation lasted for several decades after the war, widening the rift between historical research in Europe and in Iran. It was largely related to the lack of interest of Iranian politicians in developing a critical view of history. Impressed by the technological advances of European countries, they relied on academic teaching of the exact sciences at the expense of the humanities. The educational and academic reforms wanted by the Pahlavis, based on a superficial positivism, did not contribute to developing in-depth Iranian historical research.

Against this background, the professionalism of Hosseyn Zarrinkoub stood out. He was one of the rare academic historians whose ambition went beyond producing literary writings for the public at large. His seminal work on Islamic Iran entitled *Two Centuries of Silence* (*Do qarn sokout*, Tehran, 1951) was a turning point in the nationalist language of the time. It ran counter to the thesis of nationalist historians, according to whom foreign invasions were the major causes of Iranian moral stagnation and material decline. Contrary to his predecessors, he reinterpreted the history of the seventh-century Arab conquest by considering it as a fundamental event for understanding Iranian social and political organization. He claimed it was essential to realize how a foreign force could so easily overturn the Sassanide Empire and convert Iranians to Islam. He explained that this was a major historical problem whose consequences continued to the present time, just as did the thirteenth-century Mongol invasion. These great events had to be analyzed independently of patriotic passions.

While nationalist authors thought of the Arab invasion and all its consequences as a calamity every bit as repulsive as the Mongol invasion, Zarrinkoub refused to weep over the past. For him, it was more important to understand how, despite the loss of territorial sovereignty, Iran had succeeded in imposing on its invaders its own culture. Unlike the Middle Eastern countries that yielded to Arabization, Iran preserved its Persian language and literature, glorified its pre-Islamic history and, through the Muslim world, rendered its culture more universal than before.

It was not until the second half of the twentieth century that some attention was paid to the Qajar and Pahlavi periods. But, with only a few exceptions, this remained the subject of nonspecialists.[21] Of course, under nationalist domination, history was limited to propagandizing those ideas that justified the ruling political regime. Yet, the originality of Iranian nationalism lay in the fact that, contrary to the ancient religious principle that legitimacy came from "on high," it was based on national sovereignty. Under the rule of heteronymous structuring, nationalism thus managed to introduce the autonomous principles of togetherness and of liberating the country, temporarily but efficiently, from the weight of the clergy, the prime operators of heteronymous order.

In the 1930s, national feeling was so strong that it was easy to ideologically impose nationalism. Added to this was Pahlavi patriotism that ensured state support. Thus, simultaneously, on two parallel but separate registers, first ideological and then political domination were both affirmed. Neither could work without the other. The presence of nationalism on both registers gave it more credit and the strength to marginalize the clergy for a certain time.

Fury of the Clergy

All this was but an aberration for the clergy. Never having recognized themselves in nationalism, they considered it as pure fetishism, radically opposed to the Muslim religion. Filled with the illusion of an all-powerful clergy, some of them, like the Ayatollah Kashani and later the Ayatollah Khomeini, dreamed of eventual recognition as worldwide Muslim spiritual leaders and could not therefore limit themselves to Iran. But the flourishing historical writings that presented the Arab invasion reprovingly hardly contributed to the popularity of Iranian ayatollah in the rest of the Islamic world. Shiite clergy did all it could to escape from any national belonging.

Reza Shah's anti-clericalism hardly improved this complex situation; he constantly exacerbated hatred of the clergy. In 1928, when he physically attacked a seminary student who judged the queen's clothing contrary to the *shariat*, all the clergy felt themselves attacked. The shah's social policy that allowed both sexes to appear in public exasperated

---

[21] Scholarly Iranian history was not concerned with the recent past, particularly that of the Qajar period, considered too contemporary and thereby less worthy of attention. Even the Safavides period, seen as the threshold of Iranian political and cultural reassurance, was but little studied.

the clergy who considered as evil the presence of women in restaurants, hotels, cinemas, and theaters. They found it intolerable that public schools should be opened to them. The very existence of public schools, for boys as well as for girls, met with their strong resistance, since they thought all education outside *shariat* law dangerous, and particularly for girls.[22]

From the 1930s, Shiite clerical discontent reached an apex. In 1935, in the midst of the campaign against the head scarf (accompanied by compulsory Western hats for men), the clergy of the holy city of Mashad (in northwestern Iran) denounced the shah's heretical innovations, the corruption of politicians, and the heavy taxes imposed on merchants. In protest, more than a thousand men, among them the *Bazaar* merchants, took refuge in the Imam Reza's Mausoleum (the Eighth Shiite Imam) in the heart of Mashad. For four days, the police and the army refused to carry out the order to profane the holy place in order to put an end to this opposition. Finally, troops from Azerbaijan (in northeastern Iran) launched the attack, resulting in a dozen dead and hundreds of wounded. The break between the clergy and the shah was henceforth official. All those who criticized the state's repressive policy supported the clergy.

The crux of the conflict between them was of course the new judicial system. Convinced that no real change would be possible without that of the traditional judiciary—entirely under clerical control—Reza Shah did not hesitate to carry out that basic reform. Henceforth, the law required judges with university degrees. The sole knowledge of religious law (*fiqh*), as taught in the theological schools (*howzeyé elmiyeh*) of Qom or Nadjaf, was insufficient. Gradually, the clergy were removed from the courts and replaced by highly qualified judges, responsible for administering justice in the name of the state. The aim of codifying Iranian penal law was to bring it closer to laws in European countries, particularly in France, while still taking the national context into account. The penal code was thereby freed from the power of the *shariat* and the penalties it applied (flagellation, mutilation, stoning, the death penalty).

---

[22] Nonreligious school building, already begun in the nineteenth century, had quickly aroused clerical opposition. Later on, reformists and constitutionalists favored the idea of developing modern education, persuaded it would train citizens to be both free and devoted to the nation. To render the education system uniform and endow the country with competent teachers, Reza Shah committed himself to developing public schools throughout the country. *Cf.* Kasravi, *op. cit.*

The clergy, seeing the judiciary escape them, strongly denounced a new assault on their traditional privileges.[23] They then helplessly suffered the shah's massive reforms of the political and social organization of the country. Their marginalization progressed rapidly. Nonetheless, despite all Reza Shah's efforts, the anti-clerical campaign did not work as well as in Turkey. The Shiite clergy succeeded in finding underground methods for its own survival and for resisting reforms and returned victoriously to the Iranian political scene, forty years later.

In fact, the Shiite clergy are very different from the Sunnites. In Turkey (Sunni), the absence of any clerical hierarchy and economic dependence on the state weakened the clergy when the political system was modernized. The Shiite clergy, on the other hand, have a rigid hierarchy and real guild solidarity, despite the many theological differences and rivalries of custom that traverse it. Moreover, they have their invaluable economic independence, thanks to Islamic taxes (*khoms, zakat*). In Iran, these two important characteristics of the clergy give their structure a tremendous capacity for resistance. Its incredible strength makes it far more complex to impose an independent social and political organization.

This, however, did not protect the clergy from being trapped in a hitherto unprecedented situation. For the first time in the history of Shiism, politicians dared to proclaim their independence from the clergy. The legendary conservatism of the Shiite clergy could only be totally opposed to this new direction taken by the state. This antagonism left them but two choices: either to retire completely from worldly affairs, devoting themselves entirely to spiritual activity, or to unite all their forces to recover the place they had occupied at the heart of secular power.

These two choices, contrary to appearances, were closely linked. High religious dignitaries, such as the Ayatollah Boroujerdi (*Mojtahed* and source of imitation) and later on a great number of *olama* from Qom and Nadjaf, held themselves apart. They had never been interested in politics in the past. Avoiding direct conflict with the political powers, these great ayatollah preferred to devote themselves entirely

---

[23] The Iranian Civil Code, conceived in 1933, was based both on French law and on the *fiqh* (Islamic law). Its articles are based on the *fiqh*, but their definition comes particularly from French law and constitutes an interesting bit of work. It has 1335 articles. Iran's present judicial system went through great changes during the second part of the Pahlavi regime and far more drastic changes after the 1979 Iranian revolution when it returned to the *shariat*.

to the *howzeh* (religious seminaries of the Twelver Shiites). On several occasions, they failed to reply to Reza Shah's questions seeking their support despite his avowed anticlericalism. Similarly, later on, they did not reply to his son. This silence can be seen as the final proof of the integrity of these great spiritual leaders' faith, holding to the separation between the clergy and the state. But it can also be interpreted as a sign of disapproval of the Pahlavi regime. Other clergy, the Ayatollah Kashani in the lead, stopped at nothing to fight the modernizing and, above all, the anticlerical policies of the Pahlavis. All means seemed legitimate to them: inciting young clergymen to violence or decreeing the death of the intellectuals, writers, or politicians who dared to criticize Shiism or—even worse—the Shiite clergy. The situation was ambiguous because the clergy of both camps (higher clergy and radical clergy) were not so different from each other, and some of the important ayatollah could regularly be found behind the dangerous activities of the radical clergy. It must be noted that to this day hardly any of them explicitly disapproves calls to violence.

The weakening of the central government during World War II and the subsequent fall of Reza Shah gave the clergy renewed strength. Becoming more and more vindictive, they denounced the nationalist government's failures everywhere and publicized the country's problems under Reza Shah's rule. A huge body of antimodernist literature harshly criticized the reforms and called for a return to the past.[24] During a war, at a time when shortages were rampant, and while foreign influence remained a sensitive issue, this propaganda found a wide audience.

The effects of the war were destabilizing for Iran: lack of food and other basic necessities, high inflation, worsening living conditions, increasing rural exodus. The clergy took advantage of this chaotic situation to restore their power over the people. Far from satisfying themselves with the usual sermons and denunciations, the most zealous among them called for terrorism, suggesting physical attacks on those who had contributed to nationalist ideas under Reza Shah's rule.

The first thinker who drew the fire of the clergy was Ahmad Kasravi. A self-taught prolific author, he was equally severe toward the Shiite clergy and the government. A convinced partisan of democracy, his

---

[24] In particular, the first book of the Ayatollah Khomeini, *Kashf ol-asrâr* (The Discovery of Mysteries) in 1943.

positions attracted many powerful enemies, among whom was the Ayatollah Khomeini. In his excellent contribution, *The History of the Constitutional Revolution*, far from incriminating foreign countries for the failure of the first Parliament, he stressed the ambiguous part played by the clergy and the way in which they had betrayed the constitutionalists. Kasravi provides an intelligent analysis of the clergy's place in Iranian social organization, severely criticizes their love of power and their eternal desire to tame the people.

In his last book, called Shiism (*Shi'e Gari*, Tehran, 1940, still outlawed in Iran today) he analyzes Shiite beliefs point by point and reveals the means used by the clergy to maintain the people's ignorance. With sarcasm he criticizes their religious rituals as close to witchcraft. This former seminary student attacks the *mollah* and denounces their underhanded practices that take advantage of the people's naïveté. It is true that his book has certain undeniable deficiencies. He can be reproached for not seeing the spiritual riches of Shiism. Kasravi only mentions those lesser aspects common to all popular religions. He completely ignores the decisive role of Shiism in the Iranian struggle to rebuild national sovereignty after the Arab invasion. Yet, by his original approach to the concept of authority in Islam, this book goes beyond the borders of Shiism and constitutes a major event in the history of Islamic thought.

Based on primary religious sources, Kasravi questions the divine legitimacy of authority in Islam and, therefore, the heteronomy of the social order. For the first time, a thinker dared to raise this thorny question and to show the absence of any valid historical and religious reference that might justify a sacred legitimacy of social order in Islam. To the present day, nobody has yet analyzed this question with such clarity and accuracy.

Kasravi's *Shi'e Gari* caused uproar among the clergy, and the *olama* of Nadjaf accused the author of heresy. Dragged before the courts for calumny of Islam, Kasravi and one of his assistants were murdered on March 11, 1946, in the courtroom itself by partisans of Navab Safavi, a clerical extremist and founder of the terrorist organization *Fadaiyan Eslam* (The Martyrs of Islam). The tragic death of Kasravi—one among so many others—shows how the clergy react to anyone who questions their "sacred power." Far from letting themselves be marginalized, part of the clergy plotted ceaselessly to regain power.

The country's great instability during World War II revived the clergy's desire for power. It was then that the emblematic figures appeared who were later to change the course of Iranian history, such as the Ayatollah Kashani. His ambiguous positions, accompanied by unexpected U-turns, his questionable political ideas, and his negotiating talents made him one of the most dangerous men ever known in the Shiite clergy.

Born in Tehran in 1881, he rose quickly in the religious hierarchy and was noticed for his anti-British positions. In 1924, when Reza Khan thought of transforming the Qajar monarchy into a republican regime of which he naturally saw himself as the first president, Kashani was alone in supporting him. He opposed the Ayatollah Modares and other clergy who saw the Republic as a deadly threat to Islam and defended the principle of a ruling Muslim sovereign in an Islamic country such as Iran. According to them, the king is "the representative of God on earth," and he must therefore remain in place to ensure the legitimate source of the political system. At that time, the examples of Kemalist Turkey that marginalized Islam and of Russia with its Bolshevik revolution raised great concern among the clergy and the traditionalists. Although Kashani organized many demonstrations in favor of the Republic, Reza Khan finally yielded to the royalist clergy and proclaimed himself king of Iran in 1926. After that, all Kashani's efforts to draw close to the court at whatever cost ran up against the shah's deep anticlericalism.

During World War II, his anti-British positions pushed this ayatollah into the arms of Germany, and this resulted later in his being condemned to prison for complicity in war crimes. Soon after, he was forced to leave the country. In 1948, from his exile in Lebanon, Kashani opposed the creation of the State of Israel, aroused public opinion against the Israelis and raised funds for the Muslim Brotherhood of Egypt.

In 1946, when Mohammad Mossadeq launched the movement to nationalize oil, Kashani was a fervent supporter. Like the constitutionalist clergy at the beginning of the twentieth century, Kashani first encouraged the clergy and the people to support the prime minister. But shortly thereafter, he changed sides and stopped at nothing to disqualify Mossadeq and his movement. He plotted against the nationalist government, denounced its policies, and allied himself with the English and the Americans for its overthrow. Once again, the clergy's malevolence was opposed to the democratic movement in Iran.

Mossadeq: Conversion to the Nation

The postwar period was characterized by the violation of Iran's national sovereignty. Foreign occupation during World War II weighed heavily and left a bitter taste of national humiliation. The full symbolic significance of these events to the Iranian social and political scene remains unknown; yet it was decisive. With regard to specific principles, these events seemed to change little, since for decades Iran had lived through political upheavals and the encroachment of imperialist powers.

Yet, this episode was marked by a determining factor that was to redefine the balance of power both nationally and internationally. The war created a strong demand for energy supplies that reversed the market equilibrium and revealed one burning issue: oil.

Iran's realization of its oil wealth changed both *the way of being* and *the mode of collective functioning*. To the awakening of nationalist feeling under Reza Shah was added the possession of major oil reserves. The importance of the country's natural resources added a new dimension to its national identity. Henceforth, it was not only the issue of ensuring the sovereignty of an endangered nation but that of exalting its global role.

Belonging to a doubly fortunate nation—historically and economically—made Iranians prouder than ever, but also evermore sensitive to the massive presence of foreign forces on their territory. They saw themselves as a sovereign community that should not be subjected to foreign rule or administration. After the fall of Reza Shah, public opinion expressed strong disapproval of the compromises politicians had made to the world powers. It blamed those among them who failed to free Iran from foreign intervention. During the instability of the Pahlavi regime and the crumbling of royalist authority, responsibility for ensuring national sovereignty no longer belonged to the king but to the people who, identifying themselves with the state, demanded that the latter carry out their will.

In this respect, the prime minister, Mohammad Mossadeq, expressed the will of the entire people, who burned to assert their independence. But his nationalism bore a modern significance. It implied representation and had no need to be founded on a metaphysical principle. By his success in seizing the Iranian oil industry from the hands of the English, Mossadeq symbolized the nation's capacity to rid itself of foreigners and to assert its sovereignty, independent of any outside aid and *a fortiori* of transcendence. The shah, as the representative of God on earth, no longer belonged at the head of the nation.

Yet, Mossadeq was far from realizing that the more his nationalist policies strengthened the nation, the less useful the shah was to the country. For his part, the shah understood to what extent a nationalist government with a prime minister strongly supported by the people could threaten his throne. Mossadeq's nationalism gave the nation its developed form, capable of directly uniting its citizens. From then on, the country needed a power that would represent its fundamental unity and wanted this power to exist. It needed a power coming from the people and existing by and for the people. The country governed by Mossadeq called for a regime that combined authority and freedom, without any figurehead incarnating transcendence.

The height of his contradiction was that Mossadeq saw himself as a monarchist. But as soon as he succeeded in nationalizing the oil industry, the Iranians became aware of their ability to assert themselves globally without a monarchy. What was the alternative, once the monarchic system was excluded in principle? What good was a monarchy, authoritarian into the bargain, for a nation that wanted only representative power? Once Mossadeq could no longer bring the people's movement toward new horizons, his very success foretold his failure: the coup d'état of 1953, a desperate attempt by the old monarchic order to prevent the leap into modernity.

If Mossadeq meant to free the country from the old religious machinery, he also intended to enclose it in a royal framework. The result was a hybrid doctrine, attempting to rebuild the monarchy on secular and (unconsciously) democratic foundations. This is the only explanation for the surprising contrast between the vast audience gained by his nationalist action and the swiftness with which he then lost all his support. He simply found no way to overcome his own contradictions. The fact is that royalty can no more support itself on a nation than the latter can be defined only by a king.

Despite his tragic destiny, Mossadeq succeeded in one further step: the radical conversion of the political organization to the nation form. Nationalizing oil was the major event that gave meaning to the existence of a nation that yearned to assert its autonomy. This autonomy was thus able to modernize the traditionalist camp. The Iranian oil crisis opened the door to a new kind of nationalism, on the scale of a political movement. A nationalism that not only ensured the nation's sovereignty but also became the cornerstone of a social order that constituted a powerful alternative to the monarchic system.

These were the circumstances that made oil nationalization a crucial stake. They put an end to the era of foreign interventions and destabilized the very principle of the monarchy. Nationalism continued to grow in scope and in strength, in opinion and in fact. It was seen as the political shape of collective sovereignty. It became simultaneously the means of unifying a country torn by internal strife and the vector of political emancipation from domination by foreign powers. Everything in this crystallizing episode was played out symbolically.

The Protagonists of Oil Nationalization

Throughout the nationalization process, Mossadeq had simultaneously to heal internal tensions and to resist external threats. At the time, the old monarchic and religious image of society no longer enjoyed its habitual legitimacy, and there was great divergence between the nationalists and the communists. On the other hand, there was distinct complicity between the clergy and foreign powers, and all this weighed on the prime minister.

The Iranian ideological situation was divided into three main forces. On the extreme right, the clergy, deeply conservative and opposed to any change; on the extreme left, the communists, who wanted a total overthrow of society but who could not act independently from the Soviets; between the two, the nationalists, who refused to completely erase the past but who wanted essential reforms in political and societal organization. Added to this scenario was a monarchy, far stronger than suspected, and Western, particularly British, intervention, in the Cold War context.

Mossadeq's path was beset with failures and setbacks that confirmed the resistance to reform of the Iranian religious structure. It was naïve to think that oil nationalization would have a spontaneous contagious effect that would sweep away the old political and religious order. This gravely underestimated the strength of the monarchic and religious forces. Their overthrow could only be envisaged at the end of a long, slow, and gradual process.

From this standpoint, Mossadeq was wrong in 1952 in not sufficiently realizing the ambiguous game of the clergy in that complex episode. In the debris of the Second World War, and during the progress of oil nationalization, there was a phenomenon of public opinion that the clergy knew how to manipulate, proving their unequalled mastery in that art. Faced with the misfortunes that Iran suffered, their primary target was communism. The fascination of the elite for Marxism strengthened the clergy's determination to combat communism. No holds were barred in fighting it and its supposed allies. The clergy falsely denounced Mossadeq's supposed pro-Soviet leanings and took advantage of every possible occasion to undermine his popularity, sowing doubts in public opinion.

Despite these obstacles and the frustrations that made this situation so difficult to decipher, nationalist fervor did not weaken. The divergent interests between a nationalist prime minister on the one side, and the communists, British, and clergy on the other, aroused keen tensions. Compromises and alliances were constantly being made and unmade between Mossadeq and his adversaries. The scope of the conflict engendered makes it impossible to view it merely as a passing difficulty of adjustment. The intellectual and political shock provoked by those three long years that it took to nationalize oil, from the end of 1949 to the coup d'état of 1953, deserve a detailed study.

The Communists

Communist presence in Iranian politics began with the fall of Reza Shah in August 1941. At that time, the occupation of national territory by foreign forces already had spectacular consequences. Twenty years of dictatorship were ended, political prisoners were freed, and the way was opened for the clergy to preach against reforms, secularization, and communism. Censorship was abolished, and the press began to denounce the Pahlavi regime. The presence of foreign forces on Iranian soil also led to serious shortages. Cereal in the north was requisitioned for the Soviet Union, and bread was unavailable. Riots broke out in several cities. In this chaotic context, northern Iran, close to Russia, became the center of Marxist propaganda and many political groups were created.

In September, 1941, the communist Tudeh party was officially founded. In the absence of a strong government, dissident political activities developed, and the Tudeh became particularly active. A few years later, in 1944, it took part in parliamentary elections, and eight of its candidates were elected. The number of party members continued to grow, and this party became one of the major forces in Iranian political life.[25]

---

[25] In 1949, the party was banned for a failed attempt to assassinate Mohammed-Reza Shah. It continued to function underground for a time before being once again legalized during the 1950s. For a complete analysis, see the next chapter.

Many nonreligious intellectuals placed their hopes in communism, which represented both a political and an ideological legitimacy. Contrary to the 1900s, when British-type parliamentarianism was the apex of progress, the elite were now inflamed by the "revolutionary internationalism" of the communist party. But the Tudeh's systematic pro-Soviet positions at the expense of national interests, particularly with regard to oil, destabilized its sympathizers and weakened the party, faced with the rising strength of nationalist demands. These openly pro-Soviet stands, added to the military presence of the Soviet Union in the north, on the one hand, and the British control of oil production in the south, on the other, created disturbances throughout the country and harmed communist credibility in Iran.[26] Tudeh's treachery was spoken of,[27] and even its most zealous partisans found it difficult to follow their leaders' instructions.

The confrontation between Mossadeq and the Tudeh began in September 1944, when Parliament rejected the Soviet request to explore the northern oil fields. Up to several months before the coup d'état of 1953, serious differences opposed communists and nationalists on the oil issue. The latter refused any concession to the Soviets so long as Iran did not wholly control its resources. In that same year of 1944, Mossadeq passed a draft law in Parliament forbidding any negotiation with foreigners on questions linked to the oil industry without the preliminary agreement of the deputies. Mossadeq defended the principle of "negative balance," that would later become the corner stone of his foreign policy.

> What I said is in the interest of our country, that seeks its political balance. If we follow the "positive balance" theory of the Tudeh,

---

[26] In December, 1945, the Azerbaijan Democratic Party (*fergheh-yé démocrate*) announced the creation of an autonomous republic named Government of the People of Azerbaijan. At the same time, the Kurdish autonomist movement created the Republic of Mahabad in Iranian Kurdistan. These two autonomous republics had the support of the USSR, and Soviet troops occupied northern Iran. At the same time, other Soviet troops prevented Iranian national forces from returning to Azerbaijan and Kurdistan. Under the joint pressure of the United States, Great Britain, and the UN, the Soviets finally obtained a concession and accepted the departure of their troops from Iranian territory. In December, 1946, the Iranian army conquered Azerbaijan and Kurdistan, whose republican governments were crushed without Moscow's support. Soviet influence was still further lessened in 1947, when Iran and the United States signed a military agreement: from then on, the Americans trained the Iranian army and Washington began to directly influence Tehran. This episode took place at the start of the Cold War. See: *Encyclopædia Iranica, op. cit.*
[27] The expression *Hézbé kha'ené Tudeh* (the traitor Tudeh party) became so common from then on that it was taken up and used ironically by Tudeh members themselves.

we shall be obliged to cede the oil concession in the north to the Soviets for the next ninety-two years. Without mentioning the fact that Iranians are definitely against this and that Parliament is totally opposed to any concessions, the "positive balance" theory is like a one-armed person who accepts that his only remaining arm be torn off in order to create a balance.[28]

Mossadeq's strategy was to cease granting new concessions to foreigners so as to gain time for planning the nationalization of oil in the south, then under British control. As soon as Moscow's proposal was rejected, the Tudeh rose up against the government and organized a pro-Soviet demonstration in Tehran. Since all foreign countries had a sphere of influence in Iran, Tudeh proposed giving the Soviet Union what it wanted. The party's daily, *Mardom*, claimed this clearly:

> If the American government wants to be strongly engaged in postwar politics and to implant its industries in the oil fields of Baluchistan (southwestern Iran), then it is completely natural, from the standpoint of international politics, that the northern oil fields be under Soviet control.

According to the Tudeh, Mossadeq's "negative balance" was unjust. It permitted Western powers to maintain their position in Iran and refused access to oil only to the Soviets. The absolute support of the Tudeh to the interests of a foreign country, to the detriment of national interests, exposed it to virulent criticism. By pleading for "positive balance," the Tudeh placed itself on the side of those whom the Iranians then considered "foreign mercenaries."

When, in 1949, nationalizing the oil industry became a major stake, the Tudeh showed itself once again unable to pick up the gauntlet. In April, 1951, after nationalizing the British Petroleum Company (BP), Mossadeq was elected prime minister by Parliament. It was a critical moment in the nation's history. The Tudeh began this period by committing another error concerning the balance of power. The party leaders failed to understand the dynamics of the situation that opened the door to a new wave of nationalism and of patriotism.

---

[28] Parliamentary Proceedings, 16th *Majles, Ettella'at*, July 4, 1950.

Oil nationalization placed Mossadeq's cabinet in direct conflict with London.[29] Just when the prime minister was fighting the British and their accomplices inside the country, the Tudeh analyzed the situation from the standpoint of Soviet-American rivalries. From the start of nationalization, it denounced an imperialist policy, suggesting that nationalization should be limited to the south of the country. In June, 1950, *Mardom* wrote:

> We are not sure that revising the oil contract with the British is for the good of Iranians. So long as our people cannot determine its destiny, it will be unable to profit from its rights to its oil resources.

Even the rejection of the American proposal by Mossadeq in July, 1950, did not convince the party of the anti-imperialist nature of the nationalist movement. When in 1951, the nationalization of oil was speeded up, the Tudeh was already an influential party and especially supported by workers. It had a far-reaching military organization with intelligence networks within the army. The party could mobilize tens of thousands of people for mass demonstrations in Tehran. Its power was impressive, and it played a major part in trade union organizations. At the same time, its popularity with intellectuals was remarkable and many writers, journalists, and artists supported it.

Tudeh's positions toward oil nationalization were, to say the least, contradictory. At first opposed to nationalization, in defense of Soviet interests, it changed completely after Mossadeq's resignation in July, 1952, and the bloody rebellion that followed. Gradually the party lined up with the nationalists. Nonetheless, in 1953, despite its military organization and its huge capacity to mobilize the masses, the Tudeh did not stand up to the putschists. It seemed paralyzed in that situation and completely inefficient. It had been informed of the preparation of

---

[29] But not necessarily with United States interests, or a least not yet. Initially, the Americans, under a Democratic administration, had a number of differences with the British, both concerning the way the situation was managed and on the question of benefit-sharing with American oil companies. The policy of the Truman administration, developed by the secretary of state, Dean Acheson, was to try to appease the British, while attempting to convince Mossadeq to accept a compromise. Mossadeq, very aware of these differences, tried to use them for the benefit of Iran. The presence of pro-American figures, like Ali Amini and General Zahedi in Mossadeq's cabinet, is the proof. These men supported Mossadeq when he got along with the Americans but abandoned him when he disagreed with them. Zahedi led the coup d'état and took Mossadeq's place at the head of the government.

the plot, thanks to its intelligence network in the army, in particular in the Division of the Imperial Guard—which was the prime instigator of the coup d'état. It even warned the prime minister. But instead of joining him in a common cause, the Tudeh tried to overthrow the monarchy and to set up a democratic people's republic. On August 18, 1953, unable to trust the communists, Mossadeq ordered them to cease their demonstrations against the regime. He thought he could control the situation alone. The Tudeh agreed and recalled its activists, leaving the streets to the army. Thus, on the day of the coup d'état, the party remained completely passive. Following Mossadeq's request, the Tudeh renounced all resistance at the most critical moment and left the prime minister alone to cope with the putschists. To this day, the reasons why the Tudeh's military organization failed to act against the coup d'état remain a complete mystery.[30]

The Tudeh's retreat was so sudden and the imperial regime's victory so complete that several years later, the party no longer presented the least threat to the regime. Since then, questions on Tudeh's inaction when faced with the coup d'état have haunted the communist movement, raising countless queries as to the causes and motivations that led to such a strategic defeat.

In July 1957, at the party's historic Plenary in Moscow, young activists criticized the Tudeh:

> The erroneous positions concerning the oil industry's nationalization (at the start of the movement) as well as the passive policies regarding the National Front and Mossadeq's government were the monumental errors of our party during the period preceding the 1953 coup d'état. The party's position on the issue was based on an incorrect evaluation of the situation, linking oil nationalization to the opposition between the two imperialist powers, the American and the English.[31]

The party recognized its mistakes. Terming its attitude toward the nationalist government "sectarian" and "leftist," it admitted that the

---

[30] The party's assertion that its capacities had been limited in no way explained its inaction. Even if the Tudeh had been unable to overthrow the regime or to avoid the coup d'état, it might still have resisted its own destruction. The true reasons for what Tudeh later called "the strategic defeat" cannot be understood so long as the relational substance of the party and its internal structure remain unknown to us. The fourth chapter of this book is devoted entirely to the communist movement and will discuss this point further.

[31] See: *Encyclopædia Iranica, op. cit.* See also: Khosrow Shakeri (ed.), *Asnad-e tarikhi-ye jonbesh-e kargari, social delokrasi va komonisti-ye Iran* (Historical documents on the communist movement and the social democratic workers in Iran), vol. 1, Florence, Mazdak, 1974, p. 364.

demonstrations during which statues of the shah were thrown down were political errors. The party acknowledged its paralysis and blamed its leaders. It reproached them for their weakness, their lack of democratic spirit, their detachment from the grass roots, and their lack of theoretical knowledge. Overall, the episode revealed the existence of deep disagreements among the leaders at that time.

The British

Although part of the Iranian elite had begun to act in favor of nationalizing the oil fields at the start of the 1930s, this movement only came to the forefront and gained real support from 1944 on. The roots of the conflict, however, went further back than that. As of 1909, a large part of the Persian Gulf oil reserves were exploited by the British and exported directly to the United Kingdom. The Anglo-Iranian Oil Company (AIOC),[32] in the hands of the British government, sold Iranian oil and refused to share its earnings fairly with Iran. The incomprehensibility of AIOC accounts annoyed the Iranians, who spoke of "looting."[33] Toward the end of the Second World War, this feeling of being robbed incited a nationalist reaction. Intellectuals of all fields lined up under the banner of Mohammad Mossadeq, an influential parliamentarian, and several years later the National Front (*Jebhéy-e Melli*) was created. Its principal aim was to nationalize the AIOC. This party proved particularly adept at embodying the need for Iranian political representation and in uniting the peoples' national elites.

In September, 1944, the Americans and the Soviets tried to negotiate oil concessions in northern Iran. But in December, after Mossadeq's passionate opposition, Parliament passed a law refusing the ratification of all oil contracts with foreigners before the end of the war. The United States returned to its isolation, leaving the British and the Soviets to their usual manipulations. This law aroused a strong reaction from Iranian communists sympathetic to the Soviet Union and from the largely Azeri populations in the northern provinces who saw Moscow's demand to exploit local oil fields as favorable to them. In this zone,

---

[32] The Anglo-Persian Oil Company (APOC) was founded in 1909, after the discovery of a huge oil deposit in Masjed Soleyman, in Iran, on May 26, 1908. It was the first company to exploit oil reserves in the Middle East. The APOC became the Anglo-Iranian Oil Company (AIOC) en 1935, then the British Petroleum Company in 1954. See: *Encyclopædia Iranica, op. cit.*

[33] Because of the devaluation of the sterling, the royalties paid by the AIOC after the war, amounted only to 9 percent of the value of the oil exported, as against 33 percent in 1933. Public opinion demanded a review of the 1933 agreement, which it knew would henceforth benefit the British treasury more than it would Iran. *Ibid.*

occupied by the Soviets, communist propaganda was rampant, and trade union organizations flourished everywhere.

At this time, the Cold War was already underway, and the United States and the Soviet Union were in active competition. The victory of the Chinese revolution in 1949, and the start of the Korean War in July 1950, increased the intensity of independence movements in several parts of the world. In Iran, the situation was different. Without ever having been colonized, the country was fed up with foreign interventions that had persisted for 150 years. It now engaged in a fight to control its national resources. If it faced Moscow in the north, the main battle was in the south, where it opposed one of its oldest imperialist powers, Great Britain.

The nationalization of oil materialized the will of the vast majority of Iranians, in continuation of the objectives of the 1906 constitutional revolution. It embodied all their hopes and rapidly symbolized national pride. Henceforth, everything that opposed this was considered treason.[34]

In April, 1951, the new government, with Mohammad Mossadeq as prime minister, adopted an anti-British line, closing their consulates and expelling British personnel from the oil company. The conflict was begun by the refusal of BP to allow the Iranian government oversight of its accounts to determine whether or not it received the royalties it was due. Given the intransigence of the oil company, the nationalist government escalated its demands and claimed an equal share of the profits. The crisis finally came when BP interrupted its operations rather than accept the government's demands. One month after having been named prime minister, Mossadeq passed a law authorizing the government to exploit the oil resources of its own country. He thus nationalized BP, announced the expropriation of its assets and annulled the oil concession that would normally have ended in 1993. In a memorable speech before Parliament, Mossadeq declared:

> Long years of negotiations with foreign countries have served no purpose. The Iranian state prefers to control its own oil production. Thanks to the nationalization of the British company,[35] we can combat

---

[34] The assassination of General Razmara, the prime minister chosen by Mohammed-Reza Shah in 1950, illustrates this. In a long speech before Parliament, Razmara said that nothing was more dangerous for the country than a total nationalization of the oil industry. Shortly thereafter, he was assassinated by the Islamist terrorist group Fadayan Eslam. This had no effect whatever on the Iranians. See: *Encyclopædia Iranica, op. cit.*

[35] The current appellation in Iran of the British Petroleum Company.

> corruption in our country. Our oil profits will enable us to review our entire budget and to fight poverty, sickness and underdevelopment. Another important point, we will now be able to preserve our international interests from foreign influence. The British company has nothing more to do in our country, save to return its assets to their true owners.

Relations between the two countries then fell dizzily. Tehran forbade London to make the slightest engagement in the Iranian oil industry, and London in return blocked the sale of Iranian oil and oil products worldwide. In July, 1951, BP repatriated its technicians and closed its oil installations in Iran. The British government decreed a total blockade of Iran, reinforced its naval forces in the Persian Gulf, and registered a complaint against Iran with the Security Council of the United Nations. It also threatened to sanction purchasers of oil products from Iran.

In October, before the Security Council, Mossadeq in person pleaded the cause of nationalization, questioning the privileges of a European nation. An eloquent parliamentarian and a man of conviction, he succeeded in convincing the council to remit the file to the International Court of The Hague. He had to wait until July, 1952, for the court's successful decision: it declared itself incompetent in a conflict opposing a private company and a state. Mossadeq's success fired the Iranians, thrilled to finally flout European imperialist powers. Meanwhile, he had to face a major political crisis in Tehran.

The importance of oil nationalization can in no way be compared to the economic difficulties and political disorders that followed. The latter fade before the highly symbolic scope of this event's bearing on the country's national identity.

Indeed, after the departure of the BP technicians, the whole Iranian oil industry suffered from a lack of competent personnel and was no longer able to reach its annual production objectives. Production crumbled, going from 241 million barrels in 1950 to ten million in 1952. This crisis entirely eliminated oil revenues. Without money, the government was unable to continue the reforms it had begun. Yet, the prime minister was more popular than ever. He was the obvious head of the nationalist movement, and he persuaded his partisans that the radical road was the only one worthwhile.

Politically, it is not difficult to understand the reasons for Mossadeq's tremendous popular success, despite the catastrophic economic circumstances. In his favor were simplicity, clarity, and the obvious radicalism of his proposal. His entire movement can be summed up in one line: a strong and autonomous nation is the remedy for all the nation's ills.

Nonetheless, Mossadeq remained a monarchist in the strongest sense of the word. On every possible occasion, he reaffirmed his total fidelity to the shah's person and to the monarchy as an institution. He was far from realizing to what extent the modern nation to which he gave birth was revolutionary. He did not see how much this modern nation with its growing capacity to assert its independence from the hierarchical, monarchic, and traditional order, was incompatible with a royal personification. Contrary to Mossadeq, the shah clearly saw the danger represented, on one side, by the infinite potential of an autonomous nation to render null and void his heteronymous royal edifice and, on the other, its essential need to be governed by a power that represented it. The Shah could then only oppose his nationalist prime minister.

Rapidly, tensions increased in Parliament. Given the spectacular decline of oil revenues, the conservative deputies refused to finance the government's projects to solve the economic crisis. In July, 1952, when he presented his cabinet, the prime minister insisted on his constitutional right to choose his minister of defense, but the shah opposed him. More powerful than ever, Mossadeq was a threat. At the height of his glory, he was the vector of the emergence of a modern nation that refused authority and aspired to freedom. The shah sought to eliminate him from the political scene. Mossadeq was obliged to resign. He addressed the people directly, calling for support: "in such circumstances, the Iranian nation's (*mellat-e Iran*) struggle for independence can end only in victory."[36]

The shah then chose a veteran of Iranian politics, Ahmad Qavam, to head the government. On the day he was named, Qavam declared his readiness to renew negotiations with the British. These declarations aroused intense frustration on the part of the Iranians who had believed the promises of the outgoing nationalist prime minister. Nationalist fever crystallized around him, to the great chagrin of the shah and his allies. The Ayatollah Kashani strongly opposed the new prime minister whom he attacked in a public letter: "Qavam must know that the people will not submit to his colonialist policy. It is not by terrorizing people that he will manage to govern. If need be, I shall

---

[36] Ervand Abrahamian, *Iran Between Two Revolutions*, Princeton, Princeton University Press, 1983, p. 270.

call Iranians to a holy war (the *jihad*) against all foreigners and their mercenaries who want to steal our country's assets and endanger its independence."[37]

In a press communiqué, Kashani directly threatened the shah: "If, before forty-eight hours, Mossadeq has not regained power, I decree holy war." As soon as this was published, the people took to the streets. In turn, the intellectuals, the nationalists, the parties of the left—including the Tudeh party—called for a national strike and organized demonstrations in favor of the former prime minister. The movement reached all Iran's big cities and Tehran's *Bazaar* remained closed. More than two hundred and fifty demonstrators were killed or seriously wounded by the soldiers. After a five-day national strike, on *Sie-Tir* day,[38] the military left Tehran and abandoned the capital to the opposition. Fearful of losing his throne, the shah dismissed Qavam and recalled Mossadeq, accepting his terms. He granted him, in particular, total control of the army.

The triumphal return of Mossadeq to power coincided with the International Court of The Hague's decision in favor of the nationalization of Iranian oil. This double victory resulted in a spectacular rise in popularity and the massive support of Parliament. In this strong position, Mossadeq had full authority to carry out his reforms. His plan, rational and fair, to reorganize the political system, was approved by many Iranians, who saw in it the logical conclusion of what they had just lived through. As soon as he returned to his post, his will for reform asserted itself. Ministers began to work, and the administrative structure was transformed. Mossadeq gave substance to his dream of breaking with the old political and social organization. During the end of 1952, reforms progressed so rapidly that the assault against conservatism seemed fairly launched.

The Tudeh that until then had not ceased to fight the nationalist movement, changed its strategy and sought to form a coalition with Mossadeq's National Front. From then on, not only the Ayatollah Kashani—elected president of the Parliament—and his disciples, but also the Tudeh leaders, lined up behind the prime minister. The latter remained, however, very distrustful, and his relations with them were extremely strained. A great patriot and a firm defender of private

---

[37] *Ibid.*

[38] *Sie-Tir* corresponds to the thirtieth day of the month of Tir in the Persian calendar (July 21, 1952). This event is inscribed in the Iranian collective memory as The Sie-Tir Rebellion (*Qyam-e Sie-Tir*).

property, he rejected Tudeh's communism and its pro-Soviet positions. This did not prevent him from being a socialist despite himself. The social issue lay at the heart of his concerns, and he constantly fought inequalities.[39] Like his constitutionalist predecessors, Mossadeq was in love with justice and believed that without a powerful judicial system, no social progress was possible in the country.

Mossadeq therefore concentrated on strengthening the elective political institutions. He limited the nonconstitutional powers of the shah. Not only was the shah's personal budget limited, but he was forbidden to contact foreign diplomats directly. The prime minister transferred royal property to the state and succeeded in distancing from the political scene the shah's invasive and unpleasant sister, Ashraf Pahlavi. In January, 1953, he decreed the agrarian reform that established village councils and increased the portion of agricultural revenues that went to the peasants. This measure, harmful to landed proprietors, strongly destabilized Iranian feudalism.

Mossadeq's initiatives tended to sap the religious foundation of the monarchy and to place it on secular bases. Although he considered himself conservative and royalist, he clashed both with the shah and the clergy. His reforms disturbed not only the dynasty and the British: The clergy, for their part, saw nothing more threatening to their "divine royalty." By modernizing the country's political organization, Mossadeq frightened the defenders of the old order, thereby uniting the clergy, the monarchists, and the British.

The Clergy

Mossadeq's reelection thus accelerated the country's liberalization. The first to react were the *olama*, those great landowner lords. For several centuries the resources from their estates enabled them to maintain their economic independence from the state. The agrarian reform hit them forcibly, causing a colossal fall of their financial revenues. This ambitious project, also called for by the communists, ran directly counter to the interests of the great landowners, who had always held the majority in Parliament.

The great Ayatollah Boroujerdi, the principal religious authority at that time, who had always avoided any involvement in politics, then decided to categorically oppose the prime minister's agrarian reform

---

[39] Contrary to most Iranian politicians, Mossadeq paid his taxes very scrupulously and he became one of the most important taxpayers of Iran.

program, under the pretext of defending the sacred right to private property. When, several months later, the coup d'état took place, the Ayatollah Boroujerdi did not raise a finger to support Mossadeq against the putschists.

His silence could in no way be seen as a refusal to enter politics. On the contrary, it signaled his hostility to the nationalist prime minister. This hostility did not go unnoticed by those faithful to that great Shiite "source of imitation." The Ayatollah Kashani, who until then, as leader of Parliament, had served the nationalist government, realized the threats the agrarian reforms signified for his financial interests and his estates. He changed sides and began to denounce Mossadeq as vehemently as he had praised him before. It was the end of the alliance between the two.

To tell the truth, Kashani, a proud and ambitious man, had never really been able to accept the prime minister's immense popularity nor his intransigent radicalism. For his part, Mossadeq had little esteem for this manipulative cleric and had never supported his political maneuvers. Kashani fiercely criticized Mossadeq. He began a vast campaign of defamation, pointing out the Tudeh's support of the government, a support that would soon be seen as lacking. The ayatollah exaggerated the power of the Communist party, insisting on the great danger that its pro-Soviet positions represented for the country. Part of the population was frightened and convinced by this, and Kashani was quickly able to discredit the prime minister's action.

The situation lent itself to demonstrations of popular discontent. People were worn down by hardship. Poverty increased constantly. The landed proprietors and the great merchants, whose affairs stagnated, were also affected by the oil embargo, so that they hardly supported the government's radical line. Many became impatient and wanted a quick solution to the country's political and economic problems. Despite all this, Mossadeq remained popular, and the majority of Iranians were proud to have a man of his stature at the head of the government.

This was not the first time that the Iranian economy was in a bad way. Under the reign of the last three Qajar kings, save for a few rare and brief periods of prosperity, the country had gone through numerous economic difficulties. The novelty here was the communist presence. For the first time, Iranians found themselves faced with an antireligious ideology. It came, moreover, from a neighboring country with which Iran had a long history of political conflict and bloody wars. Hostile to the Muslim religion, indifferent to national sovereignty, the Tudeh party's communism[40] scarcely attracted the sympathy of believers. Far from it, it terrorized them. The Ayatollah Kashani relied on that fear of communism to undermine Mossadeq's popularity and to poison public opinion. Fear unleashed passionate reactions from a people strongly attached to its religion.

Mossadeq lost part of his popular base, his reforms began to fray, and the number of his enemies increased. Several members of his coalition turned against him.[41] The Tudeh, very divided, proved unable to play an active part in events. Nonetheless, despite all the plots against his government, Mossadeq still inspired confidence; many people believed in his sincerity, and the middle class continued to support him. The clergy, despite their skillful use of denunciation and defamation, were unable, alone, to destroy his authority. Nothing, however, stopped them from plotting against him with the English.

The Coup d'État

Mossadeq did not only annoy the clergy and the royalists. His radical actions particularly annoyed London, who never got over the loss of control of the Iranian oil industry. Their failure in that affair made them aware of the Iranians' strong anti-British feelings. Hence their desire to induce the Americans to safeguard their interests. Disappointed by the decision of the International Court of The Hague in favor of nationalization, and unable to solve this conflict alone, the United Kingdom called for the help of the United States. Washington, however, hesitated to reply favorably. The American minister, Dean Acheson, was critical, reproaching the British for their actions in Iran. He accused them of wanting to destroy the country.

Once present in Middle Eastern affairs, the Americans looked with suspicion on the English presence in Iran. The sudden occupation of that country during World War II had been undertaken without consulting Washington. The British had decided alone to arrest a number of Iranians whom they suspected of collaboration with the Germans. The United Kingdom thought it could, as in the good old days, fill the government with those members of the Iranian oligarchy whom

---

[40] The next chapter is devoted entirely to the analysis of this subject.

[41] Among whom are Mozaffar Baghaï, the pro-British head of the workers' party (*hezb-e zahmatkeshan-e iran*); Hossein Makki, one of the most distinguished heirs of Mossadeq, turned against him. See: *Encyclopædia Iranica, op. cit.*

it trusted. In January, 1942, England, the Soviet Union and Iran had signed a three-party treaty by whose terms the occupying powers committed themselves to respect the country's national integrity, to pay the costs of its troops, and to withdraw, at the latest, six months after the war's end. Despite Iran's insistence, during this Allied occupation, Washington refused to approve this agreement, avoiding intervention outside its own sphere of influence, unwilling to infringe on that of the English. Roosevelt judged, however, that the defense of Iran was vital for American interests; thus his country, without any formal alliance, supported Tehran. Many experts were sent to reorganize the Iranian army, the police, the gendarmerie, public health services, internal transportation, as well as the Ministry of Finance. The avowed aim of this cooperation was to link Iran to American interests.

Clearly, the Soviets did not appreciate an American presence in neighboring Iran. They were all the more concerned when they learned that, despite the war, Tehran was discretely approaching American oil companies with the intention of exploiting oil resources in northern Iran. The Soviets' concerns increased when it appeared that, at the same time, the English were trying to obtain new concessions.

After the Second World War, several factors contributed to a change in American policy in Iran. Both Iranian anti-British feelings and their strong mistrust of their communist neighbor favored the American entrance on the scene as a third mediating power. At the same time, in the specific Cold War situation, the fear of communism played an essential part, drawing more closely together the English and the Americans. General Eisenhower's election in 1953 marked a major turning point in Washington's Middle Eastern policy. From then on, the United States actively intervened in Iranian internal affairs.

The English resentment of Mossadeq, as victims of his oil nationalization, was immense. Despite the open hostility of the Iranian prime minister to communism, the British managed to convince their American allies that he was throwing his country into the arms of the Soviets. Both countries then unanimously condemned Mossadeq's policy, deeming it dangerous for their own interests as well as for those of the entire international community. They cited the threat of Soviet influence in Iran and pointed to the close relations of the Tudeh with the government. Meanwhile, many of the clergy, with the Ayatollah Kashani at their head, became aware that they could not fight Mossadeq alone. They did not hesitate to approach the English and the Americans to convince them that they could control the people's reaction if the prime minister were ousted. At the same time, in their sermons, they denounced ever more strongly the communist ideas that, according to them, lay behind the national reforms.

History repeated itself: with the clergy's blessings, a coup d'état was organized by the British and American secret services so as to make Mossadeq leave the government.[42] Royalists and clergy lined up under the banner of foreign countries to block the radical nationalism that had created the nation in its modern form—a nation greatly threatening to their material interests. Their aim was to weaken it and render it submissive to the monarchy.

On August 15, 1953, the shah, assured of American support, signed an imperial decree, ousting Mossadeq. This text, illegal since it lacked Parliament's agreement, was delivered by the commander of the Imperial Guard. Mossadeq had him immediately arrested. The shah, thinking he had failed, fled the country. Yet, the publication of the imperial decree in the press destabilized the government. Less than a year after the massive demonstrations in favor of the prime minister, the streets remained desperately empty. Popular support was no longer there. The clergy's anticommunist propaganda had succeeded in troubling public opinion. Nobody really understood what was happening.

On August 18, Operation Ajax was launched—a secret operation led by the United Kingdom and the United States, carried out by the CIA. Nothing less than a putsch. General Zahedi arrested Mossadeq and his partisans and proclaimed himself prime minister. A few days later, the shah returned to Iran.[43] Mohammad Mossadeq was condemned to three years imprisonment, after which he would be placed under house arrest in his native village under the surveillance of the shah's secret police. He remained there until his death in March 1967.

Nor did Tudeh members escape the dictatorship that was put in place. The five years of martial law that followed the 1953 coup d'état were fatal to the party. In 1954, the new regime attacked its military

---

[42] Barack Obama was the first American president to recognize his government's implication and to apologize for it in a speech addressed to the Muslim community on June 4, 2009: "In the midst of the Cold War, the United States played a part in the overthrow of a democratically elected Iranian government." Under President Clinton's administration in 2000, Secretary of State Madeleine Albright had already officially admitted the role played by the United States in the organization and financing of the 1953 coup d'état. *Cf. Encyclopædia Iranica, op. cit.*

[43] The head of the Ajax operation was Kermit Roosevelt, a senior CIA agent and grandson of a former president of the United States, Theodore Roosevelt. By restoring the shah to the throne, the object was to preserve Western interests in exploiting Iranian oil reserves. *Ibid.*

branch, the Communist Imperial Army Officers Organization. Its leader Khosro Rouzbeh and twelve high-ranking officers were executed. Many others were imprisoned, and some took refuge in the Soviet Union—where they were subsequently liquidated by the Soviets. The Communist Officers Organization was completely destroyed, and the Tudeh was weaker than ever. The party then lost its social basis, as well as many leaders and members. Divisions arose, and the leadership was accused of working against the grass roots.

In 1957, the creation of the secret police—the *Savak*, a Persian acronym for the National Organization of Security and Intelligence—under the command of Teymour Bakhtyar, a soldier known for his brutality, provided the regime with an instrument of terror that had a deep effect on the population. The Savak was charged with surveillance and repression in the name of state security. It was put in place with the help of the American Secret Service and the Mossad. Its agents were responsible to the shah alone, and no law controlled them. Soon opposition parties were declared illegal. Members of the terrorist group Fadaiyan Eslam—the same that had assassinated the progressive writer, Kasravi—were eliminated, and their chief, Navab Safavi, was executed.[44] Even the Ayatollah Kashani, who had plotted to overthrow Mossadeq, did not escape the repression. He was gradually eliminated from politics. In 1962, he died of cancer. The disappearance of this ambitious cleric, who wanted to be not only the Iranian religious leader but also that of the Muslims of the entire world, went completely unnoticed.

Two years after the Tudeh's elimination, the underground national resistance movement (which also included communists) was disbanded, and its members were arrested. Save for a few intellectuals who attempted to take advantage of the regime's internal divisions to have some reforms accepted, no other dissident voice was heard. The shah's regime fully embraced police repression. The page of political liberalization that Iran had known during Mossadeq's time had been definitively turned back.

Undoubtedly, Mossadeq's vacillation between two opposing worlds of thought constituted an important factor in his fall. Both a convinced

---

[44] Seen by Ali Khameney (Supreme Guide of the Revolution and Khomeini's successor) as the true precursor of the revolution, Navab Safavi is considered by the Islamic Republic as a martyr and a hero of Islam. A subway station of Tehran bears his name.

monarchist and a revolutionary nationalist, he was torn by two mutually contradictory logics. His respect for hierarchy and the monarchy were linked to his love of country, but this love was accompanied by a socialist vision of collective organization with features traditionally attributed to the Left.

It was above all his conception of social justice that soon opposed him to the clergy, "those guardians of Divine Law." Mossadeq was convinced that religion should not control the collective organization, and this necessarily implied a modern conception of society. For this reason, no lasting alliance was possible with the Ayatollah Kashani, that eager partisan of religion's priority over politics.

The nationalization of oil, with the deliberate aim of improving Iran's economic and political situation, took on a historic importance far greater than Mossadeq had imagined. It tangibly demonstrated the effectiveness of collective action and its ability to change things.

Mossadeq's action thus introduced a historic awareness, not in the sense of an eventful past that deserved to be known, as during the reign of Reza Shah, but in the modern sense: *the consciousness of the generative power of human action.* Mossadeq's success in the oil conflict, despite the mishaps and frustrations, showed that the people can voluntarily change their political destiny by their own action. That novel experience, in various ways, created in the Iranian collective spirit the hope that they could determine their own destiny. In a country still severely paralyzed by its religious structure, the power of this creative action attracted attention: it could be hoped that the present would give birth to the future, a better future, different from the past. Henceforth, nothing would ever be the same.

By wanting to wrest the independence of the Iranian oil industry from the British, Mossadeq's only aim was to restore justice to his people. He certainly had no idea of the impact that this nationalization would have on the country's political destiny. He did not realize that the practical work he had begun would end by transforming collective organization a few years later. Thus, despite his tragic fate, his action contributed to orienting society toward the future; a historic orientation that gave birth to the Iranian nation, in its modern sense.[45]

---

[45] I use this term with the meaning given it by Dominique Schnapper: "The nation as a process of integrating society by politics which, by definition, is never achieved." Dominique Schnapper, *La communauté des citoyens*, Paris, Gallimard, 1994, p. 39.

3

Modernization (1953–1978)

It was only after the fall of Mossadeq that Mohammad-Reza Shah really began to rule. Yet he neglected neither the political legacy of his former prime minister nor the country's metamorphosis that had begun under his government. Mossadeq was gone, but oil remained nationalized, and its sales abroad, renewed after the coup d'état, enabled the Iranian economy to improve. From then on, the country was given modern institutions and administration. It was affirmed as a sovereign state on the international scene. Despite the lack of freedom in public life, in the second half of the twentieth century Iran became a state whose political organization was that of a nation. Establishing autonomous principles in a nation-state framework enabled the development of political structures and led to true social progress.[1]

From then on, a true economic change took place. Quickly, the dynamics of progress were imposed on the whole of society, agriculture and the government, particularly affecting education and health. There was no aspect of collective life that progress did not begin to reform from within. The results of oil benefits[2] were also felt in the modernization of the country's administrative, legal and social structures. The need for change pushed Iranian political organization to emerge from the conservatism that had paralyzed it. The logic of progress carried the country, and the shah could but follow. Henceforth, there was real hope of a better life.

From the 1960s, the shah took a more active and central role in managing the state, both politically and economically. An ardent defender of progress—and impelled by the desire to modernize Iran—he launched

---

[1] "In any democratic nation, politics institutes the social." Schnapper, *op. cit.*, 1944, p. 14

[2] For an idea of the immense revenues that the petroleum industry gave its beneficiaries, see: Jean-Claude Werrebrouk, "Contribution to the theory of oil revenues," *Revue d'Economie industrielle*, vol. 9, no. 9, 1979.

a whole series of ambitious social and cultural reforms in line with Western models. With the support of the United States in developing the country after the war, national administrations began to function more coherently.[3] The oil manna enabled the shah to undertake more and more far-reaching reforms and, thanks to the possession of ever-more sophisticated weaponry, to strengthen the Iranian army for the defense of the monarchy and of national sovereignty. Mohammad-Reza Shah modernized industry, the economy, and finance thanks to a reform program that he called "the White Revolution" (*Enqelab-e Sefid*). Iran began a period of prosperity and accelerated economic advancement.

The economy had never been so flourishing. With the creation of modern airports, the building of big dams and factories, the opening of schools, and so on, the country gave itself modern infrastructures that clearly improved the level and quality of the lives of a large proportion of Iranians, especially city dwellers. True, the rural zones did not experience the same transformation as the urban zones, and some social strata were still poverty-stricken. But the weak, underdeveloped Iran of the start of the twentieth century, unable to protect its national sovereignty during the two World Wars, had become one of the most powerful Middle Eastern states. Thanks to strong economic growth, the shah succeeded in raising the country to the rank of a great world power and procured for it an international prestige worthy of its glorious past. Iran's geopolitical importance on the world scene was undeniable from then on.

Despite all these changes, there was no popular support. In the mid-1970s, Iranians grew increasingly dissatisfied. The Pahlavi regime found it evermore difficult to justify its policies. The more the shah modernized the country, the more popular resentment. His authoritarianism (no free elections, censorship, the single party, abuses committed by the Savak and denounced by Amnesty International) terrorized Iranians, and his exaggerated expenses (Persepolis festivities, Pharaonic projects, the purchase of sophisticated military equipment) aroused ever greater rancor.

---

[3] The fall of Mossadeq favored the arrival of the Americans in the country's great petroleum game. In 1964, an international consortium composed of French, Dutch, British, and American companies was created to manage Iran's petroleum production. In 1955, Iran joined the Baghdad Pact and thus found itself in the American camp during the Cold War. Iraq, Turkey, Pakistan, Iran, and the United Kingdom signed this pact on February 24, 1955. In 1958, the United States joined the military commission of the alliance. The pact was renamed the Central Treaty Organization or Cento and was dissolved in 1979. Its aim was to contain the Soviet Union by a group of strong states on its southern border.

To justify himself in the eyes of the Iranians, the shah stopped at nothing to raise their standard of living. He continued to advance the country's economic structures, adapting them to international needs, and by so doing he disarmed his opponents on the left. Whatever the left promised the people, the shah delivered. By depriving them of arguments, his reforms left no room for the revolutionary communists to acquire any true credibility in Iran. For their part, the intellectuals and the liberals refused to support him and remained highly critical. Lacking support from both the people and the elite, the shah resorted to force so that no democratic participation in political life was any longer possible. He set up a dictatorial regime with American backing.

Despite their massive support of the Iranian regime, the United States mistrusted Mohammad-Reza Shah's authoritarianism. They warned him against the danger of an antidemocratic political system. But it was in vain that they encouraged him to open political life to his opponents. The Pahlavi regime became increasingly firm. The shah was especially afraid of the communist militants and repressed them more than other opposition movements considered dangerous.

The situation worsened at the end of 1977. During the following year, confusion reigned and violent confrontations took place. Then came the Iranian Revolution led by the Ayatollah Khomeini, a religious leader who had lived in exile for fifteen years. The imperial regime fell in February, 1979, and gave way to an ideocratic system, called the "Islamic Republic." By what mystery did an ideological orientation succeed in toppling a firmly rooted political regime? How was the Royal Army—the fourth most powerful in the world—crushed after popular opposition? How could Khomeini's ideological Islam so easily install a far more dictatorial regime than its predecessor, setting the country back several centuries?

The Key to the Enigma

The fall of the Pahlavi regime despite great economic and political progress and the subsequent advent of the Islamic Republic are events that seem, at the least, enigmatic. Iranian historians and specialists have often tried to explain them as the legitimate rebellion of Iranians against the shah's despotism and the general corruption of the state's high dignitaries. But these explanations fall short because corruption always existed in Iran, and its long history of despotism makes it difficult to believe that the shah's authoritarian methods could be the sole trigger of popular discontent. Iran had never known any political system other than dictatorship.

True, the modernization of which Mohammad-Reza Shah was the architect caused a number of frustrations, but Iran was carried along by the dynamics of progress; the economy had never known such growth, and industrialization advanced rapidly. Nobody could deny that, under the shah's rule, the living conditions of the majority of Iranians had truly improved. True, this improvement did not reach all social classes, and a part of society remained outside it. It was also a fact that the cities developed more rapidly and better than the countryside, so that the rural population continued to migrate toward the large urban zones. It is equally true that the absence of free elections stifled Iranian public life, and the terror created by the *Savak* was such that no criticism of the regime was possible. Nonetheless, all of that does not suffice to explain the rejection of the shah's reforms by a large part of the population whose aspirations were very diverse, even contradictory.

To identify the cause of the fall of the imperial regime, it is not enough to review Mohammad-Reza Shah's administration and criticize it in detail. Because to blame its corruption, police repression, the failure or incoherence of its reforms, and the absence of political freedom is to ignore that, in Iranian history, repression and corruption were no novelty.

We need to understand why this repression became intolerable to Iranians when, before and after the shah, regimes that were even more dictatorial failed to arouse such a reaction. How did the denial of political freedom under the shah lead to a revolution, when under the worst atrocities of the regime that followed it, the Islamic Republic, Iranians seemed paralyzed by helplessness?

To understand the specific factors that contributed to the fall of one of the strongest regimes in the Middle East, we shall hypothesize that the Pahlavi regime was not a victim of its failures but of its successes. The true causes of its fall are not so much based on the faults of its modernizing policies but on the important structural changes to which these gave rise. Reexamining the ideas that dominated the political context and led to the fall of the shah's reforming regime and then to the installation of the present ideocratic regime, will allow us to comprehend the nodal phenomenon that marked Iranian history.

The Modernizing State

In 1962, the shah launched the "White Revolution" to develop and coordinate vast structural reforms that would transform Iranian society, renovating the economic and industrial system to make Iran a world power. The government financed heavy industry projects and nationalized forests, pasture lands, and water resources. The agrarian reform was a crucial undertaking, for it removed influence and power from the large landowners. At the same time, the White Revolution gave women many sociopolitical rights, the most important of which was the right to vote, which women were granted in February, 1963. It also made possible the medical profession's development and invested money in education, especially in rural zones.

At first, these changes gained popular support for the government, but they rapidly confronted the resistance of landowners and of the Shiite clergy. For long years, the higher clergy had been large landowners, and these reforms harmed their interests. Furthermore, clergy members were upset when the shah took away most of their traditional powers in the fields of education and family law. Fearing the loss of their land resources and of their influence in rural areas, the clergy opposed the agrarian reform and incited their believers to do the same. Having already lost part of their judicial power (under Reza Shah), they were in no way disposed to make concessions to his successor.

With the exception of a few rare ayatollah[4] who were not hostile to reforms in general, most of the high religious dignitaries proclaimed their opposition to the "sacred right of private property," according to *shariat,* and opposed the agrarian reform and the extension of royal power it implied. The perspective of losing control of the vast domains that provided most of the revenues of religious foundations constituted one of the principal motives for the important ayatollah to rise up against the White Revolution. They feared the elimination of the large mortmain foundations they managed, which would have represented their final failure against the secular power.

Thus, they demonized the regime's modernizing policies, pretending concern for the future of Islam and of Muslims. They painted a frightening picture of the country's future. According to the clergy, the shah's White Revolution wanted only to destroy Iranian mores and beliefs. It became the symbol of immorality, corrupt morals, and an alienated identity. Masters of manipulation, the clergy easily succeeded in rendering the legitimacy of the reforms suspect, to such an extent that shortly after the reforms began, popular discontent made itself heard.

---

[4] These were the Ayatollah Shariatmadari, a partisan of order at the expense of social justice, Rouhani and Taleqani (although the latter agreed to the principle of land-sharing, he disapproved of the methods used to carry this out).

Mohammad-Reza Shah, young and enthusiastic, never realized the great strength of the religious structure on which society was founded. A fervent admirer of the West, he thought he could modernize the country overnight, not realizing the inertia of mores and custom. His followers thought they could avoid social disorder by advancing development. Systematically, they destroyed traditional structures before new frameworks were ready to take their place. The people had trouble following, and the traditional strata were particularly destabilized. Without a global analysis, the regime's technocrats speeded up reforms, thoughtless of middle- and long-term consequences. Such conditions could not encourage true popular support of the reform movement.

By their radicalism and their efficiency, these reforms went much further than anticipated—modifying fundamental ideological and political ideas of human and social organization. The effect was a degree of upheaval unforeseen by the shah. The transformation begun by these reforms reached its apex in a political metamorphosis that radically altered the relationships between politics, the clergy, and society. These changes concerned not only the internal side of politics but its outward aspect—not only society's institutions but its way of being.

The Reversed Relationship between Politics, Religion and Society

By withdrawing most of the clergy's power, Mohammad-Reza Shah's reforms forced the Shiite clergy to abandon the official political scene and to support the regime's opponents. The way finally became clear for politics to take power over society and to become deeply entrenched in the collective organization, an area hitherto reserved to the clergy.

Henceforth, the laws codifying society were no longer defined by religious principles but by the constitution and parliamentary votes. Politics had the leading role, and religion did not infringe upon politics. It neither neutralized nor even cohabited with it, as had been the case under former rulers. Politics was now independent of religion. Thus an unprecedented situation was set up that would be difficult to reverse, even after the 1979 revolution that returned the clergy to politics.

All during his reign, Mohammad-Reza Shah relegated the clergy to the fringe of the social and political scene,[5] preventing them from taking any part in national affairs. True, the shah saw the communists

---

[5] This despite some demagogical gestures toward the clergy. He said readily that he was protected by the holy Shiite imams, and each year made a pilgrimage to the Imam Reza (the eighth Shiite Imam) in Mashad, the holy city in northwestern Iran.

as his worst enemies but, far more significantly, his policy deprived the clergy of a large part of their power. Contrary to the communists, fairly recent arrivals on the scene, the Shiite clergy had been an integral part of power for several centuries. Nothing could be done without their approval. They were the greatest losers amid the modernization that freed the country from their agelong control.

Thus the shah's policy was radically antireligious, freeing society from any metaphysical link to past tradition. This change was made possible by the political element's growing strength within Iran, a strength fueled by the nation's growing oil revenues. Mohammad-Reza Shah's reforms enabled the elimination of the religious structuring of society and reversed the relations between politics and religion. The reversal did not stop there. It also applied to the relationship between power and society. Although power still pervaded society and imposed its will upon it, the growth of political autonomy transformed the way in which people lived together.

Under the shah, Iranian society was different from what it had been before. It was aware of its strength. Political autonomy allowed human and social organization to expand in freedom. It favored the emergence of a society that organized its own evolution. At the same time, the country's flourishing economy was able to escape state control and turn toward new horizons. Installing a regime of freedom seemed indispensable to the life of a society aware that it was changing and desirous of changing itself.

But nothing took place as intended. The first factor was the economy. The imperial regime's stability depended entirely on the immense wealth from oil revenues. This allowed the regime to believe in its own self-sufficiency to such an extent that the shah was more and more careless of popular support. Convinced that he no longer needed popular support, he increased State control of the economy so that the private sector could not compete with the public sector. Simultaneously, the regime made no attempt to compromise with society, even less to grant it the least priority as compared with the State. The shah believed that his regime's survival depended more on the price of oil on the world market than on the will of the Iranians.

The second factor was politics. If traditional institutions such as the monarchy and the army were shaken to the marrow by reforms, they nonetheless remained in place and maintained their habitual spirit of superiority, deeply rooted in the Iranian bureaucratic tradition. Political leaders considered that the reforms carried out were evidence of the shah's tremendous generosity toward his country. Civil society's independence was a notable curb to these pretensions. It prevented the shah, if only symbolically, from completely taking over politics. The regime, therefore, could not tolerate the emergence of a civil society that proclaimed its independence; the price would have been too high in its eyes.

Economics and politics were both barriers that *a priori* blocked the regime's ability to put itself at the service of society, to represent it, and to change it. That explained the detachment of the shah from society and his call for police repression.

The imperial regime's downfall is less mysterious when we realize the limiting factors that are an integral part of modernity. It was precisely that crucial point that escaped the shah. He failed to realize that political autonomy unavoidably engenders civil society's freedom of expression, as well as the functional independence of the economy. He overturned politics, while restoring society's submission to power with the help of a terrorizing police repression. Without leaving the slightest room for society to assert itself or freeing the economic functions of the country from State control, the shah used authoritarianism to carry out his modernization. The more politics was freed from the clergy, the more society needed to express itself outside politics, and the more the shah made impossible any civil society free from the control of power. This fundamental paradox was the principal cause of the imperial regime's overthrow.

The shah therefore gave himself the means and the tools of a modernization that totally transformed the collective organization, but he failed to realize the meaning of this modernization; its logic escaped him. This explains why, under his regime, despite favorable circumstances, civil society never had the means or the space for its own existence. Power was never at the service of society, and he left not the least autonomy to the economic sector.

An Improbable Coalition

Civil society's inability to find freedom of expression and to assert its existence independently of the political body helped create solidarity among opponents of all kinds, despite their initial diverse motivations. Intellectuals, clergy, communists, and merchants all were caught up by one desire: freedom of public expression.

Just when the reform movement was in full swing, and Iran was asserting itself among the nations by discovering its geostrategic potential, the regime's police repression, aimed at stifling the newborn civil society, terrorized Iranians and paralyzed collective action. This repression had a baneful influence on the country's modernization. It particularly hampered the relations between politics and civil society.

Its first effect was to awaken a growing hostility against the imperial regime. More than ever, Iranians turned their backs on the regime, as well as on a modernization that had taken on police dimensions. They ignored the undeniable advances. The nationalist infatuation that had contributed to the popularity of Reza Shah, the shah's father, and fired Iranian enthusiasm under Mohammad Mossadeq's government was far away indeed. From then on, rare were those who heeded Iran's remarkable progress in the world, and even more rare those who were proud of it. The repression's second effect was felt rapidly. The stifling of civil society checked the emergence of free and autonomous agents both on the political scene and in intellectual thought. Rising against a power that refused to recognize their autonomy and independence, Iranians threw out the baby of modern political ideas with the bathwater of state-led reforms. They turned their backs on all the ideas that had contributed to the country's transformation. Henceforth, it was not only the shah's authoritarianism to which his opponents objected. In rejecting westernization, all democratic principles were regarded as evil.

A new coalition emerged. Instead of reformers on one side, conservative politicians on the other, and between them the clergy, hostile to all change and seeking only to enforce their power and spread their influence over the faithful masses, a new alliance formed among the three forces striving for power—the clergy, the communists, and the intellectuals. The country was split by a complete dichotomy between, on the one hand, the modernizing state, promising autonomy but incapable of completely following its own logic and, on the other, an alliance of the clergy, the intellectuals, and the communists, all opposed to the shah's dictatorship. Faced with the need to free society from the weight of power, the fundamental differences that divided the opposition forces paled. The fall of the shah was the one common priority. The status of women, the rights of ethnic minorities, civil, commercial, and industrial rights—all other claims seemed secondary. Communists and clergy, liberals and nationalists, intellectuals and merchants, all shared one hope with the people: the end of the monarchy. Very few indeed were those who realized to what extent this social movement was itself indebted to the success of the shah's reforms.

Thus, intellectuals, nationalists, and liberals undertook a compromise with the clergy. They opposed a modernization that, despite its internal dynamics, had prevented the birth of a free and autonomous civil society. Irony of ironies, all those who hoped for freedom, believed they could attain it under the banner of the clergy. How could such a coalition, as improbable as it was fleeting, be possible? How could such fundamentally opposing, even hostile, groups unite around a common objective to bring down a rich and strong political regime?

The Clergy's Resistance

In a society worried by the loss of its national identity as opposed to the country's westernization, the clergy feigned concern for "Iran's Muslim nation" (*melat-e mosalman-e Iran*) and thus managed to obtain a new legitimacy despite their complete indifference to the national issue. They opposed the shah's authoritarian policies with such ardor that the fundamentalist dimension of their opposition remained in the background. Through numerous sermons against the shah's despotism, they showed exemplary courage in denouncing the system and managed a revolutionary appearance that gave them a new legitimacy.

The more the shah's modernizing policies marginalized the clergy, the more the latter became important in the eyes of the people, the intellectuals, even the communists. The elite and the left-wing activists who also lacked legitimacy[6] found in the new religious discourse a last hope and thus supported it. Henceforth, the clergy were at the head of the opposition movement.

In the atmosphere of these tumultuous changes, hardly anybody paid attention to the clergy's growing hostility to reforms that improved the status of women. The vehemence of the important ayatollah's denunciation of women's suffrage aroused no reaction from the different opposition groups. Their silence concerning the clergy's reactionary viewpoints on women's place in society—relegating them to the traditional roles of mothers, daughters, and wives—revealed, it must be said, their consent, even their complicity with the clergy on this issue. The destabilized patriarchal structure resulting from the shock of the reforms engendered such a fear of moral corruption that the

---

[6] See the following chapter: "The Communist Movement."

emancipation of women could only be seen as a huge factor of disorder in the eyes of men.[7] The adherence of intellectuals and opposition groups to the misogynous language of the clergy showed the depth of the patriarchal ideas of Iranian men of all social classes.

In this atmosphere of confusion and disorder, the clergy resisted their own marginalization and, with an unsuspected skill, calmly prepared themselves to lead the opposition movement. This marginalization, following their ancient complicity with politics, could not but have an effect on their entire role. It freed them from their usual compromises with secular power; it made them emerge from their orbit and transformed them into a political opposition force. By so doing, the clergy were obliged to come down to earth to be on a par with the other social actors who opposed the regime.

The clergy expressed their resistance to marginalization by apparently contradictory reactions, which were nevertheless similar in their mutual rejection of reform. On the one hand, a few rare ayatollah defended the quietist thesis of separating religion from politics, showing their disapproval of the regime by abandoning the scene of power; on the other, most of the clergy tried at all costs to find a way to reassert their authority over politics.

In 1961, the Ayatollah Boroujerdi died (1875–1961). A great figure of Shiism, unconditional partisan of the separation of religion and politics, he consistently refused to discuss politics with the shah, as they had with his father. Spiritual Shiite leader since 1945, he strongly resisted any clerical intervention in secular power. After his death, nothing prevented the clergy from yielding to the temptation of power and from totally engaging themselves in the country's political affairs. This new commitment led them to radicalize their refusal of reforms.

The Ayatollah Boroujerdi had always strongly defended the quietist theory according to which the clergy must remain outside the affairs of this world. However, he could not help opposing the shah's modernization. Believing in the immutability of values and attached to the foundations of collective order dependent on tradition, like most of the clergy, he could not accept the fundamentally new type of government that the shah tried to install. Boroujerdi was aware that political

---

[7] This was also true for a large part of the female population who had deeply integrated patriarchal principles. On this subject, see: Pierre Bourdieu, *La domination masculine*, Paris, Points Essais, 2002.

autonomy would open the way to individual rights that would no longer be ruled by religious precepts.

Like all influential clergy who had feared the growing popularity of Mohammad Mossadeq and who had brandished the threat of communism, in 1953 the Ayatollah Boroujerdi had finally approved the coup d'état that returned the shah to power. Several years later, in 1960, strongly urged by the clergy, the important feudal lords and the *Bazaar* merchants, united both by economic interests and by family ties—Boroujerdi had determined to affirm a theological justification of property rights. By so doing, he clearly condemned the initial project of agrarian reform submitted by the government to Parliament. Most of the deputies, who were landowners, seemed happy to block an initiative that threatened their interests. By defending the old system, Boroujerdi placed himself in the camp of those who opposed the shah's modernizing policy.

His death coincided with the clergy's awareness of their increasing marginalization in the political structure. It revived the old conflict among the clergy on the political issue. But this time, it was a question of conquering a power independent of the state, within the opposition. The great ayatollah then mobilized to reflect on the role of "religious authority" in Shiism. They challenged the apolitical or quietist model of the traditional clergy, incarnated by the defunct theologian. They advanced a more active involvement in the political and social scene. Boroujerdi's disappearance liberated their appetite for power. From then on, nothing prevented them from satisfying their ambition.

In January, 1963, despite religious propaganda and the frustration aroused by modernization, Iranians massively approved the shah's White Revolution. The shah openly reproached the clergy for carrying out a "Black reaction, worse than the communists." The press multiplied attacks against the clergy, and police measures were taken against them. Having lost their role in politics, the *olama* now feared that the agrarian reform would despoil them of financial power. The Ayatollah Khomeini (1902–1989), religious dignitary of Qom, totally rejected the White Revolution. He opposed most of the shah's political reforms: universal suffrage, the right of women to vote and to be eligible for political and/or judiciary positions, the principle of popular sovereignty, the separation of the executive, legislative, and judicial powers.

Born in 1902, son of a provincial *mollah*, Khomeini was just twenty when he began his theological studies in Qom, at the time when Reza Shah's anticlericalism weighed heavily on the clergy. Immediately after the Shah's fall, Khomeini became an ardent defender of political action by the clerical corporation. Professor of Islamic law, close to the Muslim terrorists *Fadaiyan Eslam*,[8] he was rapidly confirmed as an important figure of the politico-religious opposition.

Contrary to Boroujerdi, Khomeini strongly defended the clergy's participation in politics and publicly asserted it: "This country owes everything to the clergy. History shows that throughout time, they led the popular and the revolutionary movements. They were always the first martyrs. The clergy always defended the oppressed against the oppressors."[9]

Incarnating the rejection of modernization and westernization, the Ayatollah Khomeini stood up against the shah, basing his assertions on Koranic precepts, taken as a political ideology. He opposed setting up a central judicial system, for nothing could in any way affect clerical authority in courts of justice founded on the *shariat*. He was deeply convinced that religion and power were indissociable, and that everything must yield to religious principles. According to him, the vocation of Shiite clergy was to promote social justice under a government of Islam and to protect the ignorant masses against forces of oppression of whatever kind.

In June, 1963, the Ayatollah Khomeini was arrested after an inflammatory speech against the shah; three days of revolt then shook the country, the greatest violence since the fall of Mossadeq ten years earlier. Many demonstrations took place in Tehran and in Qom, and the government responded rapidly and violently. The result was a bloodbath. The shah, aware of Khomeini's popularity, freed him shortly thereafter. The ayatollah's reaction was prompt. He promised death to those responsible, who would pay for this "massacre" with their own lives.

The failure of the 1963 revolt did not discourage the clergy and certainly not Khomeini. Well known by all, he enjoyed from then on a wide notoriety in traditionalist milieus, to such an extent that several high ayatollah named him openly as the eventual supreme religious guide, which conferred on him quasi-immunity. He became more and more aggressive, and his talks ever more radical. He abandoned the traditional theory of a legitimate monarchy as the support of religion, condemned the politics of the modernizing state, and rejected the idea

---

[8] It was they who assassinated the progressive writer Ahmad Kasravi. See preceding chapter.
[9] "Interview with Khomeini," *Ettela' at*, Tehran, June 12, 1960.

of progress. However, at that time, despite his unceasing attacks against the regime, Khomeini did not directly deny the monarchy's legitimacy nor attack the person of the shah.

In November, 1964, after having violently criticized a decree granting legal immunity to American military advisers, Khomeini was again arrested, and this time he was exiled—first to Turkey, then to Nadjaf et Karbala in Iraq.[10] He remained there for fourteen years and concentrated his statements on the rejection of modernization.

Gradually, Khomeini asserted himself as a determined adversary of democracy, repeating incessantly that it was not an adequate system for Iran. He denounced the complacency of some clerics toward democratic principles and explicitly condemned universal suffrage, saying that the people should not express their opinion. He quickly distanced himself from the nationalists and affirmed: "We shall not follow the road of nationalizing oil. Those who defend democracy are greatly mistaken. What we want is Islam."[11] An astute politician, Khomeini nevertheless knew how to ally himself with other opponents of the regime. If he symbolized the old order, he also defended the anti-imperialism and anti-Zionism dear to Iranian intellectuals. Gifted with a special charisma, master of the art of mobilizing and seducing the masses, he rapidly became the emblematic figure of the struggle against the influence of Western models.

It was during those years of exile that he worked out the thesis of *walayat-e faqih* that asserted the absolute power of the doctor of Islamic law. Whereas in Shiism the only legitimate authority is the Mahdi, the twelfth Shiite imam, the *resurrector* whose *parousia* (coming) is awaited by Shiites since his disappearance in the ninth century, this thesis claims that the clergy, heirs of the Prophet of Islam, must rule the believing community. They have thereby the right to exercise religious and political authority until the return of the Hidden Imam.[12] For Khomeini, believers must implicitly obey their religious leaders, both in private life and in the political sphere. These clerics, heirs of

---

[10] His pro-Shiite activism displeased the Iraqi regime, and in 1998 he left for France with a tourist visa. He settled in Neauphle-le-Château without requesting political asylum. It seems the shah would have refused his expulsion on the grounds that it was preferable to have him in France rather than in Syria or in Libya. *Cf.* Abbas Milani, *The Shah*, New York, Macmillan, 2011.

[11] *Cf. Sahifey-e Noor* (Khomeini's collected speeches), Vol. 1, Tehran, Imam Khomeini Foundation, 1990.

[12] In Shiism, the Mahdi, the Twelfth Shiite Imam, the Resurrector whose Parousia or "coming" is awaited by Shiites since his disappearance in the ninth century, is the only legitimate authority.

the Prophet, have the power to designate the wisest among them, the *waly-e faqih* (doctor of Islamic law), in whom is concentrated religious and political authority, an authority that is spread over all the "lands of Islam" (*bélâdé eslam*).

The thesis of the *walayat-e faqih*, after the 1979 Revolution, became the foundation stone of the new Iranian regime, what Khomeini defined as the absolute power of the clergy over the people (*omaté mosalman*). It lies at the heart of the 1979 constitution that stipulated that "the only legitimate holders of authority are the *olama* as heirs of the Prophet; the law can only come from on high and the most worthy among the erudite clergy must exercise authority until the return of the Imam of Time."[13]

Khomeini therefore defended the application of the *shariat* in courts of justice, as well as the independence of the *foqaha* (doctors of Islamic law) from the state, in particular in trials of penal justice.[14] Like other thinkers of that period, he was favorable to Western technological and industrial progress but fiercely hostile to modern political and philosophical thought.

For him, as for the other Shiite clergy, believers were incapable of understanding the true meaning of religion by direct reference to the main texts, without the mediation of religiously qualified people to interpret them. Khomeini ceaselessly stressed the importance of tradition and of the Shiite clergy's erudition. He opposed certain dissident branches of Shiism that maintained that believers could understand the meaning of Islam based on the Koran and on the teachings of the Twelve Imams. He held that the holy texts were too complex for ordinary mortals, even the Archangel Gabriel, who brought the Koran to the Prophet, was unable to comprehend the "deep meaning" of what he carried. The real meaning of the "inner layers" of the Koran could only be available to those who knew Arabic, who had studied both the ancient and contemporary works and had access to the Islamic gnosis. Only the *olama* and the erudite clergy who had reached the highest level of religious knowledge could penetrate the true essence of Islam. In other words, truth was unavailable to the profane.

---

[13] *Cf.* http://www.jurispolis.com/dt/mat/dr_ir_constit1979/dt_ir_constit1979_index.htm. The Constitution of the Islamic Republic, 1979.

[14] After the revolution, however, he found it convenient to maintain a centralized judicial structure, one that would provide an appearance of uniformity and at the same time ensure control over local judges, guaranteeing citizens a right to judicial recourse but according to the *shariat.*

If Khomeini never underestimated questions of doctrine, and if he was accustomed to the sharpest theological debates, in his public speeches he nonetheless addressed sociopolitical problems, his preferred themes being rejection of the royalist elite, expulsion of Western imperialists, and mobilization of the *mostazafin* (the oppressed) against the *mostakberin* (oppressors). Far from confusing crowds by overwhelming them with theological details, he concentrated their attention on the regime's political, social, and economic deficiencies. This refusal to approach esoteric and doctrinal issues in public was one of the major factors of his popular success. Compared with his methodical, coherent, and easily understandable speeches, the left, torn by ideological rifts, lost between Marxism, Leninism, Stalinism, and Maoism, was not on a par with him. Khomeini's speeches were indeed retrograde but powerfully mobilizing.

Condemning political modernity and asserting the intrinsic legitimacy of the clergy to lead Muslim public affairs, armed with absolutist principles, and firm in his denial of democracy, the Ayatollah Khomeini succeeded in taking the lead in the revolution that overthrew the Pahlavi regime in 1979.

The Retreat of Intellectual Thought

While the clergy, with Khomeini at their head, resisted the shah's modernization and tried to maintain the old order, a number of intellectuals abandoned politics and took refuge in poetry and literary debates, always greatly appreciated by Persian-speaking people. The intellectual elite of Iranian society despised the regime's progress and particularly criticized the shah's renewing symbols of national identity in his desire to be the defender of a prosperous Iranian nation, proud of its ancient civilization.[15] Defending national identity was judged inefficient, and its misuse by the shah seemed suspicious to intellectuals, nationalists, and liberals, those former defenders of modernization, grown suspicious of the country's westernization.

The roots of their mistrust went further back. The violation of the sovereign right of Iranian people, during the coup d'état of August, 1953, left indelible traces on the evolution of intellectual thought in Iran. Innumerable questions as to why and how the coup succeeded remained unanswered. The deepest, most upsetting, and most anguishing part of that event for Iranian intellectuals was that they felt abandoned and

---

[15] The Persepolis festivities.

betrayed by the West's failure to defend human rights and democratic principles. One of its major consequences—which persists today—was the loss of faith in democracy. This provoked a true intellectual paralysis, causing the intelligentsia to desert the social and political scene, and creating a pessimistic view of the place and future of democracy in Iran.

After a willful Europeanization that led to a general desire to learn European languages to gain access to Western political culture, the Iranian elite thereafter seemed indifferent—even disdainful—toward everything European. Indeed the intellectuals were more attracted by Western science and technology than by the philosophical and political aspects of European modernity. The clergy, for their part, were convinced that there were no moral, spiritual, or religious values in the West. They believed that people there lived in a state of moral depravity and could be of no use to Iranians.

Since then, there existed a clear dissociation between the technical progress that the clergy and the intellectuals wanted to attain and the political and moral culture that they rejected. This was a significant change compared to the elite of the previous generation, the constitutionalists. Fascination was replaced by mistrust of Western political culture. A good part of the elite judged that they could learn nothing from the West—now seen as imperialist and colonialist—and that they should rather seek the rebirth of the country's social and political organization within Persian culture itself, deeply rooted in the Muslim religion. Return to the past, resistance to forced modernization, defense of the national culture against foreigners, these themes were constant in the intellectual writings of that time. The desire was to assert an Iranian identity able to resist an invading West; criticism of modernity was their hobbyhorse. Many writers, deeply resentful of Western imperialism, suggested that the loss of the concept of a transcendent God would lead the West to degeneracy. They believed that individualism, alienation, and nihilism were problems specific to democratic systems whose political legitimacy was based on the individual—essentially corrupt and corrupting.

Iranian writers published extensively to convince their readers of the perversity of Western life. With no true knowledge of the subjects they handled, their denunciations could only be approximate. One of the well-known figures of this line of thought, whose favorite theme was criticism of the West, was Jalal Al-Ahmad (1923–1969), an author with left-wing commitments and the son of a clergyman. In a book with the controversial title *Ravaged by the West* (*Qarbzadegi*), he depicted

Iranian fascination with the West as a fatal disease, like the plague or cholera. According to him, this disease spread easily because Iranian intellectuals were "crassly ignorant" of their own culture.

Al-Ahmad thought the world was divided between countries that produced new technology and consumer countries, and he therefore advised his compatriots not to remain consumers, mere users of new products, but to become producers of technology.

Entirely self-taught, his talents as an essayist and his purely literary knowledge did not enable him to capture the stakes and the importance of social sciences in the modern world. He was particularly contemptuous of everything that escaped his limited knowledge. To him, sociology, ethnology, and anthropology—among others—were the colonizers' sciences, whose aim was to transform the least developed countries into subjects for study, like laboratory rats, the better to exploit their natural resources. His poisonous pen did not spare the great European thinkers and philosophers, who he portrayed as the thinking heads of an international conspiracy, even as spies for the West.[16]

His partial and prejudiced reading of pre-Islamic Iranian history led him to a disillusioned view of men who had marked Iranian collective memory and who were the symbols of his country's national pride. His sarcasm gave these historic figures the appearance of diabolical creatures, worthy of a cheap thriller. On the other hand, he provided a history of the Islamic period so eulogistic as to be unbelievable.

In a comparison, both superficial and unfair, between Iran and African countries, Al-Ahmad concluded that African polytheism, their primitive ways of living together and, above all, their scanty clothing, all subjected them to European colonizers and reduced them to misery. He warned Iranians against the danger of behaving like "Black savages" and called for a rude awakening: "If we want to combat foreign alienation and preserve our cultural and historic identity against Western invasion, we must return to our historic past and our tradition. The duty of each of us is to rehabilitate Islam." He concluded that only the religious discourse was meaningful for Iranians because the Shiite clergy, by its passive resistance to the country's westernization, had proved itself "the true servant" of the people. Al-Ahmad, leftist intellectual, thus greatly contributed to rehabilitating the clergy in the eyes of the people. He thought that, unlike the other opposition groups, the clergy were

---

[16] The assimilation of social-science researchers with Western mercenaries, ready to sell out their country, is still popular in Iran today.

the only ones who could play an important part in defending national identity against imperialism and the ascendancy of Western models.

A former member of Tudeh, Al-Ahmad became the inspiration of many intellectuals who thought it necessary for Islam to be the essential component of Iranian contemporary identity. Young Islamist activists—the Mojahedin of the People—later took this up, in an attempt to go beyond the alternative of Western culture and Communism. Khomeini was also one of the writer's admirers, at times quoting from *Ravaged by the West* in his sermons.

It was within this movement for rehabilitating Islam that the Movement for Liberty in Iran (*Nehzat-e âzâdi Irân*, MLI) was created by liberal nationalists at the start of the 1960s. Many former fellow travelers of Mossadeq, with clear religious leanings, then tried to understand the failure of the nationalist movement and the surprising popular mobilization in favor of Khomeini and against the shah's reforms in 1963. The MLI, led by Mehdi Bazargan, opposed reform and openly supported the clergy. The movement's leaders, seeking to conciliate Islam and the modern world, tried to "Islamize modernity" at all costs.

The Communist Struggle

While part of the elite—Muslim intellectuals and nationalists—looked askance at Western political culture and made common cause with the clergy against the shah, others favored Soviet Marxist-Leninism and sided with communist groups, particularly with what remained of the Tudeh. Whether by mistaken calculation or by a lack of long-term political vision, the shah's greatest efforts concentrated on eliminating the communists, while he underestimated the danger of the clergy. While the latter preached everywhere and criticized the imperial regime, the Savak strangled communist activists. The latter had great difficulty in organizing and facing the regime's incessant attacks. Repression on one side and modernization on the other prevented them from openly asserting themselves in the Iranian political and social arena, whose religious roots never authorized propagation of a Marxist-Leninism poorly understood by its own proponents.

The communists nonetheless soon became one of the principal figures of Iranian politics and played a key role. They fought for power and wanted to install a new world order in one of the world's most important geopolitical regions. If they did not succeed in winning nor even in surviving as a determining force, they still left their imprint on history. Opposing the state and vying with the nationalists and the clergy, the various communist groups strove to give the nation a new orientation by redefining such concepts as progress, modernization, westernization, social justice, national independence, and sovereignty of the people. Like other sociopolitical actors, they proposed their own solutions to the country's problems, but unlike the clergy and the nationalists, they failed to obtain power and implement their ideals. Of the three, the communists were the most repressed. Still, despite their failure—which we shall examine more thoroughly further on—they succeeded in introducing new ideas into public life, definitively marking the collective spirit.

True, the imperial regime could not reform traditional mores in depth; yet it created a context wherein a true questioning of standards, values, and customs became possible. Although the mores remained enclosed within traditional principles, they lost their habitual automatism.

By granting women the right to vote, by determining family rights in their favor, and by guaranteeing them access to universities and to the job market, the reforms strongly destabilized traditional patriarchy, without however defining frameworks within which new rules of men/women relationships could be worked out.[17] The shah was unable to replace the traditional patterns controlling social habits, but he inscribed them in the register of what could be reformed. A great change whose implications overturned for all time the symbolic architecture of Iranian society.

---

[17] For an in-depth analysis of the destabilization of the old patterns of men/women relationships in Iran, see: Mahnaz Shirali, *Iranian Youth, a Generation in Crisis,* Presses Universitaires de France/Le Monde, 2001.

4

Communism
(1920–1960)

The one thing on which all historians agree is the ideological confusion characterizing the Iranian left, of which nobody can clearly state the dominant tendencies.[1] There were social democrats, socialists, Marxist-Leninists, communists, Stalinists, Maoists, anarchists and believers in an "Islamist Marxism." At times within a single party, several tendencies competed. However, most often, the ideologies varied according to the country in which the politicians' university studies took place. For example, those who returned from Europe tended to be social democrats, while most of the Russian language students defended Bolshevik communism. Despite this ideological diversity, from the start until the fall of the Soviet Union, Iranian left activists considered themselves "communists." Most of them favored the authoritarian version of Marxism and called for the creation of a socialist state, if necessary by violent means.[2]

The governmental violence of which the communist activists were always the preferred targets became a factor of cohesion that made them forget their ideological differences. From the founding of the Iranian Communist Party (ICP) in 1920, by a handful of intellectuals influenced by the Russian Revolution, they were victims of harsh repression, suffering numerous and systematic attacks with heavy loss of lives. During the 1920s, under Reza Shah Pahlavi, most party leaders were forced to seek refuge in the Soviet Union when the Stalinist regime was setting up its arbitrary rule. Many ICP members perished there in the terror of the 1930s while others were arrested and executed in the

---

[1] Maziar Behrooz, *Rebels with a Cause: The Failure of the Left in Iran*, New York, I. B. Tauris, 2000. See also Abrahamian, *op. cit.*, 1982.

[2] In this book, the term *communist* is used to refer to those who consider themselves as such. In Iran, it is popularly used for all those who defend the ideas of the left, of whatever tendency.

shah's prisons. Before it could even assert itself, the ICP was eliminated as an organized political force.

Both under the reign of Reza Shah and that of his son, the repression of communists was always justified as a fight against enemies of the country or of Islam. At the same time, from its inception, the communist movement encountered a country deeply anchored in Shiite religious culture where, for more than ten centuries, the clergy had been one of the most important political actors. These roots of Iranian society in Islam, as well as the leading part played by the clergy in the social structure, constituted strong impediments to the advance of communism in Iran. Not wanting to "frighten the masses" and fearing the fury of the *olama*, during the period between the two world wars, some political parties preferred to remain discreet as to their ideological orientation. Thus, silence always ruled their relations with the clergy whose role in politics the communists largely underestimated until the 1979 revolution. The movement's founders were convinced that it would suffice to combat the ignorance of the oppressed masses in order to detach them from religion and make them adopt communism. They avoided doctrinal issues and launched the organization of the masses in order to avoid an anti-religious label.[3]

The Iranian communist movement could not, however, remain independent of international communism and had to join the international revolutionary party. At first, their adhesion to the Comintern[4] enabled them to establish their movement and express their politics more clearly. Later on, however, they drew attention to the thorny problem of Iranian activists' relations with the Soviet Union, heir to a Russia that had always threatened Iran's national sovereignty.

Their ambiguous relations with the Soviet Union, their theoretical weakness, and their fear to analyze the role and the place of the clergy in Iranian society were the main factors contributing to the failure of Iran's first wave of communism—largely dominated by the Tudeh—during

---

[3] The ICP rejected the socialism of the Second International and adopted the October Revolution as its model, based on a professional revolutionary party. *Cf.* Sepehr Zabih, *The Communist Movement in Iran,* Berkeley, University of California Press, 1966.

[4] The Comintern, from its name in Russian, *Kommounistitcheskii Internatsional* or Communist International, was born of a schism of the Workers International on March 2, 1919, in Moscow, under the impetus of Lenin and the Bolsheviks: The Communist International grouped those communist parties that had broken off from the socialist parties of the II International. *Cf.* Serge Wolikow, *L'internationale communiste (1919–1943): The Comintern or the Fallen Dream of the World Revolutionary Party,* Paris, Editions de l'Atelier, 2010.

the years from 1940 to 1960. Their dependence on the Soviet Union undoubtedly posed the greatest problem.

Iran's Tudeh Party

Communism in Iran has been linked to the Tudeh since its official inception in September, 1941. Even after its organization was dismantled in the 1950s, it continued to mark Iranian political life. In Persian, Tudeh means "the party of the masses," and it was the main political group associated with Marxism between 1940 and 1960. In the years following its founding, it rapidly became the largest and most powerful political force in the country.

Most of its leaders were young Persian-speaking intellectuals from prosperous families. Among the fifteen members of the Central Committee were a judge, three professors, a doctor, a lawyer, a theater director, pharmacists, rich landowners, and high-ranking civil servants. Critics of the Tudeh pointed to its leaders' social backgrounds, saying that "the party of the masses" was, in fact, made up of discontented members of high society. They said that the Tudeh, led by Qajar princes, was incorrectly named.[5]

The Tudeh was the legitimate successor of both the old Communist Party, founded in 1920 after the October Revolution and the group of "Fifty-Three," which succeeded the party when it disappeared in 1930. The Tudeh founders became communists during their university studies (financed by state scholarships) in Western Europe or in the Soviet Union. In Europe they met the very charismatic Taqui Arani and joined his group. Some survivors of the ICP had reappeared and organized a new party under his leadership. The Fifty-Three was made up of educated intellectuals, converted to Marxism. There is a doubt concerning their affiliations, and it is impossible to know if this was an independent grouping of Marxist intellectuals or if they belonged to the international communist movement. The group seemed to have social-democratic tendencies and, if we believe their publications, their view of Marxism was far removed from Stalinism. They did not seem to have any particular affinities with the Soviets.

---

[5] *Cf.* A. Massoudi, "The Balls of Danger," *Ettella' at*, July 31, 1943. Similarly, the Democratic Party of the then prime minister, Qavam, declared that Tudeh could not represent the workers, the oppressed and the intellectuals, because it had been created by rich landowners. Ali Mahmudi, *Irané Demokrat (Democratic Iran)*, Tehran, Diba, 1945, p. 76.

Grouped around the magazine *Donya* (the world), the Fifty-Three published primarily theoretical and philosophic essays on issues directly concerning Iranian society and politics.

Arani and his comrades were the first to open a theoretical debate on essential issues in public. Still today many observers feel that *Donya's* contribution was the most eminent in the history of the Iranian left. In 1937 the group was arrested, and in February 1940, Arani died in prison under, to say the least, suspicious circumstances.[6] It was after the fall of Reza Shah in 1941 that the survivors of the ICP and some of its former members founded Iran's Tudeh Party.

The Tudeh was thus born from the meeting of two different aspirations: the Iranian Communist Party (1920–1930), very Bolshevik, and the Fifty-Three (1930), which had evolved toward a rather social democratic line. This duality contributed to some confusion in Tudeh's ideological choices, so that, from the start, it showed little preference for the Cominterm, hesitating to present itself as a communist party whose ultimate goal would be the establishment of a socialist state. Its first secretary, Soleyman Eskandari (1908–1985), defender of the constitutional revolution and founding member of the Fifty-Three, was a highly respected Qajar prince with social-democratic tendencies. His greatest contribution to Iranian Marxism was his translation of Marx's *Das Kapital* into Persian.[7] He never claimed to be a communist,[8] even though his admiration for the Soviet Union and the October Revolution was well known:

> For us, the Soviet Union is a socialist country, the first socialist country, a Leninist country, a country that supports worldwide revolution, and lastly, a country that is the principal actor in the greatest anti-imperialist struggle that the world has ever known; and this explains our tremendous admiration for the Soviets.[9]

From the start, the Tudeh had great difficulty in asserting, in a society deeply embedded in Shiite religious tradition, its sympathy for the Soviets, as well as its ideological Marxist-Leninist tendencies. Yet the party could not remain isolated from international communism, and it

---

[6] *Cf.* Bozorg Alavi, *Panjah-o she nafar* (The Fifty-Three), Tehran, Amir Kabir, 1944.

[7] He completed the translation of the last volume before his death.

[8] Iraj Eskandari, *Khaterate siyasi* (Political Memoirs), Paris, Editions Babak Amir-Khosravi, 1987, vol. 3, pp. 162–178.

[9] *Ibid.*

very soon joined the Comintern, without however informing its members of this. The Soviets, for their part, could not allow communism to be propagated among their Iranian neighbors without interfering. They played a determining part in Tudeh's evolution and in the direction it would take.

Over the years, Tudeh's devotion to the Soviet Union and the indifference of its leaders to national interests greatly worried Iranians. Its political choices and ideological orientations, eventually highly ambiguous, were other troubling aspects. Tudeh's eventful history only increased the mystery that surrounded it. Many crises, dissidences, oppositions, and settlings of scores revealed a different aspect of the extremely complex nature of a political party systematically accused of treason and opportunism, while its real contribution to progress in Iranian society was not taken into account.

Relations with the Soviet Union

Relations with the Soviet Union were an important controversial point in the Iranian communist movement's history in general, and a decisive factor in the life of Tudeh in particular. For the Tudeh, this was an international duty toward its communist brothers. Its adversaries presented Tudeh as a spy network in Soviet pay, rather than a national and independent political party. Some former leaders, who left the party before its disappearance, mentioned the close links between its leaders and the Soviet secret police. These links led Tudeh to follow instructions dictated by Moscow. As for the independent Marxist groups, they denounced Tudeh's obedience to Kremlin orders, placing Soviet interests before those of Iranian workers, and thereby betraying the revolutionary movement.

It is undeniable that the Soviet Union's Communist Party exerted great influence on Tudeh throughout its existence.[10] The Soviets did not hesitate to support Tudeh—particularly when they occupied part of Iran—even when the Tudeh announced it had no connection with Comintern party members. In exchange, Moscow's interests became the guideline of all Tudeh activities. Ardeshir Ovanessian, the only non-Muslim member of the Tudeh Central Committee and one of the

---

[10] During the 1940s, Rustam Aliev, a Soviet diplomat, maintained numerous contacts with the party and played an important part in its evolution. He was an ally of Ja'far Baqirov, leader of the Communist Party of Soviet Azerbaijan and very close to Stalin. *Cf.* Maziar Behrooz, "Tudeh Factionalism and the 1953 coup in Iran," *International Journal of Middle East Study*, no. 33, 2001, p. 376.

party's theoreticians, spoke in his memoirs of a letter he had addressed personally to Tudeh's leadership. This letter defined the major political axes that the party should follow, such as war against fascism, by propaganda and any other means; the fight for democracy; and to lead Iranians to understand that the Soviet government desired only their good and their freedom.[11]

Both the radical and the moderate tendencies that coexisted in Tudeh shared an admiration for the Soviet Union, victorious bastion of the revolutionary proletariat. Both submitted to orders dictated by the Soviets during the 1940s, and both believed that the party should respect its international duty by following Moscow's policies.[12] However, despite their joint tendency to obey the Kremlin, the two did not share a similar perception of their relationship with the Soviet Union. The moderates reproached the radicals with being actual partners or agents of Soviet secret services.[13] The leaders maintained silence on that issue, at a time when that relationship troubled party members.[14] It was not until 1951 that Kalil Maleki (1902–1969)— one of the party's founders who had left it six years earlier—dared to openly bring up, for the first time, the thorny issue of relations with the Soviet Union. In an article entitled "What Iran's Tudeh Party Says and What It Does,"[15] he explained what led him to leave the party. Maleki accused the leadership of blind obedience to the Soviets and of acting as accomplices to those who wished to dismantle Iran.

---

[11] Ardeshir Ovanessian (1905–1995), born in an Armenian village in Azerbaijan, studied pharmacy at the American Missionary School in Rasht. After having joined the Communist Party, he spent two years in prison, where he met the "Group of Fifty-Three." Hardly had he been released than he was again condemned for ten years, during which time he translated many theoretical texts into Persian. Aged thirty-seven, Ovanessian published a series of booklets on Marxism and political organization, proving himself to be the party theoretician. He was considered the "leading brain" and one of the "dominant personalities of Tudeh." *Cf.* British Chargé d' affaires to the Foreign Office, "Memorandum on the Tudeh Congress," *F.O. 371/*Persia, 1944.

[12] We recall that during Stalin's time, the Communist Party of the Soviet Union demanded unfailing obedience from all communist parties in the world. *Cf.* Fernando Claudine, *The Communist Movement from Comintern to Cominform*, vol. 2, London, Monthly Review Press, 1975.

[13] According to Eskandari, Kianuri and Kambakhsh—two members of the party's Central Committee—were directly linked to the Soviet Intelligence Service. For further information, see: Behrooz, *op. cit.,* 2000, "Defeat and Revival, the Great Defeat of the Left," (1953–70), pp. 1–48.

[14] For example, after the first Soviet request to obtain the oil concession in the north had been rejected, three party leaders contacted the prime minister to tell him, privately, that they knew how to make him change his mind; in other words, they proposed to corrupt him. This affair deeply shocked ordinary Tudeh members. For more details, see Abrahamian, *op. cit.,* 1982, pp. 305–318.

[15] Kalil Maleki, "Hezbe Toudehyé Iran che mikhahad va che migooyad?" (What does Tudeh demand and what does it say?), *Niruy-e sevom*, Tehran, Autumn 1951.

Long after Maleki, Keshavarz, a former member of the Central Committee, reproached the Soviets with exploiting his party for the sake of the October Revolution:

> By abusing the belief that we, and the great majority of our members, had in internationalism, the Communist Party of the Soviet Union (CPSU) transformed us into its spies and agents, so that Tudeh became the tool of the Soviet Union in Iran.[16]

One of the most disputed party figures was indubitably Samad Kambakhsh (1903–1971). Officer of the air force under the reign of Reza Shah, he was a member of the Iranian Communist Party and of the Fifty-Three. He was not a theoretician but a technocrat who had very close personal relations with the Soviets. Son of a Qajar prince, born and brought up in Qazvin, he left to study in the Soviet Union and returned deeply impressed by the Bolshevik Revolution. Despite his politics, the government sent him back to the Soviet Union in 1927 to study mechanical engineering. The contacts he made during those years later proved very fruitful in forming Tudeh cells within the army.

A professor at the Military Academy of Tehran, Kambakhsh was arrested in 1937. In prison, he cooperated with the police against his comrades. After the fall of Reza Shah in 1941, he had to persevere for two years before being admitted into the recently created Tudeh party, and he only succeeded thanks to considerable Soviet pressure. Many leaders did not want him, all the more because of his collaboration with the Soviet Union's Intelligence Service.[17] Despite the unlimited admiration they all had for the Soviet Union, many considered that to work for the Soviet Secret Service was very different from the official relations that Tudeh maintained with the CPSU.

In fact Tudeh's dependence on the Soviets, both in its political choices and in the internal decisions of the Central Committee, influenced by Moscow, went far beyond the fraternal and international relations

---

[16] Fereidun Keshavarz, *Man motaham mikonam I accuse*, Tehran, MLI Editions, 1987, pp. 79–80. Keshavarz was a member of the party's Central Committee and came from a Qajar family. When he wrote his memoirs, he had broken with Tudeh. For Eskandari, who always remained faithful to Tudeh, the moderates were in favor of the party's independence while the radicals were subject to the CPSU and executed its orders systematically. Eskandari, "Hezbe Toudeh Iran va Shoravi" (Iran's Tudeh and the Soviet Union), *Fasli Dar Gole Sorkh*, no. 3, Autumn 1986, p. 25.

[17] Anvar Khameh'i, *Panjah nafar va seh nafar* (Fifty people and Three people), Tehran, Diba Editions, 1983, pp. 30–63; Eskandari, *op. cit.*, vol. 1, 1986; Abrahamian, *op. cit.*, 1982, pp. 65–66. Kianuri, one of the members closest to Kambakhsh, rejected the validity of these accusations. *Cf.* Nur-al-Din Kianuri, *Goftogu ba tarikh (Dialogue with History)*, Tehran, Negareh Foundation, 1997.

between communist parties. Under the weight of this dependence (in fact, obedience), no initiative could be undertaken without Kremlin approval. The general paralysis of the party leadership when faced with the coup d'état of August, 1953, is one undeniable proof of this. Stalin had died in March of that year, and the struggle for power raged at the top of the CPSU. Soviet leaders devoted more time and energy to their internal affairs than to intervention in the affairs of their neighbors. Mossadeq's opponents, both national and foreign, took advantage of this situation to plot against his nationalist government. Without orders from Moscow, Tudeh was at a loss and incapable of opposing the putschists. Its inaction revealed the depth of the party's dependence on Soviet leadership. It was then no longer possible to hide its total incapacity to pose as a stable and independent political organization that made its own decisions on the important events of its country.[18]

The continued presence of Tudeh in politics since the beginning of the 1940s consistently hid the existence of another pro-Soviet Iranian party, the Democratic Party of Azerbaijan (*Fergheh-ye démocrat-e Azerbaïdjan,* or the DPA). To repeat the formula of the Iranian historian Abrahamian, Iran was in the rare situation of having two pro-Soviet parties.[19] Relations between the two supplied another proof of Tudeh's obedience to the Soviet Union. The Soviet Union had occupied Iranian Azerbaijan since 1941. Unbeknownst to Tudeh, the Soviets promoted the DPA. This was first of all a secessionist party that fought for the Iranian province to join the Soviet Union. It was created in 1945, thanks mainly to the efforts of a veteran communist, Jafar Pishevari.[20] Faced with the fait accompli, Tudeh's leadership condemned the DPA, but the

---

[18] Tudeh's choice to uphold the oil concessions in the north in 1944 in order to defend Soviet interests and to create peace groups that would support Soviet international policies during the 1940s followed the same political logic. Some observers suggest that the party's anti-Mossadeq policy was partly based on Tudeh's interpretation of Soviet policy. In October, 1952, the Nineteenth Congress of the Communist Party of the Soviet Union (CPSU) suggested that the bourgeoisie had abandoned democracy internationally. It was therefore the duty of the international proletariat to uphold the torch of democracy. Tudeh's radical wing applied this line to the letter, attacking "the nationalists as representatives of the Iranian bourgeoisie." According to this thesis, Soviet policy toward Mossadeq's government was basically neutral: it neither helped nor attacked him. This could be seen as an absence of policy. Tudeh's leadership, dependent on advice from Moscow, was incapable of determining its own path. On this point, see Maziar Berooz, *op. cit.*, 2000, p. 23; Abrahamian, *op. cit.*, 1982; *Tarikhe hezbe komoniste shoravi* (History of the Soviet Communist Party), Tehran, Tudeh Party Editions, 1979, pp. 686–698.

[19] Ervand Abrahamian, "Communism and Communalism in Iran: The Tudeh Party and the Firqah-ye Demokrat," *International Journal of Middle East Studies,* no. 1, 1970, p. 291.

[20] Jafar Pishevari (1893–1947) had serious political differences with Tudeh leaders.

Soviets prevented them from expressing their discontent, even forcing them to publicly congratulate the DPA.[21] After obeying, Tudeh's Central Committee addressed an official complaint to the CPSU, but never received any reply. Shortly thereafter, the Soviets asked Tudeh to dismantle its own organization in that region and to make its members there join the DPA. Unhesitatingly, Tudeh obeyed Moscow's directive.[22]

Tudeh's obedience to the Soviets aroused strong discontent within the party, especially among the young activists, giving rise to many factions. This was one of the principal factors of Tudeh's decline in the years after the coup d'état.

Political Orientation and Ideological Choices

To formulate a program that did not upset the clergy but could attract a large number of people was one of Tudeh's principal objectives. Even if its founding members were convinced communists and admirers of the Soviet Union, they feared to show themselves as such. This discretion was not only due to the party leaders' worry concerning the *olama* and Iranian religious culture. According to them it was also due to the Pahlavi regime's twenty-five years of propaganda, which had instilled the Iranian collective imagination with hostility toward socialism, communism, and the Soviet Union. Furthermore, the Tudeh leaders' discretion in preferring to avoid the communist label was also due to their desire to attract grassroots activists of the old Communist Party without offering them important positions.

Tudeh leaders were not simply puppets[23] of their predecessors. This party was different and far more than an official branch of the ICP. Its founders could not accept the supremacy of the communist veterans because so many things separated them. First, their social-democratic tendency—the heritage of the Fifty-Three—provided a complex, even ambiguous, dimension to their political and ideological orientations. They seemed somewhat divided between European social democracy and a Stalinist version of Marxism (in the end, they showed a clear preference for the latter). In addition, the communist veterans were middle-aged, of Azerbaijan origin, and Turkish speaking; the founders of Tudeh, on the other hand, were mostly young, Persian speaking, and inhabitants of Tehran. The communist veterans were self-taught

---

[21] Abrahamian, *art. cit.*, 1970, p. 311.

[22] Keshavarz, *op. cit.*, 1987, p. 62.

[23] Abrahamian (1982) and Roozbeh (2000) oppose the idea that Tudeh was no more than the official branch of the old clandestine Communist Party.

activists who had taken the road of Marxist-Leninism by following the Russian Bolshevik party. They had a very pragmatic view of communism without caring much for doctrinal issues.[24] The Tudeh founders were young academics who had learned Marxism during their studies in Western Europe or in the Soviet Union and had a more theoretical view of revolutionary action.

Finally, the last reason for Tudeh's discretion as to its ideological positions was the undeniable fact that the industrial working class in Iran made up only a small fraction of the country's population. The party was sufficiently lucid not to launch itself into an ideological war against the *olama*. By openly declaring itself to be communist, it would clash directly with a society under religious control, just when it lacked a popular base. This was recognized by Bozorg Alavi, one of Tudeh's founders and a former member of the Fifty-Three, a man of letters and an influential writer, in a book of memoirs well known in Iran:

> A true communist must know how to adapt Marxism to the environment in which he lives. If an Iranian communist adopts the program of the German communist party or of the communist party of any other industrial country, he will undoubtedly be incapable of attracting his own people. He will only violate the elementary rules of dialectic logic and of Marxist philosophy. One must therefore say that he is not a real communist but a political provocateur.[25]

Within the party, debates on ideology raged, and the leaders were unable to shape their doctrine. They questioned ceaselessly: "Is Tudeh a communist party?" Some leaders suggested that their opponents wanted to label them as communists in order to frighten away capitalists and merchants. The party's daily, *Rahbar*, even explained that the hour for communism had not yet come:

> Tudeh is fully committed to basic laws. Why? Because we believe that communism is an ideology adapted to certain social conditions that do not yet exist in Iran. A communist party will not find popular roots in our country. We know that our immediate task is to unite a majority against the exploiting oligarchy and to consolidate the democratic forces.[26]

---

[24] George Lenczowski, *Russia and the West in Iran*, 1918–1948, New York, Greenwood Press, 1949, pp. 223–225. Also see: Abrahamian, *op. cit.*, 1983, pp. 283–284.

[25] Alavi, *op. cit.*, 1944, p. 189.

[26] "Tudeh and its Participation in Politics," *Rahbar*, May 17, 1944.

In a series of articles entitled "Revolution or Parliamentarianism? How to Modify the System?" the party doctrinaires judged that the international situation as well as the absence of organized masses did not permit Iran to prepare for a true revolution. Judging it therefore irresponsible to speak of this, they proposed the idea that in order to weaken the leading class, it was necessary to unify all the progressive forces. Thus, Tudeh's principle strategy consisted in setting up a vast campaign to organize the people of all social milieus.[27]

The "organization of the masses" then became the center of all party activities. Thus ended the internal debate on ideological orientation. Instead of formulating a clear doctrine, able to bring popular support, Tudeh developed a plan to recruit new members without offending religious sensitivities. Its slogans appealed to the working masses, who were urged to unite and take their common destiny in hand to improve living and working conditions. Aimed at the whole of society, the recruitment campaign met with real popular success, but this success was highly controversial. Without any clear ideological strategy, enabling communism to acquire credibility in Iran, the party failed to communicate its doctrine, aims, and principles to new members. Politicians, students, and intellectuals could understand Tudeh's theoretical grounding in communism, but those theories remained confusing to the rest of society.

Gradually, however, the campaign did bear fruit. If, in the beginning, Tudeh was only a group of untried intellectuals, a few years sufficed to transform it into a real political force. In 1945, it indeed became what its name proclaimed: "the party of the masses." That same year, the party's central committee declared: "We can now say that our party has penetrated the whole of the country with its organized and open branches; it ranges from the south to the north."[28]

Indeed Tudeh then numbered several thousand members, but one could not conclude from that any real Iranian enthusiasm for communism or a wider understanding of its doctrine.

The discretion of Tudeh's leaders as to their ideology did not permit communism to be shaped as a hegemonic and inspiring force of Iranian society. Its audience remained limited to the milieus of intellectuals and students. The party never risked open ideological debates and still

---

[27] H. Mostafavi, "How to Change the System: Through Revolution or Parliament?" *Rahbar*, December 21, 1943.

[28] *Rahbar*, January 8, 1945. After *Rahbar* was shut down, *Mardom* became the party's official newspaper and, in 1946, it reached a daily circulation of 120,000, nearly double that of the previous year.

less openly faced up to religious authority. It remained torn between prudence and uncertainty.

Successive Crises

Tudeh's manual, published in 1943 under the title *The Party's Organizational Foundations*, explains that the concept of democratic centralism grants rights and duties to all party members.[29] Each has the right to discuss all questions freely, to elect leaders, and to participate in determining the party line. It is also the duty of each one to apply the party's political choices and to obey elected leaders, even if he had voted against them. Carrying out decisions was thus centralized, but reaching those decisions was democratic.

Tudeh also institutionalized the principle of criticism and self-criticism—rare in a country where nobody had ever been accountable to anybody at all. Democratic centralism systematically led leaders to justify themselves and their political choices before the members. Although in fact the real decisions were made by the leaders of the CPSU rather than by those of the Iranian Central Committee, this concept of internal democracy nonetheless inaugurated a new political approach that would subsequently distinguish Tudeh from most other Iranian political parties, for which bloody purges were one means of ensuring internal "harmony." In time, democratic practices permitted successive crises within Tudeh. Many conflicts arose and destabilized the party to the extent that leaders had difficulty maintaining unity. Nevertheless, despite basic disagreements among Central Committee members, no recourse to violent measures ever took place.

In 1944, after having been harshly attacked by the government, Tudeh went through several internal crises that forced it to make structural changes. Very quickly, Khalil Maleki, who was then one of the party's key figures,[30] obliged the leaders to convoke an urgent general assembly. The post of secretary general, as well as the Central Committee and the Inspection Committee, were eliminated. A temporary Executive Committee replaced them. The new leadership

---

[29] Ardeshir Ovanessian, *Osule tashkilatiy-e hezb* (Organizational Principles of the Party), Tehran, Tudeh Editions, 1943.

[30] A German-speaking intellectual and member of the "Fifty-Three" group, Khalil Maleki (1902–1965) came from a modest Azerbaijan family. Having left for Berlin for his university studies, he had to return to Iran in 1937, his study grant having been cut off because of his political opinions. Upon his return, he was arrested by the police. A few years later, he became one of Tudeh's founding members.

closed down the daily *Rahbar* and created *Mardom*, published by Maleki and Radmanesh.[31] It also dissolved the party's extreme left-wing branches and publicly declared that Tudeh's political positions favored defending democracy, constitutionalism, and parliamentarianism to achieve social change. Finally, the Executive Committee announced that it had no intention of creating a proletariat state, but that it aimed at creating a political and economic system comparable to those existing in Sweden, Switzerland, Great Britain, France, and the United States.[32]

Yet the election of the new leadership did not put an end to internal divisions. On the contrary, sixteen months of controversy, recriminations, and factional fighting ensued. Some argued that Tudeh had failed because it had ignored the "armed path to socialism," underestimated the "class struggle," and overestimated the possibility of reform through parliamentarianism. The party's leadership was criticized for having put intellectuals in the Central Committee instead of workers. In short, the opponents accused Tudeh of having behaved more like a Menshevik than like a Bolshevik Party.[33]

Other criticisms were diametrically opposite, like those of a close friend of Maleki, the young economist Eprim Eshaq, since his return from studying in England under Maynard Keynes.[34] In Eshaq's opinion, Tudeh alone was responsible for its recent reversals, which resulted from its exaggerated populism and lack of a coherent ideological line. He claimed these were the two main factors that caused Tudeh's members to behave condescendingly toward intellectuals and to adopt a fatalistic mentality that considered the party as a defenseless victim of circumstance instead of an active agent of history. Without clear recruiting criteria, he declared, Tudeh had allowed the entrance of opportunist

---

[31] Radmanesh (1905–1994) was one of Tudeh's dominant personalities. After a PhD in nuclear physics at the Sorbonne, he taught for a long time at the University of Leipzig in Germany. He came from a well-to-do farming family of landowners. In Europe, he met Arani, and this resulted in his condemnation to five years of prison upon his return to Iran. Police reports, published after the 1979 revolution, indicated that Radmanesh had been editor-in-chief of the official newspaper, *Donya*, of the "Fifty-Three" group and that he was a political personality respected by all—even by his worst enemies—because of his sincerity and his lack of self-interest. *Cf.* British Chargé d' affaires to the Foreign Office, *op. cit.*, 1944.

[32] Temporary Executive Committee, "Proclamation," *Mardom*, Tehran, January 5 and 10, 1947.

[33] "Tabagheyé Kargar che mikhahad? Hezbé Toudeh che migooyad" ("What does the Working Class Want? What does the Tudeh Party Say?") *Mardom*, Tehran, June 4 and August 24, 1947.

[34] From an Assyrian family, Eshaq was one of the most brilliant Iranian Marxists. He quickly left Tudeh to become a professor of economics at Oxford. Abbas Milani, *Eminent Persians: The men and women who made modern Iran*, 194–1979, vol. 2, New York, Syracuse University Press, 2008, pp. 66–68.

members who shared none of its values.[35] If he congratulated Tudeh on its success in mobilizing thousands of intellectuals, workers, and peasants—many of whom had never heard of democracy and socialism before 1941—Eshaq stressed the party's institutional and ideological gaps. He criticized a leadership that preferred to recruit a greater number of members than to pay attention to their intellectual training. He condemned Tudeh's vacillation between reforms and revolution, between a parliamentary policy and street demagoguery. He suggested dividing the party by distinguishing between an avant-garde branch and a popular front. The avant-garde would consist of revolutionary activists, trained in Marxism and prepared for the inevitable armed struggle, since the countries' leaders would not give up power peacefully. The popular front would include a vast grouping of progressive organizations—trade unions, professional associations, and allied political parties.

In reply to these criticisms, the leadership admitted that Tudeh had perhaps committed some errors, that it had probably underestimated the theoretical dimension, but it took pride in having created the first mass movement in Iranian history.[36] The proposal to form an avant-garde branch was called elitist, separating intellectuals from workers and peasants. The party felt it had already created structures to welcome liberals and sympathizers, such as the women's organization, trade unions, and professional organizations. Participating in government and entering Parliament were justified as a springboard for propagating communism, like strategies employed by other revolutionary parties, particularly the French Communist Party, which had proceeded in exactly the same way.

As for the purists who wanted to avoid any political compromise, the leadership called them armchair revolutionaries, incapable of understanding the importance of participating in political institutions. It also felt that the opinions of the extreme left would frighten Iranians and alienate them from communism. Tudeh followed Lenin's advice, asserting "All communist parties in the world do not have to imitate our experience,"[37] and rejected the blind adoption of other countries'

---

[35] Alatur (pseudonym), *Hezbé Toudeh Iran sar-e dorahi* (Iran's Tudeh Party at the Cross-Roads), Tehran, Tudeh Editions, 1947, pp. 1–145. In another work, published the same year, Eshaq provides further detail on this second theme. Eprim Eshaq, *Cheh Bâyad Kard?* (What should be done?), Tehran, Tudeh Editions, 1947, pp. 1–24.

[36] Ehsan Tabari, "A Study of the Conditions under which the Tudeh Emerged, Developed, and Struggled," *Nameyé* Mardom, Tehran, April 1, 1947.

[37] Ehsan Tabari et al., *Tahlil az ozaye hezb* (A Study of the Party's Conditions), Tehran, Editions of the Tudeh Party, 1947, pp. 1–40.

slogans. The party would formulate its own political orientations in accordance with its national environment, thereby following Marx's maxim, according to which "in a capitalist society, the workers must fight to overturn the bourgeoisie, but in a feudal society, they should help the progressive bourgeoisie to overturn the reactionary aristocracy."[38] In other words, Tudeh still hesitated to publicly avow its ideology and openly assert itself as a communist political party.

In this entanglement of fear, hypocrisy, and lies, a scission appeared in the party, with two tendencies, radical and moderate, openly confronting each other. Both already existed and had cohabited for better or for worse. In that political and historical context, this difficult coexistence collapsed under jealousies, rivalries and personal conflicts between Central Committee members, and the two tendencies separated definitively. Yes, both were pro-Soviet, and to the extent that Tudeh drew closer to Moscow, they both adopted Stalinist communism, but the differences that divided them were fundamental.

The radicals' perception of Marxism was very dogmatic,[39] approving the dictatorship of the proletariat and denouncing the "petite bourgeoisie." They disapproved in general of the nationalist government. Tudeh's anti-Mossadeq positions came from their ranks. For them, the nationalist prime minister and the National Front belonged to the Iranian bourgeoisie and had close ties with the Americans, unlike the shah and those close to him who were allies of the British. This view of diplomatic relations led Tudeh radicals to see the conflict between the National Front and the British government as simply a dispute between English and American interests in Iran.[40] When the leadership proposed supporting Mossadeq, the radicals announced that no

---

[38] *Ibid.*

[39] This tendency was led by young activists like Tabari, Kianuri, Kambakhsh, Ovanessian.

[40] *Cf.* Afsaneh Najmabadi, *Land Reform and Social Class Change in Iran*, Salt Lake City, University of Utah Press, 1987. It is obvious that the petroleum nationalization movement, as we have seen, cannot be reduced to the simplistic analyses presented by some Tudeh members. It is in fact important to bear in mind the existing rivalry between the United States and Great Britain. The latter played a dominant role in Iran until the end of World War II. Yet by the end of the 1950s, the understanding between the two powers had frayed. The landowners who supported the British represented a serious obstacle for American plans. As soon as the reform had been suggested as a solution to the Iranian economic crisis, the Anglo-American coalition in Iran became problematical. In their competition, the British counted on their traditional allies, the landowners, while the Americans relied on a part of the bourgeoisie that supported them during the 1953 coup d'état. At that date, however, the Anglo-American rivalry was not yet a real problem, and their complicity made it possible to overturn Mossadeq's government. In fact, that coup d'état was a common initiative.

solidarity with non-communists could be tolerated. Another divisive issue was that the radicals considered Tudeh the "workers' party," while for the moderates, it belonged not only to all the workers but also to other deprived strata of Iranian society.

The moderate wing was led by Iraj Eskandari, Reza Radmanesh, and Fereidun Keshavarz. Initially opposed to Mossadeq, they gradually came to adhere to his cause before finally supporting him completely. They felt that the party could ally itself with non-communist forces without taking a dominant role therein. With a more flexible view of Marxism than the radicals, they felt the dictatorship of the proletariat to be unimportant. The policy of supporting the nationalists—to the point where Tudeh became an ally of Mossadeq after, July 1952—resulted in this faction's taking control of the party.[41]

The Great Split

In 1945, when the tension between party leaders and Maleki was growing worse, the party moderates drew closer to the latter and his group in order to expel non-Marxists from the leadership and to reinforce the theoretical training of party officials. However, once the delicate issues had been identified, they found themselves in the same position as the previous Central Committee. Unlike Maleki, they had no intention of breaking with the Soviet Union for two reasons. First, they admired the *first* socialist country and believed in international solidarity. Second, they felt that an independent Tudeh would push the Soviets to create a rival satellite party. In the end, the moderates accused Maleki's group of lacking discernment in its destructive criticism and of plotting to divide the party. Finally, they reproached them with refusing to conform to majority decisions.

In fact, Maleki never hesitated to criticize harshly his Central Committee comrades. During the first party congress, he criticized the leadership for what he called its "weaknesses": its pact with the Devil (USSR) in order to obtain parliamentary seats, its lack of organization, its inappropriate choices of leaders, its hasty recruitments, its ignorance of ideology, and its inability to discipline the workers' movement. Maleki's radical thought was opposed to Tudeh's pacifism and led him to attack the leadership, which he accused of blindly seeking a parliamentary road to socialism—a road that Maleki believed did not exist.

---

[41] For more information see: Behrooz, *op. cit.*, 2000, pp. 16–21; Tabari, *op. cit.*, 1947, p. 170.

However, the principal issue that divided Maleki from the leadership lay elsewhere. As a patriot, he could not accept his party's unconditional obedience to Moscow. He had no particular admiration for the Soviets and felt that the Iranian left should not receive orders from foreigners, whatever the pretext. In his memoirs he refers to his initial hesitation to join the party because, despite its members' "good intentions," the corruption and moral weakness of its founders had not escaped his notice. Since his stay in Berlin, he had been attracted by the ideas of Kautsky and the German social democrats. Furthermore, he had no sympathy with Lenin and his authoritarian communism, still less with the Russian Bolsheviks.[42]

It was on the Azerbaijan issue, in 1945, that the tension between Maleki and Tudeh reached its crisis. Sent by the party's Central Committee to study the situation and prepare a report, he declared that the Soviets were behaving like an army of occupation and that their officers treated Iranians with a good deal of arrogance and contempt. Maleki wrote that Tudeh should not have supported the Azerbaijan separatist and pro-Soviet movement, which was primarily opportunistic. This conclusion greatly annoyed party leaders.

After this report, Maleki and other dissidents decided to resign from the party just before being expelled. This was the most important split in Tudeh's history.[43] Maleki then created the Tudeh Socialist Foundation (*Jame'ey-e sosialisti-e Toudeh*), intended to be communism's progressive wing and to criticize the errors of the party he had just left. However, this foundation was rapidly dissolved, since the Soviet Union would not recognize it.[44] Maleki then lived through a period of political inactivity and made several attempts at suicide. Some years later, the exclusion of the Yugoslav Communist Party from the Cominform[45] brought him back into politics. He founded a new group to which he gave the significant name of *Niruy-e Sevvom* (the Third Force). This group adopted Titoism as its ideological line and objected to Tudeh's doctrine, denounced as a mere copy of Soviet Bolshevism.

---

[42] Milani, *op. cit.*, 2008, pp. 222–226.

[43] Among these "separatists" were some renowned intellectuals, of whom several were members of the Central Committee. Among these were Anvar Khame'i, Jalal Al-Ahmad, Nader Naderpour, Eprim Eshaq, Ebrahim Golestan.

[44] Years later, Khalil Maleki returned to politics, thanks to the Workers' Party. *Cf.* Behrooz, *op. cit.*, 2000, pp. 31–34.

[45] The Cominform was the centralized organization of the international communist movement from 1947 to 1956. It was, in a way, the successor to the Comintern. *Cf.* Wolikow, *op. cit.*, 2010.

At the start of the 1950s, when the fight to nationalize oil was at its peak, Maleki began publishing the magazine *Niruy-e Sevvom*. The editorial committee, committed to scientific socialism, tried to work out a new version of socialism, one that could be adapted to the country's social/economic conditions. The magazine was equal to its founders' political and ideological ambitions and also reflected Maleki's capacity to attract talented people to him. The editorial committee was composed of the most influential writers. Eprim Eshaq, Jalal Al-Ahmad and his wife, the famous novelist Simin Daneshvar, the poet Nader Naderpour, and other leading people in the world of Persian literature wrote for the magazine. An idea of its contents is the best indication of Maleki's cultural and political aspirations. In 1951, for the Iranian New Year, the magazine's special issue included an article on the English Chartist Movement, the translation of a poem by W. H. Auden, a criticism of daily life in the Soviet Union, a laudatory essay on the contribution of Muslim scholars to fundamental physics at the start of the twelfth century, a criticism of Soviet genetics, a short novel by Thomas Mann. Finally, in an essay signed by him, Maleki pointed out the common features between the Soviet Union and Nazi Germany, describing the pro-Soviet Iranian communists as "the fifth column of an imperialist government." The back cover announced the forthcoming publication of the Persian translation of Arthur Koestler's famous novel, *The Zero and the Infinite*, on the Soviet Union in the 1930s and the establishment of Stalin's totalitarian vision. This work's translators were regular contributors to the magazine. It was then hardly surprising that the Iranian Stalinists should have accused *Niruy-e Sevvom* of being a tool of "imperialist propaganda."

The country's current problems and the fate of Mossadeq's government were also discussed. Despite deep disagreements with the head of government, Maleki was an ardent defender of oil nationalization. He supported the prime minister until the very end. One year before the 1953 coup d'état, Maleki wrote: "If Mossadeq does not change his policy, the fall of his government is imminent." He particularly criticized the lack of any concrete program for solving the country's internal problems. His prediction soon came true, and yet Mossadeq's fall annihilated him. He wrote to Mossadeq, aging and exhausted: "I will follow you to hell."

On August 23, 1953, just before surrendering to the police, in a public and impassioned letter that was never published, Maleki addressed the Iranians, explaining in detail the circumstances that had led to Mossadeq's defeat. In this letter, he accused the United States, England, and the Soviet Union of having plotted against the nationalist government. He called upon his partisans to maintain the life of the movement and not to allow themselves to be demobilized by the childish radicalism of the left nor by the brutality of the right. He felt that the only legitimate way to transform Iran was through "legal and peaceful reforms" like all the world's civilized countries. He pointed to Tudeh as the Iranian people's most dangerous enemy—worse than the shah's regime. Shortly thereafter, Maleki and his comrades were arrested. After his liberation, in despair at the shah's return to the throne and the repression that followed, Maleki fell into alcoholism and depression. In 1969, he died in complete solitude.[46]

Settling Accounts

The study of Tudeh's documents reveals that most of the factional differences came from rivalries and antipathies between activists rather than from true political and ideological disagreements. Between 1953 and 1954, the Central Committee that had remained in Tehran sent five letters to the leadership, then exiled abroad. They provided a general view of Tudeh's internal situation and revealed the extent of the divisions and paralysis suffered by the party during the years of strong police repression that followed the coup d'état.[47]

In these letters, the Central Committee requests the arbitration of the exiled leaders concerning a member, Nur-e-din Kianuri (1915–1999). Grandson of the famous religious *sheikh* Fazlollah Nuri—in his time the great enemy of the constitutionalists—Kianuri was the first secretary of the party and one of its theoreticians. Professor of civil engineering at the University of Tehran, he had studied at a German university. His many facets and his varied ideological leanings made him one of the most complex figures of Iranian communism. Unlike the party radicals, fervent admirers of Stalin, his sympathies lay with Mao. Yet his devotion to the Soviet Union was such that he did not hesitate to assert publicly "if the Soviets ask something of a Tudeh member, the latter must obey, even without informing the party or at the expense

---

[46] See *Khalil* Maleki *be ravayat-e asnad-e* Savak (Khalil Maleki according to Savak documents), Tehran, Markaze baresye asnade tarikhye vezarate etela'at, 1379/2000, p. 507. Quoted in Milani, *op. cit.*, 2008.

[47] These letters were first published in Europe and later included in Kianuri's memoirs. *Cf.* Kianuri, *op. cit.*, 1997, pp. 307–335.

109

of his country's interests.[48] Whether partisans or adversaries of Tudeh, numerous were those who denounced the relations that Kianuri and his friend Kambakhsh maintained with the Soviet secret services. Just before dying, after having spent long years in the Islamic Republic's prisons, Kianuri asked his comrades to forgive "the erroneous orientations" of his youth.[49]

The Central Committee's letters blamed Kianuri and his faction for all the party's failures, saying that he had created an irreparable situation. He was reproached with wanting to take control of the party and with sectarian, bureaucratic, and opportunistic acts. He was said to be responsible for Tudeh's deplorable situation. The letters then attacked his personal life. The signers denounced his "morally corrupt behavior" and condemned his wife Maryam Firouz (1914–2008) for her infidelity. They claimed to have shown written proofs of this to Kianuri, which he denied ever having received. At the head of the Tudeh Party's women's organization, Maryam Firouz was one of the first Iranian feminists. From a Qajar family, a cousin of Mossadeq, she was called the "red princess." Her broad-mindedness and her keen fight against machismo brought her many enemies in the very heart of Tudeh.[50]

This example clearly reveals the prevailing patriarchal patterns of a communist party's leaders, all of whom came from upper class families. True, the rigidity of Iranian mores is hardly a novelty, but that such issues appear in Tudeh's secret correspondence shows a serious deterioration of personal relations, as well as a very lowering view of men/women relations. During the party's fourth plenary, Kianuri was harshly criticized for his lack of "revolutionary character" and his "corrupt mores." In fact, the rumors of his wife's infidelity blackened his image far more in the eyes of his comrades than his suspect relations with the KGB.

Despite their pretension to broad-mindedness, the communists were no different in their practices from other Iranians on the question of

---

[48] Keshavarz, *op. cit.*, 1987, p. 45.

[49] In 1995, Kianuri testified before the United Nations Human Rights Commission on the conditions endured by political prisoners in Iran. He was at that time the only detainee who dared to officially denounce the torture and other inhumane practices carried out in the Islamic Republic's prisons.

[50] Kianuri was Maryam Firouz's second husband. She was condemned to death by the shah's regime after the coup d'état but fled Iran, first to the USSR and then to the German Democratic Republic. The day after the 1979 revolution, she returned to Iran after twenty-six years of exile. Two years later, the Islamic regime threw her into prison where she was tortured and raped for many years. She remained under police surveillance until the end of her life.

respecting the honor codes dictated by patriarchal culture, as defined by traditional principles.[51] Very few women managed to rise in the hierarchy of Iranian political parties, whatever their faction or ideological leaning;[52] even fewer were those who escaped calumny or a bad reputation as soon as they wanted to assume their activist roles independently of their family ties (whether to father, brother, or husband). Nonetheless, despite women's secondary place in its internal organization, Tudeh always defended their rights, and in particular the right to vote that had been granted them by the shah. And this, when the clergy fiercely opposed it.

Disappearance

The growing tensions between the Soviet Union and China toward the end of the 1950s divided Tudeh more and more. Many factions—Cuban, Maoist, Stalinist, anti-Stalinist—arose within the party, without anyone really knowing what differentiated them. The personality cult reigned supreme, and impassioned arguments about the figures of Stalin, Mao, Castro, and others rent activists apart. Contrary to what might have been expected, the real disagreements were neither doctrinal nor ideological. They concerned above all personal rivalries or organizational details.

Deprived of any legal existence since the 1953 coup d'état, in the 1960s Tudeh was a party torn by internal struggles for power and weakened by the departure of the Maoist activists. These separatist groups, in spite of pretending to be substantially different, strongly resembled each other. They had the same internal organization, close to the Stalinist model, but admired China and Albania more than the Soviet Union. Like Tudeh, their view of Iranian society and of the shah's reforms were idealistic. Similarly, they tried to organize the people to combat the imperial regime but quickly failed.

The best example of these unrealistic splinter groups was the attempt by "The Revolutionary Organization of Iran's Tudeh Party" (ROITP) to form a peasant army. Created by former Tudeh activists between 1961 and 1963, the ROITP gathered all Iranian communists who contested Tudeh's pro-Soviet line. Fascinated by the Chinese experiment, they promoted Maoism, which considered third-world countries as

---

[51] Personal differences and rivalries, perhaps somewhat less intense, also marked young Marxists. On this, see: Behrooz, *op. cit.*, 2000, p. 144.

[52] The singular case of Maryam Rajavi's presidency of the Mojahedin of the People's Organization will be analyzed further on.

"semi-feudal" and "semi-colonial." Although Iran had no urban proletariat, they called on the rural areas to rebel. They wanted to repeat the Chinese experiment, ignoring the living conditions of Iranian peasants.[53] In those years of industrial reform, peasants were more and more attracted to the cities with their factories and large industries, and their only desire was to leave their villages quickly to reach what seemed to them a real El Dorado. They were naturally indifferent to the ROITP activists' calls. Such efforts were bound to fail.

In the 1960s, Tudeh therefore tried to reorganize, but it remained very weak. Finally, it proclaimed openly its official Marxist-Leninist ideology. Its exiled leaders had great difficulty in reinforcing their ties with members who had remained in Iran. The Savak had largely infiltrated their organization. Even abroad, where the party seemed more active, it did not succeed in taking the opposition's lead[54] and was rejected by activists of the National Front and by rival communist splinter groups. During the troubles at the start of the 1960s, it played only a marginal role. From then on, Tudeh was but a shadow of its former self. It was unable to adopt a coherent line against the imperial regime. Its analyses of reforms and of social and political problems appeared contradictory and showed no clear view of the Iranian situation. Less popular than ever, it still pretended to be "Iran's true communist party" or "the authentic workers' party" (*hezb-e taraz-e novin-e tabaqey-e kargar*).

Tudeh's successive crises only weakened and atrophied it. Members separated from the leadership, some of whom sought refuge in the Soviet Union and others in European countries. In the course of time the leadership frayed. Gradually the party fell into general indifference. Absent from the Iranian scene, it was no longer referred to as a political actor and slipped into the collective unconscious. From time to time, some former leaders were heard of, through their criticisms or analyses of events. After the 1979 revolution, they returned to Iran to reorganize the party, but this attempt was swiftly crushed by the Islamic regime. Until the fall of the Soviet Union, part of the organization still remained active, and underground cells continued more or less to

---

[53] *Cf.* Bijan Jazani, *Capitalism and Revolution in Iran*, London, Zed Press, 1980, pp. 148–151; Tabari, *op. cit.*, 1947, pp. 234–238.

[54] The most important of these was the Confederation of Iranian Students. In the 1960s, Iranian students studying in foreign countries founded communist groups of various tendencies and openly criticized the shah's economic and social policies. In 1960, the Confederation was rapidly politicized and transformed into a radical group opposed to the shah. It supported movements whose set aim was to overthrow the Pahlavi dynasty.

function. Tudeh even tried to secretly introduce some of its members into the Iranian administration, in an attempt to influence leaders of the Islamic Republic. The fall of the Soviet regime was the final blow to the party and eliminated it from the Iranian stage. Is Tudeh really dead, however? Will it not, once again, manage to rise from its ashes?

The Imprint of Tudeh

Tudeh's obedience to the Soviet Union, its refusal to assume its ideological choices, and its strategic errors at key moments of Iranian history gave it a reputation for treachery. Yet its enigma remains. The question is: Can one sum up the symbolic weight of a communist party, that lasted for several decades in a country deeply rooted in Islam, in its mistaken political choices and strategic errors?

Nothing allows one to claim with any certainty that, without Soviet help, Tudeh would have survived the hostile context of the years from 1940 to 1950. Nor does anything support the supposition that, had Tudeh detached itself from the Soviet Union, its future would have been better than that of Maleki and his group. But to go further, it is highly probable that a frank declaration of its anti-religious ideological line from its inception would not have enabled it to survive the repression. An openly communist Tudeh would undoubtedly have been swept away by both the imperial regime and the clergy.

Tudeh always avoided a direct clash with the religious beliefs of Iranians. On the other hand, it prudently encouraged them to make changes that could improve the present and orient society toward the future. Party theoreticians were convinced that preparing individuals to build a better future would draw them from their religious and traditional past. Deeming it useless to directly confront the *olama*, most Tudeh members tended to believe that religious tradition was fated to disappear by itself. They never suspected that it could be legitimized anew and used again by the new religious actors. By categorically opposing religion to reason, they were too quick to believe in the imminent success of the latter.

In spite of the internal conflicts that divided it from the start, the external dangers that threatened its existence, and the many vicissitudes of its history, the party never turned to violence. Its structure was essentially based on democratic principles and on the assertion of the rights and duties of each member. As fascinated as they were by the Soviet Union, its leaders did not want to use the same radical means—dear to Stalin—to solve their internal problems or to settle accounts with external adversaries. Brought up in Iran's upper class and having studied in the finest universities in the world, party leaders systematically tried to achieve their goals by political means.

The practice of criticism and self-criticism, necessary to all democratic organizations, held an important place in the party. Members often accused the leadership, and the latter always felt obliged to reply to every reproach. Nothing ever shook the party leaders' conviction as to the efficiency of rational solutions and the virtue of negotiation.

It was true that Tudeh never asserted itself as an independent communist party, but it did introduce respect for democratic principles into its members' political culture. Tudeh's merit lay primarily in the political modernity of its popular organizations. Its members were trained to use democratic thought in their political relations and in their exchanges with others. Tens of thousands of Iranians thus learned the usefulness of, and the need for, active rational participation in their country's political debates.

Tudeh claimed that its activists included about a third of civil servants and workers.[55] This enabled it to introduce a thoughtful and controllable relationship to politics and to society, a reflection on how to live with dignity. It drew the attention of thousands of its members to their individual rights as well as to their living conditions with reference to political and social rules.

If Tudeh did not know how to adapt communism to the Iranian context, if it was unable to work out a clear ideological position, it went perhaps further than that in introducing a new relationship to politics. It changed the view of many Iranians on politics. In the 1940s, two decades before the shah's reforms modernized politics, Tudeh deployed all its efforts to rationalize relations between society and politics. When the shah's reforms were still only embryonic, Tudeh began laying the groundwork for the changes that were to mark Iranian history. It is true that Tudeh was unable to carry its projects to conclusion, and the steps it had so well begun were crushed early on. Still it succeeded in blazing the trail of a rational relationship to politics for Iranians. Nothing could efface that rational, even democratic, imprint left on Iranian politics by the party's more than forty years of activism.

---

[55] In 1946, Tudeh was at the height of its glory with three ministers (Keshavarz, Eskandari, and Yazdi) in the government. The circulation of its official journal *Rahbar* had reached 120,000 copies. It numbered some 100,000 active members and more than 335,000 sympathizers. The majority lived in the cities, since the party's success was limited among the villagers. One year earlier, in 1945, the Iranian population was estimated at less than fourteen million people, hardly 30 percent of which lived in the large cities. For details concerning the origins of Tudeh members, see: Abrahamian, *op. cit.*, 1982, p. 303.

5

Revolutionarism (1960–1978)

From the 1953 coup d'état to the mid 1960s, the communist movement was marked by a long history of crisis, dissidence, opposition, and exclusions that tore it apart. The young communists, well educated and activist, no longer believed in the possibility of a political intervention. The incapacity of the parties—National Front, MLI, and Tudeh—to confront the event and their difficulties in adapting to the new environment created by the imperial regime all contributed to the despair of the young. Many left Tudeh to invent a new communist movement.

While the world blazed with wars of independence and popular rebellions, their movement tried to develop in a social context strewn with obstacles. Fascinated by world events, Iranian communist activists were borne along by the revolutionary spirit that inflamed the entire planet. Their enthusiasm was contagious and exalted the whole of society. Never before had Iranians been so attentive to what happened beyond their borders; never had they been so concerned with world-shaking events. Yet, the young communists' revolutionarism quickly led them to favor political action over theoretical reflection. Neither serious analysis of the ideologies they proclaimed nor the least adaptation of these to their country's specific context strengthened their action. Their disdain for theoretical reflection greatly weakened a movement that was, of course, essentially ideological.

The New Communist Movement

The new communist movement that asserted itself after Tudeh's decline was born from the debris of the crisis of confidence that shook the preceding generation. Several years later, the young were still unable to comprehend the reasons that had led Tudeh to what its leaders called "the strategic defeat" when faced with the putschists. The young strongly denounced the party's erroneous choices. Ideologically and sociologically disparate, they nevertheless organized themselves against the leadership to break the party's unity and to create a new party. At first, the task was hardly obvious. Imbued with the same line of thought as their predecessors, the young communist activists resembled, far more than they thought, those whose treachery they denounced. Despite all the bonds linking them to their elders in the 1960s, these young were a new generation of militant communists, more revolutionary, less Bolshevik, both greater in number and less educated than the preceding generation. They seemed deeply impressed by the struggles for independence taking place throughout the world, but they were rebellious to the Cominform and detached from the Soviet Union. Preaching revolutionary action and the armed struggle, they created a communism different from that of Tudeh in its relations to society and to politics. The distinction between the two generations was important.

During the period between Tudeh's decline and the 1979 revolution, the new communist movement had a rebellious spirit and militarist tendencies, while the old generation had been pacifist and essentially rational. At that time, the dominant feature of the movement was its great diversity,[1] both in ideology and in organization. Following numerous exchanges with foreign groups, Iranian activists were familiar with the various left-wing trends of thought. There followed endless theoretical political arguments and serious misunderstandings in the movement. To this was added the unexpected opening up of Iranian politics at the start of the 1960s. After the election of President John F. Kennedy, the American government insisted that Iran apply democratic reforms and obliged the shah to institute changes. The National Front took advantage of this to have some of its members enter Parliament. The Marxist-Leninist think tanks comprising students and former Tudeh members met and functioned openly. The promotion of communist ideas was on the agenda, and hundreds of books and articles from all sources were translated into Persian, contributing to a new dynamics in the public sphere.

---

[1] The new communist movement consisted of about one hundred different groups. We can cite, for example, the four following: *Sazman-e enquelabi-e Komunisti-e Iran* (SAKA), the Organization of Revolutionary Communists of Iran; *Gorouh-e perosa* (Trial Group), founded by a former member of the Tudeh Party who had had to leave the party in 1933 because of his opposition to Mossadeq; *Sazman-e rahaïbakhsh-e Iran* (Liberalizing Organization of Iran), a Maoist group; *Gorouh-e Nikkhah* (Nikkhah Group), a Marxist formation bearing the name of its founder. The members of this last group wanted to inscribe themselves in the line of the Revolutionary Organization of the Tudeh Party of Iran, but they were accused of having organized an attack against the shah in 1965 and were all arrested. After long years in prison, Nikkhah, the group's founder, abandoned his leftist ideas and supported the shah's government. He was executed immediately after the 1979 Revolution.

The Iranian intelligentsia showed a real infatuation for communism, and the finest writers of Persian literature began to translate ideological texts. However, lacking any methodical process, they did not succeed in providing their Persian language readers with a coherent and complete view of Marxism or of Marxist-Leninism, and even less of the international communist movement. The choice of books depended on the translators' tastes and preferences, and side by side with certain basic texts—such as the *Communist Party Manifesto*—the various ideological tendencies of the communist movements were, at best, ambiguous. As much as the intellectuals and the students admired the rationality of Marxism, whose anti-religious side seemed to them the only road to modernity, so much did devout in popular milieus fear communists and think themselves in danger.

Very quickly, moreover, the regime again limited cultural and political activities, and repression once more closed the public sphere. In 1963, renewed tension between the shah and his opponents, the *great* ayatollah in the lead, succeeded in stifling dissident voices. The shah dissolved the National Front, prohibited opposition group activities, and showed particular hostility to the young communist activists.

Despite the repression, many writers and intellectuals continued their work of popularizing communism.[2] An underground intellectual network of Marxist-Leninist thinkers was set up. Given the ideological domination of the revolutionary left in a large part of the Third World in the 1960s, the concept of revolution attracted the intelligentsia and seemed the only solution to Iranian society's problems, freeing it from the shah's control. Henceforth, revolution alone seemed able to emancipate the Iranian proletariat from "capitalism," "liberalism," and the "bourgeoisie." Those three themes were repeated systematically in the writings of the elite who, nonetheless, never defined the proletariat they wanted to free. As for "liberalism" and the "bourgeoisie," those terms still have no equivalents in the Persian language.

Yet, the young communist activists believed in the infinite potential of the proletariat and tried, first of all, to educate it so that it would take its destiny into its own hands. Communist propaganda texts invited the popular class to rebel against the "bourgeois system" or against "capitalism" and its "blood-thirsty liberals," three expressions

---

[2] Among them were interpreters and academics like Manouchehr Hezarkhani and Merteza Ravandi, the poet Ahmad Shamlou, the novelists Siavosh Kasraï, Mohamad-Ali Afghani, and Samad Behrangi.

used synonymously. Activists spoke of the "economic struggle of the proletariat against the "bourgeois" and the "petite bourgeois." This implied that revolutionary action should be led against the opportunists who made common cause with the "unjust class system." Some groups began to speak of the need for armed action (*jang-e mossalahaneh*) as the legitimate way to free the oppressed people (*toudey-e zahmatkesh*) from "blood-thirsty capitalism."

In a country not yet emerged from a traditional economy and, as yet, only very slightly industrialized, not only were the afore-mentioned capitalists not generally detested, but in fact they stood for prosperity and economic modernization. The "blood-thirsty capitalism" that the communist activists asked people to combat only existed in an embryonic state and would take a long time to mature and, eventually, become detested. But the worst confusion of the communist activists concerned the "Iranian proletariat," still deeply imbued with religious culture. Without having measured the influence of religion over this proletariat, the communists deplored the "ignorance of the masses." This undeniably objective fact was not followed by any attempt to really educate these masses. At the same time, like their Tudeh predecessors, fearing the reaction of the *olama*, the young communist activists made no attempt to undertake a true critical analysis of religion and the clergy's role. Paradoxically, it would take the appearance of new Muslim thinkers to finally question religious authority over society.

While imperialism and the bourgeoisie were considered the people's worst political enemies, the clergy and their influence over the impoverished classes were greatly under-estimated. The communist activists saw the clergy as a disappearing species, against which no effort, not the slightest pedagogical work, would be required: "Religion is the opium of the people and is fated to disappear by itself. It is not for us to insult popular culture,"[3] they explained. They did, however, deem it necessary "to emancipate the proletariat from the ideological influence of the bourgeoisie,"[4] even if the term bourgeoisie remained opaque in a country whose structure was still tribal. Thus, they accused the media and the press of being under the control of the poisonous ideology of the "bourgeoisie," of "social chauvinism," and of "right wing opportunism." These concepts, always

---

[3] *Cf.* http://mobarez.web.surftown.se/?cat=166, Archive of Organizations of Iranian Communist Activists (1965–1979).

[4] *Ibid.*

written in Latin in Persian texts, were not really clarified in communist activist writings. In spite of the nearly mystical influence they had over intellectuals, they remained incomprehensible to the proletariat that these men sought to attract. On the other hand, thanks to the incomparable eloquence of the *mollah*, religious speech continued to bewitch the people, to whom it seemed far more understandable—therefore efficient—than the ideological speech of the communist activists.

As for the intellectuals, their attraction to Marxism, and especially to Stalinism, seemed more emotional than rational. It was the popular side of Marxist speech that appealed to them. One of the remarkable properties of ideology, according to Marcel Gauchet, was that that type of speech could be reduced to a few simple ideologemes, while filling out that elementary theme with erudite demonstrations and sophisticated analyses.

By definition, ideology is a two-faceted speech: popular and erudite. It is popular when serving as propaganda. It must be filled out with scientific pretension to serve as an explanatory and normative discourse. Some authors are able to play it both ways and to go from one register to the other. But it is the existence of this skillfully worked out language that can carry conviction on crucial issues and be the object of learned recognition, ensuring the plausibility of what would otherwise be reduced to insignificant slogans. The combination of both aspects is necessary to really occupy the ideological space.[5]

Having studied science or technology, favoring the practical and theoretical aspects, totally foreign to the tools of philosophic thought— and indeed contemptuous of these—rare were the Iranian communists who understood the learned side of Marxism. Still more rare were those who felt the slightest desire to submit their dogmatic belief in communism to the test of critical reason. In addition, most of them had but a very approximate idea of their country's history, of the society in which they lived and of its productive forces. In fact, it was through Marxism that they began to study, albeit in a disorganized way, politics, society and history. Lacking distance, they had no overall view of the social context and could not therefore apply adequate theories. Their communism was clear only as to its principles, and the question of procedures remained completely open. Their knowledge of the world of thought, speech, and representations that characterized Marxist

---

[5] *Cf.* Gauchet, *op. cit.,* 2011–2012.

ideology suffered from many misunderstandings. Among others, their admiration of Stalin was startling. Not knowing, or not wanting to know, what went on in the Soviet Union, Iranian communists identified Marxism with Stalin's person and maintained an unconditional sympathy for him, without according the least importance to the criticisms expressed by the Soviets themselves on the Stalin era.

The emotional relationship of Iranian activists to communism was one of exaltation and adoration. Like the clergy who adamantly quote Koranic verses, rejecting the slightest discussion or the least doubt, Iranian communists spoke of Marxism religiously: Marx, Lenin, and Stalin replaced the Prophet of Islam and his holy Imams. Their faith seemed so unshakeable that one might believe them able to move mountains.[6] To hear them, the "dogmatic closure of Islam"[7] extends to Marxism as well, so that any critical approach or rational analysis would be punished by God.

However, unlike the clergy, the discourse of the communists did not enclose them in the past. It opened the horizons of the future and oriented its adherents toward new prospects, toward a better future in which hope was possible. Marxism gave them a new explanation of the world in which they lived, divided between the dominant and the dominated, shaped by class struggle, and in which injustice would be righted. These ideas were received favorably by those who had known only the paralyzing speech of the clergy, which invited them to forget the present world for the promises of the world to come and accept suffering here to be the better rewarded in Paradise.

---

[6] The certainty with which they quote Marx or Lenin seems, at the least, baffling. Even today one can hear new communists say: "Freedom is one of the forms of bourgeois dictatorship," "When freedom reigns, there will be no more State," or "Religion is the sigh of a dejected creature . . . the opium of the people."

[7] "The Islam of dogmatic closing" means that the intellectual field—in which human reason is permitted to carry out its research—is closed by the Muslim theory of revelation. Since the thirteenth century, the implacable solidarity between political power, writings, and the official religion has imposed a permanent dogmatic closure on the entire Muslim world. Attributing the exclusive right to interpret the Koran to the *olama*, this dogmatic closure has removed religion from rational inquiry and contributed to the dispersal of free thinkers. Still today, it is imposed on a large part of the Muslim world and encloses it in the rigidity of a canonized knowledge that prevents critical reading of religious texts. It has quickly reduced the Koran to a series of definitions, of dogmatic standards of enforced behavior. For more details on the dogmatic closure, see Mohammed Arkoun, *Penser Islam aujourd' hui*, Neuchâtel, Unesco/La Baconnière, 1977.

The clergy's speech was overborne by the strength of the ideological language of the communists, pushing them to act for a better life here and now. People did not need to know more about an ideology that led them to a better future. In Iran after the coup d'état, Marxism was not merely one choice among others; it was the one and only path enabling intellectuals to situate themselves in the world. It supplied the tools needed by those unable to make sense of what had happened to them. It provided the keys for interpreting the balance of power that seemed beyond them. It helped them to believe that it was possible to live differently and to unite for this purpose. Theory engendered practice, and the time had come to find adequate means to achieve change. Action then became the logical choice for those who no longer accepted submission and forced silence. The communist militants' will to act led them to a dizzying and unprecedented experience: revolution. This required blood and sacrifice. They would now learn to give their lives in order to change the world.

With a victorious revolution in Cuba, Algerians having won their independence, and Americans checkmated in Vietnam, a revolutionary fever set Iranian activists ablaze. They took as their models the emblematic figures of Mao Zedong and Che Guevara, stressing the communists' role as armed and educated pioneers against a repressive state dominated by capitalism and imperialism.

Among the events that both favored and conditioned the revolutionary movement, the shah's reinforced power after the 1963 rebellion marked a real turning point. Repression took over in Iran and stifled the public sphere. Unable to participate legally in politics, the revolutionaries decided to move into action and rapidly chose the most radical solutions. Guerilla groups were organized in Iran, as in many countries in Asia and Africa. They wanted to prove themselves worthy of their idols and to radically change their country. The young communists broke with their milieu and went underground, learning military training in the mountains and the forests.

The 1960s were marked by the appearance of armed groups whose common denominators were disorder and disorganization. Composed of former Tudeh members or of intellectuals newly converted to Marxism, their ambition was to strengthen the communist movement. They lacked, however, any clear and coherent theory and thus any real action strategy. Faced with a repression that crushed all opposition, the armed struggle and the systematic use of violence became their only means of combating the imperial regime and of thereby asserting their existence. Reduced to reacting to political events, they followed them without in any way controlling them. The armed struggle became the movement's only strategy, leading the country's most gifted youth to perish in urban guerilla battles or in the shah's prisons. By the end of the 1960s, the communist movement's return was completed. All the Marxist groups were engaged in fighting a regime that was then at the height of its power.

The Remodeling

The 1970s were a glorious decade for the imperial regime. The reforms of previous years bore fruit and consolidated the shah's power. The United States ensured the regime of its backing and provided it with valuable military support. The Iranian army thus benefited from the latest technological innovations. Oil revenues gave the shah the means with which to modernize the country. He triumphed over his adversaries on the international political stage.

During those same years, relations improved between Iran and the Soviet Union. While Brezhnev was in power, the two countries grew much closer together. For the Soviets, the disappearance of Tudeh, their principal ally in Iran, the absence of any alternative to the shah, and, above all, purely economic considerations favored the dialogue with Teheran. For the imperial regime, the Soviet Union still represented a threat not to be underestimated. It was therefore important to normalize relations with that powerful northern neighbor.[8]

The shah was convinced that the success of his reforms entailed strengthening his power and completely crushing all opposition groups, Islamic and Marxist. Between 1965 and 1970, the Savak managed to eliminate many underground cells that were preparing armed operations. At the start of the 1970s, all the power was in the shah's hands; Parliament was no more than a figurehead and the government a simple middleman between the two.

Yet that period saw the restructuring of Marxist groups and the revival of their activities. The harsh repression pushed many political activists into the armed struggle. Unable to establish a base within the country, what remained of Tudeh and of its Maoist splinter groups faded into the background. From 1970 to 1979, the revolutionary

---

[8] Thus, in 1966, the two countries signed a pact according to which Iran supplied natural gas to its northern neighbor and, in exchange, the Soviets sold it military supplies and participated in certain industrial projects. The most important of these was the Ispahan ironworks complex, the country's first. The operation was followed in 1967 by a five-year agreement.

units returned to the foreground, carrying out armed attacks in the large cities. The last Tudeh members and pacifist intellectuals were incapable of preventing the young communists' headlong rush to ruin. Nobody seemed able to propose an alternative to violence for changing the country's political orientation. Defenders of the armed struggle felt any other option to be unacceptable, accusing their opponents of conservatism and servility. The events that followed only strengthened their choice of armed combat. Caught between the young communists' radicalism and a repression that left no room for any free expression, those thinkers or political groups who, for one reason or another, did not belong to guerilla groups, soon abandoned all political activity and fell into despair.

The period was marked by guerilla warfare, by urban riots, by the heroism of young activists, and, in general, by increasing violence. The impact of the armed struggle was such that even the shah could not hide his astonishment: "The determination with which they fight seems incredible to me," he admitted in an interview on January 13, 1976. "Even the women fight tooth and nail. The men carry cyanide pills and prefer to commit suicide rather than to be arrested."

Very quickly, the Marxist groups faced new problems, both theoretical and practical. They were obliged to find rapid solutions to escape the impasse in which they found themselves. But never having worked out concepts on the individual, society and the historic processes of modernization, nothing helped them to make rational choices; nothing prevented them from yielding to emotional reactions. Without the tools of rational thought, without any in depth analyses of the country's recent history, these young people had no global view of the social and political events that marked their epoch. Strongly attracted by revolutionary fever and anti-imperialist feelings, they were unable to put together a coherent political reflection on the shah's reforms, the nature of his reign, and even less on the role of foreign powers in Iran. Heirs to an autocratic political culture, impregnated with an omnipresent religion, and under the ideological hold of the revolutionary left, the young activists had no way of envisaging any path other than that of armed struggle.

The Origins of Guerilla Warfare

The two most important Marxist groups of the 1960s were Jazani-Zarifi and Ahmadzadeh-Puyan. They were the first to go into action. Although few in number, they succeeded in launching armed attacks against the imperial regime. The Jazani-Zarifi group bore the names of its two founders, Bijan Jazani (1937–1975) and Hassan Zarifi (1937–1975). Its history began at the start of the 1950s. Its members had been active in the Tudeh Youth Organization that had developed underground activities even before the coup d'état. The new group became active at the very beginning of the 1960s. With the defeat of the popular uprising of 1963, they quickly decided that the only way to confront the regime was by armed combat.

In 1967, Jazani and Zarifi signed and disseminated a document defining their strategy for revolutionizing Iran, an actual urban guerilla manual that was to inspire their successors. Yet the group was more used to open political action and had hardly any experience in armed combat. This enabled the Savak to arrest its principal members before the least military operation had been carried out. In 1968, those who had managed to escape the Savak succeeded in reorganizing themselves. Some left for Lebanon and joined the Palestinian movement in order to obtain military training. The youngest of them, Hamid Ashraf (1946–1976) remained in Iran to recruit new members and to keep the group alive. In 1970, the expatriates returned with arms and munitions.

The Ahmadzadeh-Puyan group differed from the first in that it comprised young activists from religious backgrounds and from the old National Front who had no political experience and little knowledge of Marxism. From the start of the 1960s, Massoud Ahmadzadeh (1947–1972) and Amir Parviz Puyan (1947–1971) set up several political-religious cells in their native city of Mashad, to fully engage in the opposition movement. In 1965, Ahmadzadeh and Puyan came to Tehran to study at the university. Very rapidly and contrary to all expectations, they were attracted by communist speech and its opening toward the future. They converted to Marxism, in its Maoist version. Some years later, the group decided that the Chinese model was not adapted to the Iranian situation. It then tried to work out its own vision of armed struggle and to present an analysis of the shah's reforms.

In 1970, the two groups merged to create the organization *Fadaiyan-e Khalq*, convinced that armed struggle was the only way to combat the imperial regime. Despite the important ideological and political differences dividing them, they felt it necessary to remain in solidarity to resist the shah's repression.

Theoreticians of armed struggle

In the history of the Iranian communist movement, Jazani, Ahmadzadeh, and Puyan are considered the theoreticians of guerilla warfare. Authors of a whole series of theoretical analyses, both of the programs and objectives of their group—which later became the Organization of the Fadaiyan of the People (*Sazman-e cherikhay-e fadaiy-e khalq-e Iran*)—as well as of other armed groups in general, they became known as the brains of the communist movement in the 1970s.

All three praised armed combat without really explaining their reasons or the circumstances that had led them to that choice. All three were assassinated in prison. Their brutal and premature deaths gave their writings a particular legitimacy in the eyes of their readers at the time. Arousing vocations, supporting tireless activism, encouraging unlimited military devotion, their texts present a theory of action, contemptuous of human life, that pushed their followers to the abyss of collective suicide. Far from bringing victory or power, the armed struggle strategy knew only bitter failures. The human loss was inestimable. Yet it had the strength to attract people and to turn them toward the future. This call to action, however blind it might be, renewed that call to the future in the collective thought of a society stifled by disappointment and paralyzed by pessimism. Such a society could not be indifferent to the heroism of young communists, ready to fight to the end to defend their ideas. In fact, despite its undeniably premature aspect, the heroic activism of these young people recalled the old Shiite sacrificial pattern that asked people to fight and to die for it. It was this surprising mixture of a modern worldview with the sacrificial heroism deeply rooted in religious thought that made these young communists' experience so eloquent for their period.

Through their writings in the 1970s, a new type of historic character was born: active and reactionary, reflecting little, but ready to lose all to achieve his aims.

The Necessity for the Armed Struggle and the Rejection of the Theory of Survival signed by Amir-Parvis Puyan was the first theoretical work,[9] scarcely twelve pages long, on armed combat written by an Iranian Marxist. This work was tremendously successful with students

---

[9] Amir-Parviz Puyan, *Mobarezey-e mossalahaneh va radd-e teori-e baqâ* (The Necessity for Armed Struggle and the Rejection of the Survival Theory), Tehran, Organization of the Fadaiyan of the People, 1971. All of this editor's books are available at www.iran-archive.com.

and intellectuals, affecting them deeply. Its activist style, colored with an avenging fury, does not today allow one to understand the scope of its success at the time. The awkward application of Marxist theories to Iranian society and its view of the shah's regime bear witness to its theoretical weakness. It is a "fascist" regime, "thirsty for the blood of the people," a "mercenary of foreign powers," and the shah is an "agent of the American secret service whose mission was to hand over his country's wealth."

At a period when, for the first and last time in Iranian history, oil resources were devoted to modernizing the country, when the Iranian standard of living was at its highest, Puyan was surprised at the complacency of the proletariat toward the regime and at its lack of enthusiasm for the communist movement. Blaming government repression for the left's failure to attract the people, he thought the workers were victims of a double strategy: on the one hand, the Savak terrorized the "working classes," and on the other, it poisoned them by the vulgar leisure of bourgeois culture. With baffling candor, he wondered why the workers stood for such a situation. His opinion of this proletariat so easily corrupted into idleness was bitter: it was a *lumpenproletariat*," with no political conscience, and, like the revolutionary theorists, Puyan warned against trusting it.

According to his theory of the "two absolutes," the crushing power of the state confronting the ignorance of the working class created a situation in which *absolute* force confronted *absolute* weakness. The responsibility of the "revolutionary intellectual" was to make the working classes aware of their strength and to encourage them to believe in their capacity to resist the "blood-thirsty police of the Shah's fascist regime." That would only be possible through the "spiritual bond that would link intellectual revolutionaries to the proletariat." He invited the working classes to overturn the "bourgeois system of production." The armed struggle would therefore destroy the false idea the proletariat had of its own weakness. In this context, asserted Puyan, the intellectuals, pioneers of the proletariat, must impose armed struggle on the working class, at whatever cost.

Aside from these theoretical errors, the heart of Puyan's thought was clearly defined: "To achieve a better future," he wrote, "one must not wait for the best time or for better conditions. It is now or never. We must act today; tomorrow will be too late."[10] If, for Tudeh, survival came

---

[10] *Ibid.*, p. 12.

first—"We must not be aggressive; we must ensure our survival"—for Puyan, submission was synonymous with disappearance—"Nothing is more comforting for our enemies than to see us behave like defenseless victims." True, the armed struggle does not ensure the survival of the combatants. "It invites them to revolutionary action and promises them sudden death as the most painful solution." Yet in the years that followed the coup d'état nothing could have been more seductive to the disillusioned intellectuals, undermined by deadly Shiite fatalism, than this heroic call to armed combat.

Shortly after the appearance of Puyan's pamphlet, Massoud Ahmadzadeh published a theoretical work that, in its turn, had a tremendous effect on the intellectuals and the young communists. *Armed Combat, Tactics and Strategy* presented a whole series of socio-economic analyses of Iranian society and of the shah's reforms, based on Marxist theory and attempting to understand the role of revolutionary intellectuals in relation to the proletariat. The Iranian people's principal enemy was imperialism, which Ahmadzadeh, like Puyan, tried to present as a greedy and bloodthirsty figure that wanted to seize the country's wealth and to exploit its people. The shah was but a vile mercenary paid by imperialism; a marionette without a soul, content to obey the dictates of foreign countries. The author concluded that the real struggle must be directed against imperialism, since the shah was but a simple representative. Nonetheless, despite the great importance the author accorded it, imperialism remained an abstraction, and nothing explained to whom or to what the word referred. The book was carried along by the revolutionarism of the time. Its analyses, filled with equivocal Latin expressions, lacked objectivity and suffered from as much superficiality as those of Puyan. Ahmadzadeh believed just as sincerely in the efficacy of armed struggle. To replace each communist martyr, tens of trained warriors would rise up.[11] Affected by the radicalism of the Latin American guerilla theoreticians, the author considered armed warfare as the only way to sensitize the workers and free their historic force. From the guerilla would arise a mass army to lead the revolution to its final victory.

Clearly, the thesis of armed struggle of Ahmadzadeh and his comrades was in contradiction with Tudeh's rationalism. The latter, no more

---

[11] Massoud Ahmadzadeh, *Jange mossalahaneh: ham strategi ham taktik* (The Armed Struggle: Tactics and Strategy), Tehran, Organization of the Fadaiyan of the People, 1970.

than the ghost of its former self, was highly critical of the radicalization of the communist movement into a guerilla organization. Tudeh had indeed no longer any visible or significant activity in Iran, but its long political experience enabled it to analyze the situation more lucidly than the young communists. It rejected the armed struggle and believed that the communist movement should support the imperial regime to accelerate the country's march toward modernization, industrialization, and development. This support would reduce the regime's dependence on imperialism and enable the country to assert its sovereignty. Tudeh felt that the time for armed struggle had not yet come, since the democratic means toward political reform remained undeveloped. According to Tudeh, for the time being, communist parties should organize the popular classes and incite the imperial regime to more democracy. The aim of the communist movement, at that particular moment of history, was not the fall of the regime or the dictatorship of the proletariat, but the transformation of the shah's regime into a democratic one. Tudeh warned young communists against the exaggerated and inopportune revolutionarism of their doctrinarians. It judged that the Organization of the Fadaiyan of the People was made up of a handful of unaware people, anti-Leninist, petit bourgeois revolutionaries who wanted to throw themselves into an armed struggle while the proper revolutionary conditions did not exist.[12]

For their part, the guerilla doctrinarians felt that Tudeh's conformism was merely a way of hiding its incapacity to act. They remained totally convinced that "Now was the time to act or never." Their virulent criticisms of their predecessors also revealed the depth of the trauma suffered by the young communist activists following Tudeh's political errors in the 1950s and 1960s. "Its treachery was extremely harmful to communism in Iran," asserted Ahmadzadeh, for whom Tudeh was but a caricature of a Marxist-Leninist party. At the same time, his view of the National Front was no more lenient. For him, the nationalists were merely petit bourgeois, indifferent to the interests of the working masses and thinking only of their personal profits.

In his writings, Ahmadzadeh insisted on the absence of theoretical and practical politics of the young communist activists. His revolutionary radicalism did not prevent him from being aware of the factors paralyzing the movement. According to him, the greatest danger that

---

[12] *Cf.* Behrooz, *op. cit.*, 2000.

threatened the new communist movement was the incapacity of revolutionary intellectuals to make themselves heard by the workers. "If we cannot attract the sympathy of the working masses to our cause, the blood-thirsty regime might quickly eliminate our movement." With a whole series of instructions, he explained in detail how to train the proletariat and to familiarize it with communist doctrines—a proletariat that had never yet shown much interest in the ideas of leftist activists. Aware of the workers' indifference and of their minimal desire to change their living conditions, Ahmadzadeh attributed this to the shah's "fascist regime's" repression. The shah was considered responsible for all the country's misfortunes, including the absence of protest in the working-class milieu. His solution was to propose that communist activists prove their revolutionary courage by immediate action. All plans to wait for the best moment when the oppressed and the workers would join the communists were but evidence of opportunism.

Ahmadzadeh's thesis might be summed up in one sentence: "On with the revolution despite everything, including all unfavorable circumstances." This constituted the theoretical basis of the Fadaiyan during long years of armed combat. The unrealistic aspect of this idea did not escape Jazani, who warned his comrades against revolutionary radicalism.[13]

Bijan Jazani was the oldest, the most skillful, and above all the most methodical of the three thinkers. He alone perhaps deserved to be called a theoretician. His aim was to combine militancy with political activity. But at that time of devotional activism, the thoughtful and temperate nature of his ideas did not touch the communist revolutionary militants as much as those of Puyan and Ahmadzadeh. His ideas took a long time to be appreciated, and his line was not adopted until 1976, a few months before his death in prison. He was often suspected of connivance with Tudeh or charged with opportunism or conformism. Only a few years before the revolution, circumstances demonstrated the credibility of the analyses of this thinker, who tried to remain objective and rational despite the generalized frenzy of the times.

Unlike most of the Marxist and Muslim militants who had technical training, Jazani had a degree in philosophy. He was born in a militant family. His parents were Tudeh members, and from age ten he belonged to a youth organization. When he was arrested in 1968, while preparing

---

[13] Bijan Jazani, *Pishahangan-e enqelab va rahbari* (The Pioneers of the Revolution and Leadership), Tehran, Organization of the Fadaiyan of the People, 1973.

an armed operation, the Savak congratulated itself on having captured one of the principal Iranian Marxist ideologues. Condemned to fifteen years of prison, it was there that he wrote most of his texts. His writings concerned diverse issues from analyzing society to organizing armed struggle, and included a series of theoretical essays on democracy and revolution. Impregnated with the pedantic style of that period, deeply influenced by Marxist literature, they contained a mixture of theoretical confusion and ambiguous expression. His efforts to distinguish between "bourgeois democracy" and "the people's democracy"—meaning the dictatorship of the people—were one example. According to him, all means were valid to prevent the people's revolution from being recuperated by the bourgeois whose firm intention was to set up their democracy. The aim of the communist movement was to set up the dictatorship of the people so as to achieve "real" socialism; hence the importance, in his view, of the communist activists' leadership.

The originality of his thought lay in his being certainly the first left-wing thinker who sought to comprehend the unpopularity of communism in popular milieus where the clergy's influence was uncontested. His objective was to understand the decisive factors of their popular success. He was therefore able to perceive the clergy's importance in general and that of the Ayatollah Khomeini, in particular. At the beginning of the 1970s, Jazani was indubitably the first to foresee that the latter might lead the movement that would overturn the shah. "With his experience," he wrote, "Khomeini is very popular among the masses and, thanks to a relative freedom in his political activities, he stands a great chance of succeeding."[14] Indeed, while the communist activists were the favorite targets of repression, the clergy—although they were outside politics—enjoyed a relative freedom of expression. This was a determining factor in the popularity that enabled the ayatollah to take power after the imperial regime had been overthrown. Yet, neither Jazani nor any other communist or nationalist thinker could have imagined that, one day, the clergy might install themselves comfortably at the head of the country and crush all dissidence. The Iranian intelligentsia was then so attracted by the revolutionary left that hardly anybody was concerned with the speeches and the writings of the clergy in the 1960s. Yet, Khomeini had very clearly exposed his intentions in his books: his thesis on government by the clergy, his opposition to women participating in social life, and his open hatred of nationalists

---

[14] Jazani, *op. cit.*, 1980, pp. 51–64.

130

and communists. But the communists did not stoop to concern themselves with the "old fashioned" thoughts of this extraordinary cleric. Even Jazani did not seem to have fully realized his political plans and let himself be attracted by Khomeini's anti-imperialism.

Through a series of too-subtle arguments, Jazani examined the role of the clergy in what he called the people's revolution (*enqelab-e khalq*). Later on, this analysis proved to be a serious historical error of the Iranian left. He thought that the clergy's long experience in popular revolts and their deeply anti-imperialist leanings would ally them with the communists against the shah's imperialist regime. Jazani thought it necessary for communist activists and clergy to combine forces to overthrow the shah, and he erroneously believed it would be easy to marginalize the clergy once the dictatorship of the people became a reality.[15]

Hypnotized by the "superiority of Marxist ideological speech over that of the clergy, outmoded and backward," Jazani could not see the clergy's capacity for resistance. He never imagined that the left would not easily eliminate them. With no historic perspective, he could not see that, with very rare exceptions, most of the clergy had systematically sabotaged Iranian democratic movements. Jazani did not suspect that the presence of a few noble minds among them changed not a jot of their substantial resistance to reform, to change, and to whatever comprised, in any way, anything new. They were and would always be anti-imperialist; they were similarly hostile to the shah's regime. Yet Jazani did not realize that they were even more hostile and more ill disposed toward communists, liberals, and reformers.

Like Puyan and Ahmadzadeh, Jazani praised Tudeh members' courage but reproached its leadership with not having known how to use the force of the people who supported the party to resist the August, 1953, coup d'état.[16] He also thought that, if Tudeh's relations with the Soviets had helped it develop, its close identification with the Soviet Union had harmed it. In his eyes, during the 1960s, Tudeh had been a non-revolutionary force, and its efforts to appear as the working-class party were in no way credible. The strategy of resorting to purely political means to confront the imperial regime seemed insane to him: "Tudeh" he wrote, "lives in the expectation of a political opening without making the least effort to bring this about."

---

[15] *Ibid.*
[16] *Ibid.*

Jazani was even more severe than his comrades toward Tudeh's Maoist factions. While they were generally accused of being dependent upon China, incapable of organizing themselves to act inside Iran, and indistinguishable from Tudeh, the factions' doctrinaire members drew Jazani's most vehement criticism. He reproached them with relying on the Chinese model and refusing to recognize that, after the shah's reforms, the Iranian feudal system had become a capitalist system.[17] Jazani was, furthermore, one of the few Iranian communists critical of the Stalinist period, denouncing the way in which the Soviet Union had left the Marxist-Leninist revolutionary path. His analyses, however, did not dissuade his comrades from resolutely calling themselves Stalinist. Like other communist groups, their view of Marxism was solely determined by the Russian revolutionary experience as disseminated by Stalinist propaganda.

His assassination in prison in 1975, together with six other founding members of the Fadaiyan, was a severe blow for the movement. It had, however, other consequences. The murders tarnished the imperial regime's image and aroused popular sympathy for these young people who devoted themselves to the last drop of their blood. If communist ideology left people cold, the young activists' sacrifice struck a popular chord. The assassinations discredited the regime and gave birth to the cult of the revolution.

Theoretical differences

Without a coherent analytical view of the Iranian communist movement's history, Puyan, Ahmadzadeh, and Jazani all agreed that past defeats were caused by Tudeh's opportunism. They hoped that the revolutionary heroism of the guerilla would give the movement a new legitimacy that would efface those unpleasant memories. On the other hand, their analyses diverged on the strategy and objectives of the armed struggle, as well as on the meaning of recent events.

Their main point of divergence concerned the shah's reforms. Ahmadzadeh, for his part, felt that American capitalism had imposed the reform program the better to intervene in Iranian affairs. He was convinced that the Iranian comprador bourgeoisie was closely allied to the international bourgeoisie and that it was, therefore, just as imperialist. Consequently, the reforms, far from attenuating the class conflicts in society, intensified them, preparing the ground for the revolution.

---

[17] *Ibid.*

Jazani's analyses of the reforms ran counter to those of other Marxist thinkers. According to him, the regime's resolve to carry out changes should be seen in the convergence of internal and external factors. The blocking of pre-capitalist Iran's socio-economic relations in the 1950s was the principal motivation for reform. Jazani saw the role of imperialism as altogether secondary. Unlike Ahmadzadeh and Puyan, Jazani affirmed that, beginning with the 1960s, the reforms had lessened class conflicts and therefore, the objective conditions for revolution did not exist in Iran. He was nonetheless convinced that the nature of the capitalist system was such that these conditions would arise in time. Meanwhile, he warned his comrades against blindness and impatience. "Their organization," he said, "is threatened by adventurism." His ideas, however, found no favorable echo among the revolutionary activists absolutely convinced that the time for revolution had arrived.

Ahmadzadeh's and Jazani's analyses also diverged on the nature of the shah's regime. For the former, the shah was a mere puppet of imperialism, created and maintained by it. For the latter, the regime was despotic, founded on the shah's absolute and supreme power, whatever the support given by imperialism. Unlike Ahmadzadeh and Puyan, Jazani did not stop at attributing the absence of opposition in society to police repression. He was aware that the shah's reforms had largely contributed to improving Iranians' standard of living and saw therein one of the reasons for the weakening of opposition movements.

The essential point in Jazani's ideas was the importance he accorded political activity. For him, the armed struggle was a process at once political and military. He reproached his comrades with scorning the political aspects of their movement and warned them of the dangers of a blind and frenzied activism. His ideas of the end of the armed struggle seem scarcely orthodox. For most Marxists, Lenin among them, the use of violence is legitimate when the objective revolutionary conditions exist. In his theory of "armed propaganda," Jazani suggested, on the contrary, that the avant-garde use the armed struggle to establish itself on the one hand and to prepare the movement for revolution, on the other, whether or not the objective conditions existed. This allowed him to conclude: "The armed struggle is not a means for overthrowing the shah but a strategy for creating a popular opposition movement.[18]

---

[18] *Ibid.*

As methodical and rational as he might have been, Jazani could not escape the revolutionarism of his era. Aware of the absence of the objective conditions that made revolution a necessity, he tried to justify the armed struggle at the risk of contradicting his own ideas. By very different and excessively involved theoretical reasoning, he finally arrived at the same conclusion as Ahmadzadeh and Puyan: the objective conditions for revolution would come about thanks to violence.

The Fadaiyan of the People: Conversion to Revolution

The fusion of the Jazani-Zarifi and Ahmadzadeh-Puyan groups around the figure of Jazani at the end of 1970 gave birth to the *Fadaiyan-e Khalq* (literally, those who sacrifice themselves for their people) that immediately adopted a Marxist-Leninist revolutionary line, giving a central role to the armed-struggle strategy.[19] The Fadaiyan sought to supply themselves with the means to succeed—training and equipping shock troops to be substituted for the barricade tactics, creating an insurrectional General staff, working out battle plans, choosing the right moment to attack, and so on. Their offensive strategy tirelessly sowed terror among the regime's allies and aroused the admiration of the masses. Yet the Fadaiyan never managed to transform those feelings into a force capable of overthrowing the shah.[20]

The Fadaiyan harassed the shah's regime by multiplying attacks on banks and assassinating well-known people, usually high-ranking Savak agents. The bank attacks helped to finance arms purchases, but the repression devoured them. At least 172 members were killed between 1971 and 1976. The public admired their courage but withheld its support. Their Marxist references, theoretical weakness, and ideological divisions distanced them from the day-to-day concerns of Iranians. Plagued by unpopularity, the Fadaiyan engaged in ceaseless self-criticism.

Despite their great admiration for China and for Mao, the Fadaiyan rejected the Chinese model, which they judged inapplicable to the Iranian context. All during their fight against the imperial regime, they tried at all costs to remain independent of Beijing and

---

[19] Abrahamian, *op. cit.*, 1982, p. 485. Their tactics, against the police penetration in their organizations and infiltration in their networks, consisted of forming small cells and preparing limited military operations.

[20] The armed struggle strategy experienced serious failures in Germany (1923), China (1927), Asturias (1934), Brazil (1935), and elsewhere.

Moscow.[21] Tudeh's attachment to the Soviets had so harmed its reputation that this independence seemed the *sine qua non* for obtaining
a popular base, given the historic hostility of Iranians to any foreign
intervention in their national affairs. Like Tudeh, they saw the Soviet
Union and China as progressive socialist countries but, unlike Tudeh,
they placed national interest before communist international solidarity.
On the contrary, following Jazani, who was very conscious of political and ideological differences between the Chinese and the Soviets
in the 1960s, the Fadaiyan were careful not to declare themselves in
favor of either.[22] They also took part in other liberation movements,
and members of the organization fought and died with Palestinians
and Dhofar revolutionaries in the Oman Sultanate.[23]

Between 1971 and 1979, the Organization of the Fadaiyan of the
People was the most active of all the guerilla groups in the country.
It chose its targets, not only for their political importance but also in
accordance with the psychological impact they could have on the security forces of the imperial regime. Under the leadership of Hamid Ashraf
(1946–1976), the Fadaiyan prepared and carried out their attacks with
care and precision, showing great coolness. They targeted the imperial
regime's symbols of power and those military and political leaders who
were known for their role in the repression.[24] They assassinated heads
of industry accused of having enlisted state support to repress workers,
as well as a considerable number of Savak torturers.

---

[21] According to the Iranian historian Behrooz, the Fadaiyan never had any direct affiliation with
any socialist state. Yet, they had links with other movements (the Palestinians, for example) and
received financial aid from a country like Libya without however accepting any intervention by
them. *Cf.* Behrooz, *op. cit.*, 2000.

[22] Contrary to the political line of the founders of the Fadaiyan who preached the group's independence of the Soviet Union and of any other country, in 1972, those members who were abroad
received the order to approach the Soviet government for financial aid. It seems that the Soviets
who, *a priori*, were not inclined to help the Fadaiyan, asked them in exchange for information
on the Iranian army. Hamid Ashraf refused violently and the exchange with the Soviets went no
further. This reaction was an example of Fadaiyan sensitivity against any outside influence. In
June, 1976, Ashraf's death left the Fadaiyan with no charismatic leader, and this greatly weakened
the group. The Fadaiyan never completely recovered. *Ibid.*

[23] Dhofar's separatist rebellion, supported by Egypt and several other countries, claimed a hard
Marxist line from 1964 to 1976. It was conquered with the help of the Iranian army and the
support of the special British forces.

[24] 1971, the assassination of General Farsiu, head of the military tribunal and responsible for
political trials, was one example. *Cf. San Francisco Chronicle*, April 12, 1971. Aside from that,
the Fadaiyan targeted foreign interests in Iran. It is, however, important to stress that they never
killed any foreigners and, contrary to the Mojahedin, they did not consider foreigners as legitimate
targets. This subject will be handled completely in the following chapter.

Each operation was accompanied with a distribution of explanatory documents, but when Ahmadzadeh's line was finally adopted, political action was marginalized in favor of military action. The Fadaiyan paid dearly for their armed struggle and suffered heavy losses, but they returned blow for blow.

The lack of clarity of their organizational structure considerably complicated their relations with other Marxist groups. During the first three years of their existence, it was difficult to know whether they were a communist group with a well-defined theoretical structure or a front organization for other Marxist groups united to combat the imperial regime without having drawn up a common doctrine. For Jazani, the Fadaiyan were to be seen as a united platform, comprising all Marxist-Leninist activists who believed in the armed struggle.

Later on, this ambiguity gave rise to terrible internal settlings of accounts, such as the expulsion of Mostafa Shoaian (1936–1975). At the start of the 1970s, Shoaian was a founding member of the Democratic Popular Front (*Jebhey-e democratic-e khalq*), siding with other well-known intellectuals of that time. The Democratic Popular Front defended the armed struggle and joined the Fadaiyan in June 1973. Like Jazani, whose ideas took time to be adopted, Shoaian denounced Stalinism and considered Leninism a deviation from Marxism. Thus, both groups united despite their doctrinal disagreements. Their collaboration did not last long. Shoaian was soon expelled from the Fadaiyan. A skillful theoretician, he tried to integrate and systematize the analyses of Marx and Engels in accordance with Iranian guerilla conditions. He invited the Fadaiyan to a confrontation of their ideas in order to defeat their "personality cult" and their "elementary Stalinism." But the Fadaiyan were not used to that sort of exercise. Their leadership was primarily composed of activists—not theoreticians—whose primary concern was to conduct day-to-day combat and ensure the members' survival. This left neither room nor time for ideological reflection. Forced to accept the challenge, the Fadaiyan entrusted the task to Hamid Momeni, their only mastermind left alive. A dogmatic Stalinist, he replied to Shoaian's questions and criticisms throughout the year 1974, by a series of letters never published. The death of both in 1975 put an end to that exceptional episode of ideological confrontation.[25]

---

[25] See Mostafa Shoaian, *Pasokhhay-e nasanjideh beh qadamhay-e sanjideh* (Injudicious Replies to Judicious Steps), Florence, Italy, Publications Mazdak, 1976. Shoaian was killed in a confrontation with Savak agents, when the latter attacked his hiding place. There are still doubts about the Fadaiyan's role in this, but to date nothing enables us to confirm these. After his expulsion, the rest of the Democratic Popular Front adopted the Fadaiyan ideology.

Shoaian's expulsion was an example of the recurrent use of Stalinist methods in the Iranian guerilla movements—both Muslim and Marxist—in accordance with which internal democracy had no place.[26] After the disappearance of the Fadaiyan founders in 1971, these methods were again used and became commonplace. Many members were thus eliminated by order of Hamid Ashraf.

Among the Fadaiyan, Ashraf was known for his organizational ability, his unshakeable optimism, and his exceptional courage. His extraordinary ability to foil police traps turned him into a legend, and he was at the top of the most-wanted list of the Savak. During his lifetime, the Fadaiyan nicknamed him "The Great Comrade," and he was without doubt the idol of an entire generation of militants.

It is difficult to evaluate his role in the group. In 1968, after Jazani and his comrades were arrested, his organizational capacity was a determining factor in the survival of the Jazani-Zarifi group. Similarly, he saved the Fadaiyan from probable extinction after the disappearances of Puyan and Ahmadzadeh in 1971 and 1972 respectively. Yet under his leadership (1971–1976), the Fadaiyan fell into Stalinist practices, using dangerous methods against the advice of their founding members, Jazani and Ahmadzadeh. Nevertheless, nothing can justify the summary execution of those with divergent opinions.

The radicalization of the Fadaiyan to Stalinism gave rise to bloody purges between 1972 and 1976. With the death of the principal protagonists and the silence of survivors, it is difficult to obtain information on these purges. Yet there remain some overwhelming documents.[27] Under the leadership of Ashraf and his deputy, Ali-Akbar Jafari, the Fadaiyan executed all those who wanted to leave the group.[28] The idea of physically eliminating undesirable members was already an issue of controversy between Ahmadzadeh and Ashraf at the start of the 1970s.

---

[26] The Fadaiyan had welcomed the Democratic Popular Front although they were perfectly aware of their declared hostility to Leninism. For further details on Fadaiyan history, see Behrooz, *op. cit.*, 2000, pp. 48–94; Mehdi Khan-Baba-Tehrani, *Negahi az daroon beh jonbesh-e chap-e iran* (An Internal Look at the Iranian Left), Saarbrücken, Hamid Sholat, 1998.

[27] Interview with Mostafa Shoaian, in Irvine, California, February 1, 1992. Madani, an active *Fadaiyan* militant in the 1970s and a member of the Central Committee from 1979 to 1980, confirmed the bloody purges without giving details, explaining that he was in prison at that time. *Cf.* Behrooz, *op. cit.*, 2000, p. 202.

[28] Hassan Masali, "Influence of Insight and Conduct on Social Struggle," in *The Results of Wiesbaden Conference on the Crisis of Iran's Left Movement,* Frankfurt, 1985, p. 55; quoted in Behrooz, *Ibid.*

During Ahmadzadeh's lifetime, any violent action against those who wanted to leave was forbidden. But after his death, Ashraf gave free reign to his criminal tendencies.

At the price of heavy sacrifices and many military operations, the Fadaiyan succeeded in establishing itself as a military-political force. Yet they still lacked popular support and remained essentially a guerilla group whose members came mostly from the intelligentsia.

The Fadaiyan's combat reached a dead end fairly soon. Despite their violent attacks, the shah's regime did not crumble, and Ahmadzadeh's thesis that "the small motor would cause the big one to start" proved completely wrong. As a result, by the end of 1974, while the group seemed at the height of its power, and its leader, Hamid Ashraf, was still alive, it seemed clear that a reevaluation of its tactics and strategy was necessary. But it was not until 1976 that the Fadaiyan Organization changed its political line, because two severe blows profoundly destabilized the organization. The first was in March, 1976. Jazani was assassinated in prison with six other founding members of the Jazani-Zarifi group, as well as two members of the Mojahedin of the People. The second occurred after a series of setbacks in June, 1976. Hamid Ashraf and nine other Fadaiyan leaders lost their lives in a long battle with the police.

In 1976, shortly after Ashraf's disappearance, *Nabard-e Khalq*, the Fadaiyan newspaper, officially announced the rejection of Ahmadzadeh's line and the adoption of that of Jazani. The Fadaiyan then changed their strategy and began according greater importance to political action. The armed struggle remained central, but they invested more in what Jazani called "the movement's second phase." They worked to arouse the revolutionary conscience of the masses and to organize them politically and militarily. In October of that year, there was a split in the Organization. Those who no longer believed in the armed struggle left the group and finally recognized the correctness of Tudeh's rational approach. Apparently most of them were killed a few months after having left the Fadaiyan. The new Fadaiyan leaders never ceased tearing each other apart.[29]

---

[29] The leaders of the Tehran branch feared the increased membership of the Khorasan branch, under the leadership of a militant called Panjeh-Shahi. They were convinced that he and his comrades were plotting against them and wanted to take control of the Tehran branch. The Tehran leaders then decided to prevent the development of the dissident faction. At the end of 1976,

The adoption of Jazani's line coincided with the first signs of revolution in Iran. Just when the Fadaiyan were trying to neutralize the dissident groups, the revolutionary tide swept through the country. Despite its limited capacity, its bloody internal crises, and the very heavy losses it had suffered, the Organization of the Fadaiyan of the People was the only armed group to effectively participate in the revolutionary struggle in an organized way. Like other guerilla groups, the Fadaiyan joined the people in February, 1979, when the latter launched assaults against military barracks. They proved themselves the best prepared for combat until the shah's overthrow.

The Appearance of the Revolutionary Actor

The conversion of political action to armed struggle had not brought the popular support for which the communist activists hoped. In the history of social movements, that strategy has known only failures: one does not arouse the masses without organizing them. The guerillas led an army of young Iranians to perish in the shah's prisons or in urban combats. They gave their lives in the hope that others would follow them, but their dogmatism and their radicalism falsified their view of social reality. The hasty recourse to armed combat aggravated an ideological confusion the cost of which proved extremely high.

The armed struggle harmed the cohesion and the credibility of the communist movement. It never enabled its partisans to develop a clear, coherent conception of Marxism or to adapt it to the Iranian context. They never succeeded in justifying their choice of armed combat to the people. Everybody knew that these young people were fighting the shah, but their real motivations remained a mystery. The presence of a few "brains" among them was not sufficient to link their theoretical steps to their activism. Their refusal to think out their action was so absolute that Jazani's thesis of conciliating political action with armed combat never found a real audience among his comrades.

Contrary to the Ayatollah Khomeini, who as of 1942 had worked out a real political plan for Shiite clergy rule, these young militants envisaged nothing but heroic acts, military operations, and martyrdom. Their misunderstanding could not have been greater. To the Fadaiyan—as

---

Panjeh Shahi was summarily executed, although nothing indicated that he was really favorable to a break. Apparently his disappearance left his branch under the control of the new leadership. Interview with Ali-Reza Mahfuzi, quoted in Habib Lajevardi (ed.), *Iranian Oral History Collection*, Cambridge, Harvard University, 1981–1996.

139

well as to many other actors or observers of the Iranian scene—it hid the political preeminence of the clergy.

Lacking political experience, the communist militants were quickly removed from any power. The ease with which Khomeini and his companions were able to "confiscate the revolution" was in large part due to the weakness of an ideology that came from outside and was never understood or assimilated by the local actors. How could this ideology, imported from the Soviet Union and reduced to its urban-guerilla form, confront an Islam strongly entrenched for several centuries in the maneuvers of power and in the very depths of society?

Given the chaotic condition of the communist movement, their thesis of the "usurpation of the revolution by the clergy" did not stand up to analysis. The internal crises, the ideological confusion, and, above all, the absence of any political program, left them no chance of gaining power after the shah's fall. In fact, the clergy had no rivals.

The premature call to armed combat gave the political actors free reign to violence, both in their relations with the imperial regime and in their internal relations—the bloody purges in the Fadaiyan Organization were one example. The radicalism of the armed-combat doctrine limited its audience. Just as its denunciatory virulence discredited the imperial regime, just so much did its ability to create solidarity among the masses for the communist activists remain limited, indeed infinitesimal.

Armed combat must not, however, be summed up by its political failure. Despite its ill-fated consequences, it had important dimensions that deserve consideration. The most remarkable was surely to break with the passivity inherent in the Shiite clergy's discourse, inviting the faithful to "resignation to the will of God." When death became a choice, the victim became a hero, and the living became actors who could decide their own fate. Of itself, this break gave a new luster to armed struggle in Iran. Thus, young communists, violent and reactionary, disdaining theoretical reflection and celebrating militant activism, were able to resolutely mark the country by their devotion and sacrifice.

If Mossadeq took the first step, the genesis of the nation, the communist militants carried out the second—a consequence of the first—that of the appearance of a new actor in society, the revolutionary actor. It was by other agents and in favor of other groups that this became decisive, but it was the young communists who gave birth to it.

6

Ideological Islam
(1960–1978)

The tormented context after the coup d'état, the intensive modernization of the 1960s, not to mention the 1963 blood bath, created deep
disillusionment in the nationalist ranks. Nothing would ever be the
same again. The idea of a nation of nationalists as a means for recreating
a traditional social order in a new framework of modernity did not make
sense anymore. The desire to close as quickly as possible the parenthesis
of the coup d'état was stronger than the will to understand the lessons
of that event. The denial of responsibility for the failure of nationalist
ambitions was added to the denial of defeat. Once again, the intellectuals' denial and resentment sought their eternal excuse in demonizing
foreign countries. This time the English and the Americans were
blamed. Surprisingly, even in the religious camp, frustration regarding
the role of these two countries, authors of the coup d'état, seemed the
most important. Even more surprising, scarcely anybody blamed the
clergy for their instigation of these events. There was a feeling of *déjà vu*:
the nationalist defeat recalled that of the constitutionalists.

Among the public, disappointment was just as great. Confused by
the politicians and by the hypocritical arguments of the clergy, public
opinion was totally uncomprehending. Most Iranians retired into
their legendary distrust of politicians and of foreign powers, seeking
an explanation to all the country's problems in conspiracy theories,
always popular in times of chaos.

Frustration and disappointment amplified the national crisis until it
became a burning issue. The disillusionment aroused by the colonialist behavior of Western countries was injurious to the plausibility of
modern political thought among the elite and made the faults of the
democratic system seem even more glaring in the Iranian context.
Some Iranians turned to the religious and historical past, in the hope
of finding a reply more adapted to the originality of Persian culture.

Return to the Past

The shah's reforms had modified the traditional distribution of political opposition forces. The left that should normally have developed an autonomous view of society and politics drowned itself in details and busied itself in pointing out the slightest weakness of government action. It had a surprising lack of objectivity and was completely destabilized by this modernizing state that went further than the left itself in its desire to overthrow the old forms of social and political organization.

The clergy also opposed the reforms. Fearful of change, they called for a return to the past and the defense of religious principles, attempting to highlight the advantages of Islamic laws. Their resistance aroused the admiration of many disillusioned intellectuals and led them to work out a religious theory that could conciliate the modern world with Islam. They invented "Islamic democracy."

Disappointment gave ear to those conservative doctrines that had previously been ignored. The old liberals rejected reforms in the name of rejecting westernization and sought to Islamize modernization through ideas calling for the rehabilitation of Islam's political thought. They hoped to remake politics with religious principles.

The 1963 crisis had the effect of replacing faith in the nation and hope for the future with the return to favor of traditional values and principles. Conservative alternatives that had, too quickly, been thought definitively disqualified by the modernizing whirlwind of the postwar years found their most salient expression in the antimodern and antidemocratic discourse of the clergy preaching a return to the past. The intellectuals' identity crisis rehabilitated the religious structure, which had seemed to disappear gradually in all its aspects: domination, hierarchy, inclusion and tradition. Their disillusioned view of the West lessened the luster of the ideas and principles of a modern structure based on representation, equality, freedom, the individual, and progress. Since modernization was suspected of intrigue and treason, salvation seemed to lie in promoting a "modern Islam" in harmony with democratic values. This was the start of the liberal nationalist movement's conversion to Islamic democracy and the appearance of what were later called the "Muslim intellectuals." Starting with the White Revolution, Islamic democracy became the principal source of inspiration and reflection of most politicians nationwide, save for a part of the left. It became the main political actors' claim in the name of history and of cultural and religious roots.

Disappointment and disillusionment drew intellectuals and liberal nationalists to ally themselves with the clergy.

The Rehabilitation of Islam

The significant transformation of the clergy's role was shown by important modifications on the ideological scene. Their marginalization by the modernizing state had changed the way in which they reacted to social reality. The marginalized clergy were different from those who had been in collusion with secular power. They had now acquired the status of dissidents and proved they could gather opposition forces, independently of their ideological or political leanings. A powerful movement called for the return to the religious past and to tradition.

The withdrawal of intellectuals who no longer believed in democratic values favored their reconciliation with the clergy. Having lost their privileges in political power, the latter sought more than ever to strengthen their societal base. This alliance between two previously opposed forces produced a major turning point in political and social organization. Within a few years, the ideological and political stage was taken over by a coalition of former enemies. Disappointed reformers, having lost faith in democracy, converted to the clergy's conservatism. Together they would create a political ideology that claimed to be free and autonomous but that was completely bound to religious principles.

Against the ascendancy of the modernizing state, while the communist activists were in a state of open crisis, dissidents proposed to rekindle the flame of cultural independence and to return to founding principles. Former nationalists and Islamist activists organized underground networks whose ability to resist the state was impressive. The union of these opponents not only favored challenging the reforms of the regime and of its political structures but also democratic principles. It was thanks to that union that the idea of rehabilitating Islam began to flourish.

The two great figures of this movement to rehabilitate Islam were undoubtedly Mehdi Bazargan (1907–1995) and the Ayatollah Mahmoud Taleqani (1911–1979). Both were totally convinced that "true Islam" was perfectly compatible with modern values and democratic principles. They devoted their lives to erasing the superstitions and irrational aspects of religion, in order to present the "authentic Islam" (*eslam-e râstine*) to the whole world.

Islamic Democracy

Mehdi Bazargan was the first thinker to develop a theory of Islamic democracy. His aim was to "ideologize Islam." A thermodynamics engineer, graduate of the Ecole Centrale des Arts et Manufactures de Paris, he returned to Iran in 1933 after six years in France. Upon his arrival, he was named head of the engineering department of the University of Tehran. In 1951, after the nationalization of the oil industry, Mehdi Bazargan became the first director of the *National Iranian Oil Company*. After the fall of Mossadeq's government, he was one of the founders of the Movement for the Liberation of Iran (*Nehzat-e âzâdi Irân*, MLI), together with an enlightened cleric, the Ayatollah Taleqani, and a geologist with a degree from the Sorbonne, Yadollah Sahabi. His political activities and, above all, his categorical rejection of the shah's reforms, resulted in his being imprisoned several times.

Some considered him a great democratic thinker and a true specialist of Islam. However, Bazargan was primarily a technocrat, completely self-taught in the social sciences and in religion. His reflections on Islam and democracy were the result of his personal observations among Parisian scholars before World War II. He sought his inspiration in science. Throughout his intellectual life, he tried to develop a concept of religion and politics inspired by the theories of fundamental physics and especially by the notion of general equilibrium in thermodynamics, which he had studied at the Ecole Centrale in Paris.

His first writings showed the keen enthusiasm of the young Iranian that he was—born into a traditional family—and confronted with Western life. Bazargan was impressed with the democratic dynamics of Parisian society between the two world wars; it was so different from what he had imagined. Very quickly he discovered the existence of religious trends in France, specifically Catholicism. In his memoir he spoke of that extraordinary discovery with admiration and thrill: "Europeans believe in God!" Whereas, like the liberal intellectuals of the constitutional revolution, he had been convinced that religion had no place in democracy, this discovery opened new perspectives, and he backtracked on his ideas. After meeting with partisans of the Christian Democratic Movement, he was convinced that democracy was no enemy of religion and declared: "It is the European's faith in God that mobilizes so much progress in the West." From then on, he wanted to prove that Islam, like Christianity, was perfectly compatible with science, modernity, and democracy. In the mid-1950s, he wrote a number of articles defending the compatibility between Islam and science. His ideas attracted a remarkable audience among science students of religious backgrounds.

Later on, his books bore witness to the sincere efforts of a believing and intelligent writer who wanted to save religion in a world that was destined to change. He was one of the first Muslim thinkers to realize that religion could not survive in its old forms, and that certain changes were imperative for it to find its place in the modern world. Yet, his theoretical gaps in the humanities and in social science prevented him from gaining a deep knowledge of the subjects he dealt with so passionately. His viewpoints were incomplete, and his analyses superficial. He attempted desperately to solve the dilemma between modernity and tradition, but the task was impossible. It was by trial and error and by personal experience that he tried to progress on a theoretical ground of which he had little or no command. His rejection of the shah's reforms was based on his radical refusal to obey any but God: "Our faith," he wrote, "constitutes our human dignity." He believed that the true object of the reforms was to subject the people to the shah's regime, although no rational thought supported that assertion.

Bazargan was a man of conviction who believed that by clinging to the Muslim religion and to Persian culture, his country could resist the invasion of the West and preserve its national originality. His return to the principles of the religious past distanced him from the nationalism that had motivated him at the start. He was, henceforth, in the conservative camp.

His first ambition was to ideologize Islam. His attempts to open a path from the religious universe to that of ideology were motivated by the need, felt by religious thinkers, to find a place for religion in the future. But Bazargan's undertaking was modest. It was more a theorizing of the political aspects of religion than a real "ideologization" of Islam *per se.* He always remained attached to the Islamic discourse without ever really entering into the world of ideological speech.[1]

---

[1] *Cf.* Gauchet, *op. cit.,* 2011–2012. According to Marcel Gauchet, the fundamental difference between the religious and the ideological discourse lies essentially in the fact that the former legitimizes itself in the name of the past and the latter in that of the future. Ideology is a universe of thought, discourse, and representation that takes up where religion leaves off to explain and justify the social and political order: Ideology is what society says of itself and that historically follows what religion has said. In contrast to societies ruled by tradition, today's societies establish and organize themselves to project themselves through time, in the direction of the future. They leave religious structuring, whose patterns are imposed by the past. Ideology thus enables actors to explain the movement of societies toward the future. Ideological discourse answers the questions that they must ask: what is to be done and in the name of what?

His thought was never truly oriented toward the future, and despite his distance from the orthodox clergy he remained closely attached to the principles inherited from the past. For this reason, he never achieved his goal. It would be, as we shall see, Islamist militants—the Mojahedin of the People—whose idol he was—who would succeed in emptying the Muslim religion of its spirituality to make of it a political religion in tune with the world of ideology. As a good engineer, specializing in thermodynamics, Bazargan sought only to rid religion of its irrational aspects—superstitions, he said—and to transform it into a conceptual whole: coherent, rational, harmonious, and logical, accessible to all. He did indeed rid religion of its spirituality but failed to link it to ideology.

In his book, *Resurrection and Ideology* (*Be'sat va idéologie*), Bazargan explained that the separation of body and soul was an erroneous idea that came from ancient Greece and had no Islamic basis. *The Road Traveled* (*Râh-e tey shodeh*), his most well-read book, revealed another aspect of his engineer's mentality. He doubted there was any afterlife: "So long as nobody returns from the kingdom of the dead to prove its existence to us, we have the right not to believe in it." The originality of his work lay in the fact that he based it on the same sources as the clergy—the Koranic text and the tales of the life of Islam's prophet (*Hadith*)—and yet developed a reasoning counter to those traditionally accepted.

Convinced that ideologizing religion would guarantee its survival in the modern world, Bazargan tried to simplify Islam's political doctrine and to use it in a democratic framework. But this was far from obvious. First of all, he had no clear idea of the process of democratizing modern societies. For him, democracy was a given—like universal suffrage—that he described in an affirmative rather than a demonstrative way: "Democracy is good, it is necessary," and so on. Secondly, his free interpretation of Islam did not stem from an intellectual process with a critical study of religious thought. Other partisans of Islamic democracy close to Bazargan, the Ayatollah Motahari (1920–1979) and Beheshti (1928–1981), would prove more capable than he in approaching the issue, redefining the notion of authority in Islam, and trying to set up a collegiate leadership at the head of the clergy in order to institute basic changes within the system.[2]

---

[2] These tentative attempts unleashed the fury of the orthodox clergy. Those two ayatollah, assassinated by Islamist extremists, shortly after the 1979 revolution, had a relatively more open and far more critical view of religion and of the world than other clerics, which put them at odds with the concepts of the traditional clergy. Yet, in no way could they be considered as intellectuals or reformers.

Very quickly, a cleavage arose between the defenders of Islamic democracy and the conservative clergy, attached to the divine legitimacy of political power, who rejected any form of power sharing. "Democratizing" Islamic principles seemed absurd to them; it would mean tacitly accepting the idea of democracy and thus renouncing their ideal of divine legitimate political power. The concept of a democratic system based on universal suffrage and citizens' votes could only be totally rejected.

Thus, the clergy defended their monopoly on religious thought and also began to invade the fields that usually belonged to the intellectuals, such as the contemporary world, the debate on political values and ideological discourse. The Iranian elite, who were primarily technocrats, lacking the theoretical tools required to develop a solidly constructed critical thought, abandoned those fields that belonged to the clergy and rapidly became mere auxiliaries.

After the revolution, Bazargan was named prime minister by the Ayatollah Khomeini. He was, however, considered one of the leading figures of the "Islamic democracy movement." He very soon opposed the Assembly of Experts and contested the regime's intention of calling itself an "Islamic Republic." His conflict with Khomeini was therefore nearly immediate. He and his entire cabinet resigned in November, 1979, at the start of the Iranian hostage crisis and the takeover of the American embassy by Islamist students. This resignation was considered a protest against the hostage taking and, when added to his liberal views, set him at odds with the Ayatollah Khomeini. Convinced that he could not carry out the slightest improvement in the Islamic regime, Bazargan retired from public life. He died of a heart attack in January 1995.

Thanks to the help of his friend, the Ayatollah Taleqani—a nonconformist cleric and convinced Mossadeq supporter—Bazargan founded the MLI or the Movement for the Liberation of Iran (*Nehzat-e âzâdi-e Irân*) in 1961. Taleqani was a remarkable cleric in many ways. Son of a provincial *mollah* who had preferred to earn his living as a watchmaker than to live on the revenues of religious endowments, Taleqani grew up in a family proud of its poverty. Born in 1911, he remembered the time when the religious dignitaries had openly justified the feudal system and Reza Shah's despotism. At the end of the 1930s, he had been arrested for refusing to carry an identity card. His keen intelligence and curiosity enabled him to tolerate political diversity and to explore new concepts. In prison, he had been impressed by the ideas of the young Marxists. Years later, he asserted himself as the reformist preacher of the Hedayat mosque in the center of Tehran, and his two books entitled *Islam and Property* and *The Concept of Islamic Government*[3] found a new audience among students. According to him, "true Islam" protects legitimate property, unlike feudalism and capitalism. He also supported the idea that religion was synonymous with social justice because it opposed flagrant inequalities and defended the rights of the exploited masses: peasants, workers, craftsmen, and small shopkeepers. His second book was, in fact, the re-edition and translation into Persian of a classic written in 1909 by the Ayatollah Mirzay-e Naiini, a famous constitutionalist cleric who lived in Nadjaf. In his preface, Taleqani took up the author's argument on representative government, stressing the agreement of this concept with the fundamental teachings of Shiism. The essential point of this idea was its rejection of clerical political power. Taleqani, like Naiini, felt that the *olama* should not govern and that their sole political role was to protect the people against the tyranny of men in power.

Taleqani often asserted that the most dangerous despots were kings and clerics. His political thought was a combination of nationalism, socialism and constitutionalism. Defense of liberty was his leitmotiv. When pronouncing his funeral oration in September, 1979, Bazargan declared that by his defense of modern ideas, political pluralism, and social reform, his old friend held a unique place among contemporary clerics.[4] It was, therefore, not surprising that Taleqani's fervent admirers were found among young activists and intellectuals rather than in the ranks of the clergy.

The Movement of Liberation of Iran was created by the combined efforts of these two men whose friendship grew from their shared convictions. They wanted at all costs to conciliate Islam and democracy, proving to the world that it was plausible to associate those two concepts.

The shah's regime, which feared the communist activists, authorized the Movement of Liberation of Iran to function freely and to act openly. However, two years after its creation, the June, 1963, rebellion put an end to the relative freedom it enjoyed, and its leaders were imprisoned.

---

[3] Mahmood Taleqani, *Eslam va Malekiyat* (Islam and property), Tehran, Sherkat-e Enteshar, 1975; *Hokoumat az Nazar eslam* (The Concept of Islamic Government), Tehran, Sherkat-e Enteshar, 1953.

[4] Mehdi Bazargan, "Eloge", *Ettela'at*, Tehran, September 12, 1979.

Bazargan and Taleqani were each condemned to ten years imprisonment for attacking the monarchy.

After that uprising and the unprecedented repression that followed, incredible rumors circulated in the capital. The population was indignant at the behavior of troops who were said to have massacred thousands of unarmed demonstrators. Those events had a traumatizing effect on young people interested in politics. Just like the new communist generation that asserted itself in the beginning of the 1960s, a new wave of activism appeared among young Muslims from traditional and, at times, even modest backgrounds.

While the old liberal and nationalist politicians who had grown up during the reign of Reza Shah had always preached the rule of law, the separation of powers, and the 1905 constitution, the new arrivals whose political baptism took place in the bloodbath of June, 1963, tended to see their predecessors as irresponsible. Those latter, who had participated in the campaign to nationalize oil and had witnessed the treason of the great ayatollah, had no confidence in the clergy and preferred secular and nationalist ideas rather than those with a religious tinge. The young, impressed by Khomeini, were prompt to espouse religious symbols and to see in each anti-regime *mollah* a "progressive cleric" and a "lover of freedom." If the older people feared British colonialism, the younger ones saw the greatest external danger in American imperialism.

The elders, forged in the experience of the political movements of the 1940s and the beginning of the 1950s, tended to speak in terms of nonviolent struggles: political parties, trade unions, professional organizations, street demonstrations, mass meetings. The young, deeply influenced by the communist activists' ideas, spoke only of armed struggle—underground cells, heroes, martyrs, propaganda. In short, the elders were secular, reformist, anti-British, and nonviolent, while the young were more religious, radical, anti-American, and, above all, ardent proponents of violence.

The June, 1963, events provoked a generation split within the Movement of Liberation of Iran, as within other political organizations with religious tendencies. If those events convinced the communist militants of the inflexibility of the imperial regime and led them to take arms to try to weaken it, their impact on the clergy and its place in society was particularly decisive. From then on, the clergy were catapulted to the head of the opposition movement.

In 1965, three young students founded a small discussion group to explore new ways to combat the regime. In a secret letter addressed to the MLI leaders, they reproached them with not knowing how to resist the shah's regime effectively. This discussion group would later become the Organization of the Mojahedin of the People. They were profoundly influenced by a Muslim intellectual, Ali Shariati.

Ali Shariati: The Religious Ideology

Kill if you can: Jihad;
If not, die as a martyr: Shahâdat;
Ali Shariati

Ali Shariati (1933–1977) was the Muslim intellectual who most marked the spirit of Iranians in the 1970s. He was considered, quite rightly, as the ideologist of the 1979 Iranian Revolution. Mehdi Bazargan wrote: "Shariati contributed greatly to the success of the revolution under the guidance of the Imam Khomeini. Had he not so enhanced the role of the *imam* and stressed the need of an Islamic people (*ommat-e eslam*) for a strong leader, the Imam Khomeini and his doctrine of *walayat-e faqih* (the absolute power of doctor of Islamic law) would never have enjoyed such a success in Iran, a success that bordered on holiness."[5]

A man of conviction, Shariati attracted the youth by his novel approach to Islam, his innovative ideas and unequaled eloquence. Inflamed by his passionate love for religion, his nation, and his country's destiny, Shariati knocked over the anthill of Shiite religious thought. His national feelings led him to want an "Iran reconciled with its national identity." Born into a clerical background, he was severe toward it. Without compromise or concession, he virulently reproached the conservative clergy. His critical analysis of its role led him to denounce the abuses and errors of which it had been guilty throughout Islamic history. Shariati contested the clergy's monopoly of religious discourse at a time when, paradoxically, it was being rehabilitated for its resistance to the imperial regime, as well as by some writers, such as Jalal Al-Ahmad, who praised the *mollah's* anti-imperialism.

In 1959, Shariati left Iran to prepare a doctorate at the Sorbonne—a doctorate that he never completed. Upon his arrival in Paris, he associated with Algerian independence activists and became friendly with Frantz Fanon. He was soon convinced that to fight imperialism and colonialism, it was necessary to rely upon the immense capacity of the Muslim religion in order to mobilize the oppressed people.

---

[5] Mehdi Bazargan, introduction to the book of Jafar Saïdi, *Shakhsyat va andishey-e Shariati* (The Thought and the Personality of Ali Shariati), Tehran, Chapakhsh, 1987.

Upon his return to Tehran in 1964, his favorite place became the Hosseyniy-e Ershad Foundation,[6] where his seminars attracted a large number of young students in search of a "modern Islam." He became very popular among intellectuals. His new ideas, presented through the old religious forms, also pleased devout Muslims who sought for a harmony between their religion and the modern world. From then on, Shariati was appreciated both by the Iranian people and the elite—even communist activists admired his courage. Only the clergy could not stand him. More and more virulent, he accused it of conniving with the imperial regime and tarnishing the image of "authentic Islam" (*Eslam-e râstin*).

Shocked by his virulent criticisms, some ayatollah, who felt themselves to be "open to modernity" (Motahari, Béhéshti), sided with the conservatives and left the Hosseyniy-e Ershad Foundation. In 1972, the police closed it down and, after several months of clandestine activity, Shariati was arrested and remained in prison until 1975. He was liberated thanks to the intervention of the Algerian government but was not authorized to speak in public. Nobody ever again saw him on a podium. In 1977, after his death, his writings were tremendously successful, and his posthumous audience rivaled Khomeini's influence.

Shariati's originality, in the context of that time, lay in his historic and philosophical reading of religious thought. He supplied the basis for a systematically anti-conservative thought and proceeded to modernize religious discourse. Shariati separated it from its attachment to the past and its nostalgia for a static order. He resolutely projected it into historic immanence and into the dynamics of a universe in motion; he made it adopt the realizations of the modern world and turned it toward the future. In other words, Shariati transported religious discourse onto the ground of the Marxists, the progressives, and the liberals, that is, the ground of ideology in the full meaning of the term. He used the tools of ideological thought to propose a revolutionary version of religion or, as he said: "the religion of today." His ambition was to define a religious alternative to Marxism.

---

[6] The foundation of Hosseyniy-e Ershad was a religious institution not under the contrôl of the traditional clergy, In the beginning, some ayatollah close to the founders of the MLI and particularly to Khomeini who wanted to be "open to modernity" like the Ayatollah Motahari or Beheshti, had great authority et gave Hosseyniy-e Ershad a relative theological legitimacy. The institution was financed by rich merchants of the *Bazaar*, reassured by the presence of these clerics in the association.

The dominant note of his thought was revolution. He wanted an antidemocratic revolution and opposed the "idolization of democracy." Contrary to his predecessors—the nationalist intellectuals and the liberals of the constitutional movement—he was hostile to democracy and felt that human rights would push Iranian society into decadence. His ideas reflected those that were dominant in the Iran of the 1970s. They were at once revolutionary, ideological, utopian, anti-imperialist, and antidemocratic, influenced by Marxism and by a simplistic interpretation of Heidegger's thought.

His revolutionarism prevented him from comprehending the elevated mystic thought that had permeated all Persian literature for more than ten centuries. He fell into an activism that ignored the essence of Shiism and minimized the significance of spiritual Islam. He ridiculed the mystic authors of the seventh and eighth centuries who had chosen to concern themselves with the esoteric world rather than to combat unjust monarchs, wasting their time in producing a "saving knowledge" while the country was on fire. He thought himself authorized to eject Sufism to the borderline, forgetting that by this hasty judgment he was forbidding spiritual Islam to be Islam.[7]

Marxist in spirit, he thought that what Islam and Marxism had in common was the class struggle to abolish capitalism. His ambition was to transform the Muslim religion into a weapon to be used in the combat of the dominated against the dominant. Like Marx, who said that "the emancipation of the working class should be carried out by the workers themselves.[8] Shariati's leitmotiv was the Koranic verse: "God will not change a people's destiny, so long as the people do not change it." If his aim was to transform the Muslim religion into an ideology, he yet never clarified what he meant by ideology: "In my opinion, the best definition one can give of religion is that it is an ideology," he wrote, "and the best definition of ideology is that it is the continuation of intuition."[9] Based on this most unclear definition, he began to work out a "religious ideology," close to an "ideology of combat," that conformed more to Marxist plans than to religious precepts but that gravitated around the Muslim doctrines of holy war (*jihad*) and martyrdom (*shahâdat*).

---

[7] *Cf.* Corbin, *op. cit.*, 1971.

[8] *Cf.* Karl Marx, *Inaugural Address to the International Association of Workers*, Paris, Librairie de l'Humanité, 1921.

[9] Ali Shariati, *Majmou-e asar* (Complete Works), vol. 1, Tehran, Hosseyniy-e Ershad, 1979, p. 209.

The Right to Kill

Shariati's Islam was no religion of peace but of war. He extolled martyrdom as the weapon of the dominated against the dominant. When there was no longer any way to obtain one's fundamental rights, when life was unjust, the oppressed must fight the oppressors by risking their own lives: "Kill them if you can: *jihad* (holy war). If not, do not accept an inferior life; choose heroically to die as martyrs (*Shahâdat*)."[10]

The doctrines of holy war and of self-sacrifice came from sacrificial logic and obeyed the ancient principle of control and social regulation founded on the rule of an arbitrary absolute imposed on a sovereign's subjects, on the conquered, on serfs. It ignored the real interest of the people and was explicitly justified in the name of an order dictated by transcendence. Shariati invented a new interpretation to introduce this into the dialectics of the class struggle. The martyr, far from a victim, became a hero whose death was his life's work. He cited the example of the Imam Hosseyn, the Third Shiite Imam who died in Karbala during the war against Yazid, the caliph of that time. Whereas throughout Shiite history the Imam Hosseyn had symbolized defenseless victims, a weak and resigned person who lost his life in an unjust war, under Shariati's pen, he became the symbol of courage, the emblematic figure of Islam refusing injustice and daring to fight his enemies unarmed, in order for Truth (*haq*) to be recognized. The Prophet of Islam and his descendants, as depicted by Shariati, resembled anti-imperialist heroes more than holy figures upheld by the spiritual and tending toward a unity with the divine. In his famous book *Fatemeh, Fatemeh ast* (Fatemeh is Fatemeh)—his book most read by young Iranians—he described the daughter of the Prophet, the Imam Hosseyn's mother, as if she had been a twentieth-century feminist fighter, more closely resembling a Rosa Luxemburg than a saint of Islam's golden age. Without the slightest reference to the spiritual nature of this icon of Islam, the saint's personality is revealed to readers through a keen psychological analysis of her relations with her father and her husband—Ali, the First Shiite Imam. In an unforgettable speech given at the Hosseyniy-e Ershad Foundation, Shariati cried out with the greatest eloquence: "I want to say that Fatemeh is not the daughter of the Prophet; she is not the wife of Ali, nor is she Hosseyn's mother. She is what she is! She is a

---

[10] *Ibid.*

free woman! A woman capable of causing the bastions of injustice to tremble! Fatemeh is Fatemeh!"[11]

These few lines sum up Shariati's conception of woman and her place in society. He removed her from the hold of traditional patterns (daughter, mother, wife) and gave her a prime role in the heart of the combat against the world's injustice. He saw no difference between the sexes and, with the dark humor that typified him, criticized the clergy's limited conception of the role of women in society and politics. While sensitive to women's beauty,[12] he appreciated their capacity to transform themselves into revolutionaries, even into warriors. According to Shariati, woman is an Amazon more courageous and determined than man.

Shariati saw Islam as a permanent war for truth (*haq*) against injustice (*bâtel*). The relationship between violence, the sacred, and truth might be considered as a sort of sanctification of violence. What Shariati's thought had in common with that of the clergy was its enclosure in a fossilized conception of truth. The danger with extremists is that this truth is presented as "absolute," as the "truth of God's word": because God revealed law and just knowledge to men, they have the right and especially the duty to impose it on others. Shariati's truth was the revolution, the war of the oppressed against the oppressors. It was on this categorical conception of truth that the decisive closeness between Shariati and the orthodox Muslims, Khomeini at their head, was based.

It is precisely the incompatibility between the founding principles of modern democracy and the belief in a transcendent truth that prevents those who believe they possess the latter from living in harmony with their times. They must find themselves outside democratic logic and opposed to it. It is thus that all adherence to "absolute truth," proclaimed as such, inevitably gives free rein to violence.

The Right to Die

> *We live without reason;*
> *They die for a reason.*
> Ali Shariati

Insisting on the value of martyrs' blood, renewing the traditional concept of sacrifice—horizon of the individual's accomplishment in the

---

[11] Excerpt from his speech on the daughter of the Prophet, in 1975. The stress on certain words is from Shariati.

[12] See: Ali Shariati, *Kavir* (The Desert), Tehran, Ershad, 1974. In this book he praises femininity.

154

loss of his life—Shariati awakened the most impassioned feelings of young Iranians and invited them to shed their blood on God's mission, combating those who did not share the same conception of truth. He presented sacrificial rites as the foundation of religious faith and, in defending this truth, he "sanctified" violence and solemnly legitimated the undertaking of war whose necessity always arose from purely political and strategic interests.

In a world where "it was no longer natural to die"[13], the choice of a martyr's death, by its strange singularity, challenged those values on which social life was established. The martyr said "no" to the world's order, "no" to all those conditions that made him a victim, "no" to a world that did not let him live in dignity. He refused it and spurned it, turning his death into the final proof of his rejection, like the Imam Hosseyn.

True, the concept of martyrdom no longer had the old legitimacy that the function of regulating violence gave it in traditional societies, but the martyr himself was able to define his death differently: to die for something. The martyr died because he refused to live a life that he esteemed unworthy. That death gave a meaning to his life, a life without basis or support, alone with oneself, enclosed in solitude, a solitude transformed into despair. The martyr turned his despair into a heroic act, both for himself and for his community, an offering to the "road to Truth." Since nothing had ever allowed him to feel useful in his life, he felt able to be so in a death that served a cause: the survival of his ideas. He gave himself death so that his ideas would remain alive, so that others would follow him. By doing this, he did not suffer death, he chose it. "In opposition to death that is but every man's lot," wrote Weber, "a destiny that strikes everybody without one's ever being able to say why him and why now; in opposition to that merely inevitable death, a death on the battlefield is distinguished by the fact that here, and here alone, the individual thinks he knows he is dying for a reason."[14]

The insertion into the sequence of events of death with meaning, and a sacred meaning, gave religious doctrines a specific legitimacy that disposed them to respond to all calls for violence. By choosing to die for something, by making death one's life's work, the martyr broke the circle of absurdity. His belief in a life after death opposed the absurdity

---

[13] This expression is taken from André Gorz. *Cf.* André Gorz and Michel Bosquet, *Ecologie et Politique*, Paris, Seuil, 1979.

[14] Weber, *op. cit.*, 1996, p. 427.

of the world and, by defending it to the ultimate degree, he sacrificed an existence doomed to failure to defend the absolute and intangible truth of God's Word. The martyr scorned a world where death no longer had any meaning; he thereby defied all those who did not share his conception of truth.

As weak as they might be, the dominated, the marginal, and the abandoned, by choosing a martyr's death, transformed their despair into the most redoubtable weapon possible against those who did not recognize their fundamental rights and who excluded them from any active participation in social life. They henceforth believed themselves to be God's instruments, imposing his laws and his truth on a world to which they had never belonged: "We live without reason, wrote Shariati, while they, they die for a reason."

It was thus that Shariati's ideas on a martyr's death and on holy war, a war against injustice, fired young Iranians and led several hundred thousands of them to the precipice of death.[15] They all dreamed of dying as martyrs.

The Cult of the Guide

Like the communist militants, Shariati was an adept of a materialist conception of history. But it was with an immeasurably superior competence that he approached philosophy and sociology to develop an analysis, both historical and economic, of the dominant forces of Iranian society and, to a lesser extent, of Muslim societies. From religious discourse, he extracted the necessary motives to constitute a coherent example from which his "project of revolutionary Islam" appeared a free and egalitarian society, liberated from social injustice, the salary system, capitalism, states, and borders. Thus he spoke of a "classless monotheistic society" (*Jamey-e bitabaghey-e towhidi*). It must be led by a leader, an imam (the guide) whose authority could be questioned by nobody. Excluding any opposition force, Shariati's monotheistic classless society was a system that asked for complete totalitarianism.

Reducing religion to ideology led Shariati to the conclusion that "democracy is incompatible with religion, because democracy is an anti-revolutionary system and thus opposed to the ideological leadership (*Imamat*) of society." According to him, a social and political organization needed a guide (imam) who ruled supreme and governed it according to

---

[15] That logic prevailed not only during the 1979 Revolution but also thereafter, during the Iran-Iraq war and under the repression of Khomeini's regime.

the dominant ideology. Contrary to the democratic system, the imam's legitimacy did not come from the people but from on high: it was a cognitive legitimacy granted by divine grace. The ideological leader not only represented political power; he was the incarnation of Truth since this power was not based on the people's choice but on God's will. He was the representative of God on earth. The role of the people was to discover who had received this specific grace, to place him at the head of the community of Muslims (*ommat*) and thereafter to obey him religiously. *Believe, obey,* and *combat* were the three words that summed up the people's role in Shariati's religious ideology.

He thought that the imam's responsibility was to guide "the amorphous and ignorant masses." Contrary to democratic systems whose political leaders listen attentively to their people, the religious leader, the imam, did not need to be receptive to people. He must lead them, change their decadent mentality, push them, at times even against their will, toward horizons of development and progress. Contrary to leaders of democratic countries, the imam was not a demagogue or a populist leader who, in order to ensure his reelection, did not dare to take radical measures to make his people advance. Shariati considered that that was what made modern democracies so weak, totally unstable, and even dangerous. He felt that the problems of modern democracies came from that incapacity, inherent to the democratic system, to impose order and direct the people.

In *Omat va emamat*,[16] the book that so delighted the Islamic Republic's leaders, he developed the theory of leadership in Islam. He described the religious guide as a totalitarian dictator, to whose orders the entire people must submit. It was he who would install an "authentic Islam" (*eslam-e râstine*), heroic, endowed with the sense of belonging to the nation, able—by his own action—to forge history by integrating himself in a state that assumed its aspirations. This should be done by radically transcending individualism. The individual must not express himself egotistically, in competition with other subjects, but in an orderly and disciplined manner, accepting himself as part of the collectivity. The Muslim community must be incarnated by the person of the imam, turned toward a common objective and not divided by class hatred. The socialist concept of class struggle was thus transformed into love between

---

[16] Ali Shariati, *The Oumma and the Imanat: The Muslim community and its spiritual and temporal leadership*, Beyrouth, Albouraq, 2007. This book was later used by the Islamist leaders to justify their repressive social policies in Iran.

the classes. To this end, the need to strengthen the feeling of belonging to the community of believers through the exaltation of religious faith was asserted. In such an ideological context, the state was conceived as ethical, an end therefore and not a means. Its interest took precedence over that of the individual, in the name of the common good.

Opposed to democracy, parliamentarianism, individualism, liberalism, capitalism, and civil society, Shariati's thought was above all revolutionary, but it was also authoritarian, totalizing, and nationalist; it disdained individual freedom. Its social model was centered more on communitarian patterns of society than on those of the individuals who compose it. It sought to create a group united and in solidarity, endowed with a strong sense of identity. For this purpose, the collectivity had to share a common history and destiny and be built on the will to perpetuate its cultural consolidation. It was therefore essential to preserve the homogeneity (ethnic, religious) of the national collectivity.

The whole ideological apparatus that would support Khomeini's thesis of *walayat-e faqih* (the absolute power of the doctor of Islamic law)—the basis of the future Islamic regime—was thus in place. The exaltation of religious feeling, the rejection of democratic and liberal institutions, the repression of opposition, and the extensive political control of society carried out after the 1979 revolution found their roots in Shariati's thought.

The Mojahedin of the People: an Ideology of Combat

The start of the 1960s was placed under the sign of rehabilitating Islam. The desire to provide an image of religion in harmony with the modern world occupied people's minds. Recurrently, intellectual writers used expressions such as "true Islam" or "the authentic religion." These designated two different conceptions of classical and orthodox Islam, but the borders between the two approaches remained very ambiguous. Moreover, any attempt to break the traditional religious framework could not escape from the ideological dominance of Marxism.

It was at the beginning of the 1960s, around this fuzzy image of "authentic Islam"—and with the idea of proposing a modern interpretation of religion—that three students of the University of Tehran met together. In 1965, this small group became the Organization of the Mojahedin of the People of Iran (OMPI)[17] dedicated to armed struggle against the shah's regime. Just like the young communist activists, their

---

[17] *Sazman-e Moudjahidin-e khalqe Iran*, "Organization of the Iranian People's Fighters," OMPI.

call to arms was lost in space and did not receive the popular support so hoped for. The novelty was that this group wanted to place its theoretical objectives in a military perspective. Thus, theoretical work and political action became the melting pot of an urban guerrilla that later revealed itself as so terribly bloodthirsty.

As we have said, the Mojahedin's founders (the combatants of Islam)[18] met at the start of the 1960s at the University of Tehran. Several years later, they formed groups of theoretical reflection, but armed, in different cities. Devout Muslims from traditional families, these young people were nonetheless strongly attracted by Marxist programs. In 1964, Shariati's revolutionary ideas, very popular among students, impressed the Mojahedin and confirmed their hope for an "authentic Islam." They called for *jihad* and martyrdom to combat the world's injustices. Like Shariati, the Mojahedin wanted to build a "monotheistic classless society." This utopian society—led by Muslim intellectuals, without clerical participation—became the ambition at the heart of their commitment.

The Mojahedin felt that the shah's parliamentarianism, his reforms, and his ambition to modernize the country would end in nothing. Like the Fadaiyan, they believed that no political solution was foreseeable and that armed combat was the logical reply to the tyranny of an authoritarian state. They determined to go into action and sent their members to Palestinian training camps in Jordan or Lebanon after the Six Day War (1967). They showed solidarity with anti-colonialist movements in Arab countries and ardently defended the Palestinian cause. This contributed to the rapid radicalization of their organization and to their commitment to urban guerrilla warfare.[19]

Very quickly, the ardor and sincerity of these young believers gave them a fine reputation. Their fidelity to Islam aroused the people's sympathy. They became one of the most visible of the opposition forces in pre-revolutionary Iran, without however really rallying Iranians to

---

[18] The three founding members of the Mojahedin of the People were Mohammad Hanifnejad (1939–1972), Ali-Asghr Badizadegan (1940–1972), and Saiid Mohsen (1939–1972). Hanifnejad, the group's ideologist, was a mechanical engineer. Although he was a practicing Muslim—unlike most traditional Shiites—he refused to follow the advice of any *marja'e taqlid* (source of imitation), arguing that one did not need a *mollah* to understand God's word. Mohsen, the group's organizer, from a middle-class clerical family, was a civil engineer. Badizadegan, born into a traditional family, was a weapon's expert and a chemical engineer. All three were active in the National Front and the MLI. On May 24, 1972, after being tortured, they were executed in the Evin Prison in Tehran.
[19] Abrahamian, *op. cit.*, 1982, pp. 489–93.

their cause. Nobody knew why they fought, but everybody understood that they wanted to "please their God"—or, as one says in Persian, be in God's path. Everywhere people spoke of the young Muslims who died in street fights or under torture in prison. The reasons that led them to armed combat remained just as enigmatic as those of the communist militants but, unlike the latter, the Mojahedin's religious beliefs made their action, their devotion, and their sacrifice far more understandable in the eyes of all. If the death of communist activists led nowhere, the Muslim martyr, according to Shiite eschatology, was destined to live in Paradise.

The will of the Mojahedin to reconcile Islam with scientific theories soon drew them close to Bazargan, but their relations with the MLI remained ambiguous. Both groups defended more or less the same ideas: respect for Iran's national sovereignty, political freedom, social justice under the banner of Islam, respect for human rights, and so on. But the Mojahedin had gone into armed combat against the shah's regime,[20] while the MLI preached peaceful methods and tried to obtain political freedom by democratic means, such as negotiation and compromise. "The Shah's barbarous crimes," wrote the Mojahedin, "forced many young MLI members to seek new ways of combating the regime. Henceforth, the question is not *if* but *when* and *how* to take up arms."[21] Despite the radical differences of method and of ideology, MLI members considered that the young Mojahedin were on their side and generously aided them financially. Both groups were rather popular in the 1970s and would play important parts in the 1979 revolution.

The Mojahedin also maintained strained relations with Shariati. Despite the undoubted influence of his revolutionary thought on their organization's formation, they mistrusted him, thought him an idealist disconnected from reality and with bourgeois inclinations. Some went so far as to accuse him of complicity with the shah's regime. Shariati, for his part, did not at all appreciate the crystallization of the Mojahedin's

---

[20] The Mojahedin were convinced that peaceful means were useless: "The June 1963 insurrection was a turning point in Iranian history. It revealed not only the political awareness of the masses but also the fundamental flaw of the old organizations that wanted to peacefully resist the regime and its imperialist clients by street demonstrations, strikes and parliamentary reforms. After June 1963, political militants—whatever their ideology—realized that one could not fight tanks and artillery barehanded. Thus, we had to ask ourselves: What should we do? We had only one answer: armed struggle." Mojahedin Organization, "The armed struggle is a historic necessity," *Mojahed*, no. 1–4, Tehran, November 1974.

[21] Mojahedin Organization, *"Akharin défa'iyat"* (Last Defenses), OMPI, 1972, p. 7: quoted in Ervand Abrahamian, *The Iranian Mojahedin*, New Haven and London, Yale University Press, 1989.

political action in armed combat and felt it was premature. He asked them not to go into action before thorough theoretical reflection, the better to comprehend "the authenticity of revolutionary Islam."[22] But the Mojahedin paid more attention to the theoretician's concepts than to his advice. Glorifying the call of Shiism to rebellion, Shariati always legitimized violence in the name of God. It was neither their rationality nor their knowledge of social science but their highly emotional dimension that gave the "idealist thinker's" ideas such a large audience among young Iranians and, in particular, among the Mojahedin. Although they did not admit it openly, he was their main source of inspiration.

Just like the communist activists, the Mojahedin were young and enthusiastic; their intellectual knowledge was rather limited, but their ideological and political pretensions knew no limits: they wanted to change the world. Attracted by anti-imperialist and anti-colonialist movements, deeply influenced by Marxism—or "the science of revolution," as they said—they were in their turn carried away by enthusiasm for the Cuban, Chinese, or other revolutionaries and found in Che Guevara their undoubted idol. Their attraction to Shiism crystallized around the aspect of contestation that Shariati had particularly known how to highlight.

The Mojahedin drew closer to the Fadaiyan, to the extent of entering into negotiations with them to form a front against the shah's regime. The existence of common strategies did not prevent tactical differences from creating trouble and causing the negotiations to fail.[23] This led the Mojahedin and the Fadaiyan to engage in an ardent ideological debate on Islam and Marxism, the first ever in Iran. It turned out to be very enriching. From his prison cell, Bijan Jazani, the Fadaiyan theoretician, made this surprising observation, extremely lucid for his time:[24] "These attempts to revive Islam are highly dangerous, for they can bring fuel to the fire of the reactionary clergy."[25] Indeed, the Mojahedin movement, with its emphasis on sacrifice and devotion, greatly contributed to renewing the image of Islam in the part of Iranian society that was

---

[22] Shariati, *op. cit.*, 1979.

[23] On the one hand, the Fadaiyan refused to sign proclamations beginning with "In the name of God . . ." They criticized the Mojahedin's choosing to assassinate foreign advisers posted in Iran, arguing that their main targets should be governmental civil servants. They reproached them with playing "the martyr's complex," sanctifying their dead heroes by giving them holy halos. On the other hand, the Mojahedin refused the possibility of any formal alliance with communist activists, in order not to risk losing the systematic help they received from the *Bazaar* merchants and from the MLI. *Cf.* Abrahamian, *op. cit.*, 1989, pp. 145–169.

[24] Bijan Jazani, "Marxist-e eslami ya eslam-e marxisti?" *Jahan*, no. 34, Tehran, September 1985.

[25] *Ibid.*

not close to the clergy. Jazani criticized the new intellectuals who attempted to "modernize Islam" and to launch a "protestant reform" in the Muslim world, whereas the Iranian context was very different from that of European countries. Such an attempt, he believed, could only restore religious obscurantism. The Koran and the *shariat* belonged to seventh century Arabia, and it was impossible to update them so as to respond to the needs of today's world: "Islam, like all religions, being based on divine truth and revelation, is in fundamental disagreement with reason, science, and modern thought."[26]

More directly, Jazani criticized the Mojahedin's conception of Marxism and felt that religion and the teachings of the Prophet were not eternal truths but a superstructure, fated to change. He also warned the Mojahedin that Iranian merchants formed a retrograde force and that only the working class—and not the national movement—was the true driving force for revolution in contemporary Iran. The Mojahedin's stubborn efforts to attract the *olama* seemed absurd to him, for the latter were linked to the ruling classes and were very rigid on issues concerning individual liberties—such as the consumption of alcohol, wearing the headscarf, enjoying the cinema and music, and infringing on sexual taboos. The use of religious emotion, Shiite symbols, and Koranic terminology seemed dangerous to him, for it would inevitably strengthen the position of the retrograde clergy. To avoid this, Jazani suggested that, while continuing to fight the regime, the left should undermine the ayatollah's authority by educating the masses on the true nature of religion. This the Iranian left never did.

Jazani's criticisms came at a time when the Mojahedin were in conflict with the opposition clergy and led them to rethink fundamental ideological issues. Completed shortly before his assassination by the regime, Jazani's reflections were the first systematic analysis of Islam developed by an Iranian Marxist.[27]

Ideological Confusion

The Mojahedin said they were both militants and Muslims. To justify their leaning toward dialectical materialism, they tried to Islamize the philosophical foundations of Marxism. The obvious philosophical

---

[26] *Ibid.*

[27] In the 1940s, when the communist movement was at its height, the Tudeh had carefully avoided that type of theoretical reflection on Islam, so as not to incur the clergy's fury.

162

gaps of their ideologists, who had, for the most part, been trained as engineers, prevented them from understanding the exact meaning of Marxism. As for Islamizing it, the undertaking was well-nigh ridiculous. Their writings and their speeches on the subject, a mixture of incomprehension and superficiality, were sprinkled with pseudo-scientific expressions and remained greatly inferior to those of the *mollah*. The latter at least were past masters of the art of eloquence.[28]

The Mojahedin saw themselves as the catalyzing agents in the evolution of Iranian society in which social changes had to go through class struggle. "Class antagonisms are the driving force of any change affecting the functioning of society and modifying the course of its history," they said, adding some verses from the Koran, which they claimed had the same meaning. They presented the class struggle "to abolish capitalism" as a cultural feature of society. This was where the difficulties began: these clichés borrowed from Marxism bore no relation to the Muslim religion nor to Iranian society, whose internal structure was closer to tribal divisions than to an actual class society. The idea of class in Iran could only apply to a recent period, no more than a few decades, while family background still dominated social organization.

Vaguely conscious of features that differentiated their country from others, the Mojahedin chose armed combat for the emancipation of oppressed peoples. They spoke of combat as the driving force of important social change. Their revolutionary project that aimed at creating a free and egalitarian society, freed from paid employment and from capitalism, took no account of the fact that paid employment hardly existed in Iran and that the country's traditional economy was far from comparable to world capitalism. For that reason, they indulged in their ideological claptrap, linking Marxist concepts to those of Shiism as used by Shariati.

Aware of their gaps, they began to study religion, history, and theories of revolution. They studied the Koran, the Nahjol-balaqeh,[29] as well as the principal works of Shariati, Taleqani, Bazargan, and revolutionary literature—Russian, Chinese, Cuban, and Algerian. *The Best Combat* by Amar Ouzegane became one source of inspiration. A former-communist-turned-nationalist, Ouzegane fascinated the Mojahedin with

---

[28] On this subject, see: *Tabïn Jahan* (The Origin of the World), Massoud Rajavi, Lectures at the University of Tehran, 1958–1959.

[29] Nahjol-balaqeh (The road of eloquence) is a long collection of aphorisms attributed to the Imam Ali, the first Shiite Imam. This book is the principal reference of Shiite Muslims, after the Koran.

his theory of compatibility between Islam, revolutionary religion, and socialism. They agreed with him that the only way to combat imperialism was by armed struggle and by appealing to the religious feelings of the masses. At the same time they studied the economic theories of Marxism, carefully avoiding its philosophical content in order, they said, to protect "their religious sensitivities." After three years of theoretical reflection, the Mojahedin created a Central Committee to develop a revolutionary strategy and to define their organization's ideology.[30]

Their theoretical publications proclaimed a cloud of ideas that can be described as a mixture of Islam and Marxism. Some years later, they were to explain: "Our initial purpose was to reconstitute Islamic thought with the help of Marxism's scientific theories, for we were convinced that "true Islam" was compatible with theories of social evolution, historic determinism, the class struggle."[31] They divided Marxism into two component parts, scientific and philosophical and asserted that "scientific Marxism" was compatible with "true Islam."[32]

The Mojahedin were convinced that God had not only created the world. He also had created the law of historic evolution. This had set up private property and class inequality and had given birth to the first unequal communities. Class divisions had favored the appearance of oppressive regimes, false ideologies, and fundamental contradictions between owners and workers, as well as between methods and relations of production. These fundamental contradictions were inherent in all obsolete social systems, such as feudalism and capitalism; they would disappear with the eventual appearance of the just and egalitarian society, in which, as the Koran promised, "the masses (*mostazafin*) would inherit the earth." This was, promised the Mojahedin, the law of evolution of historic determinism

---

[30] Most of the early Mojahedin leaders were young; they had studied in universities, particularly in the country's engineering schools and came from middle-class traditional provincial families who shared the religious mentality of the *Bazaar* merchants. The fifteen members of the Central Committee and the ideological team were born between 1938 and 1948. Many of them were therefore adolescents at the time of the 1963 insurrection and young adults when the first discussion group was formed. Thirteen of them were university graduates, nine of whom were engineers. Ervand Abrahamian, *The Iranian Mojahedin*, New Haven, Yale University Press, 1989, pp. 81–125.

[31] "Interview with Hosseyn Ruhani and Torab Haqshenas," *Peykar*, no. 79, November 3, 1981. Similarly, a Mojahedin manual, published on the eve of the Islamic Revolution, asserts: "We say *no* to Marxist philosophy, especially to atheism. But we say *yes* to Marxism's social thought, particularly its analyses of feudalism, capitalism and imperialism." *Cf.* Mojahedin Organization, *Les Politiques actuelles de l'Organisation des Mojahedin du peuple*, Tehran, pp. 10–12, 1979.

[32] *Ibid.*

(*Jabr-e Tarikhi*), which, like the concept of the class struggle, was an integral part of the Muslim religion: "To separate the class struggle from Islam was to betray Islam."[33]

They believed that the Prophet Mohammad had come to establish not only a new religion but also a new community of believers (*ommat*) perpetually advancing toward progress, social justice, and final perfection. The Prophet's purpose was to create the *Nezam-e Towhidi* (the monotheistic system), a classless society sheltered from all misfortunes. "The Prophet was sent to free mankind from all forms of oppression: class exploitation, political repression, corruption, war, and social injustice."[34] The essence of their discourse consisted in saying that the Prophet's legitimate successors, the Imam Ali, the Imam Hosseyn, and other Shiite Imams were opposed to the Sunni Caliphs, not because of power rivalry or theological differences but because the latter had betrayed the true cause of the community of believers.

Those ideas were developed in detail in their work *Nehzat-e Hosseyni* (Hosseyn's Movement). That text was based on a variety of sources—Shariati, Taleqani, Ouzegane, Maxime Rodinson, and others—and presented the golden age of Islam in a very particular, even debatable way, to say the least. If one believes this book, the Ommeyade Dynasty usurped political power after the Prophet's death and forged an alliance with corrupt personages to create a sterile clerical body, diluting Islam's dynamic and revolutionary message through static concepts borrowed from Greek philosophy. This "high treason" of Islam gave rise to social inequalities and fed popular discontent, leading the Prophet's companions to oppose the caliph. However, after the class conflict had exploded, the popular rebellion against the Caliph Muawiya and his son, Yazid, convinced the Imam Ali's family that to take up arms was a sacred duty and that they should put themselves at the head of the rebellion, even if it had no chance of succeeding.[35] The Holy Imams therefore sacrificed their lives not because they wanted power (as certain non-Muslim authors claimed) nor because the caliphs had deceived

---

[33] Mojahedin Organization, "Excerpt from the Will of Mohammad Hanifnejad," quoted in Abrahamian, *op. cit.*, 1989, p. 93.

[34] Massoud Rajavi, "What is to be done?" *Mojahed*, no. 87, Tehran, June 14, 1980.

[35] The Imam Hosseyn and his seventy-two companions perished as martyrs in a battle near the city of *Karbala*, on the eighth day (*Ashura*) of the month of *Moharram* in the lunar calendar, sixty one years after the beginning of the Hegira and twenty-eight years after the death of the Prophet in 680: whence the famous Mojahedin slogan: "Each day is Ashura and each place is Karbala," inviting Muslims to give their lives in combating their enemies, like the Imam Hosseyn.

them (as some Sunnis thought) nor because they were following a road predetermined by God (as the Shiite fatalist theologians theorized) but because they were motivated by their "revolutionary duty" to fight the oppressors in the name of the oppressed, even if the chance of winning the battle was slim.

Nehzat-e Hosseyin ended by stressing that the eternal message of Karbala and the sixty-three martyrs signified that human beings have the sacred duty to combat oppression. The tragedy of Karbala proved that it was necessary to sacrifice oneself by martyrdom to obtain justice and liberation; it showed that those who live under oppression are already dead while those who die fighting for freedom live forever. According to this book, the Shiite martyrs are thus modern individuals who choose death to honor their revolutionary duty. Thus, the armed struggle against oppression is the duty of every committed person.

Upon reexamining the history of Islam, the Mojahedin developed an unorthodox—and, according to some, totally heretical—method of interpreting religion. In the book *How to Learn the Koran* (*Cheguneh Qor'an biamusim*), they explain their viewpoints:

> Our way of understanding and interpreting the holy texts, in particular the Koran and the Nahjol-balaqeh, is qualitatively different from that of the traditionalists. We have developed a scientific and realistic approach that enables us to capture the true essence of these texts. For us, they are not static dogma but sources of inspiration for change and revolutionary action. Unfortunately, the clergy take them literally, in order to manipulate the masses, hiding the truths concerning science and technology. Thus, they succeeded in repelling the progressives, the intellectuals and those with a scientific spirit. This traditionalist clergy transformed Islam into a conservative ideology that allows it to tame believers. In fact, it did to Islam what, according to Lenin in The State and the Revolution, the revisionists did to Marx, transforming his radical ideas into harmless commonplaces, placing a halo above his head and depriving his revolutionary message of its meaning.[36]

How to Learn the Koran applies this observation, described as objective and scientific, to slavery, polygamy, gender inequality, and other

---

[36] Mojahedin Organization, *Cheguneh Qor'an biamusim* (How to Learn the Koran), vol. 1, Tehran, 1980, pp. 8–13. Among other things, the book explains that the right way of studying Islamic texts is to respect the following directives: "One must, first of all place the holy texts in their historical context, particularly socio-economic. Then one must be ready to learn from the experience of revolutionary movements elsewhere in the world, to interpret the world in order to change it and to put in place the monotheistic system that is the basis of a classless society." *Ibid.*, pp. 25–26.

practices mentioned in the first Islamic texts. These phenomena are therefore not compatible with all eras nor with all societies. They refer to unjust practices that existed in Arabia and that reappear throughout history, but that have now become null and void. The most striking idea in the book is its conclusion, more assertive than demonstrative: "Absolute equality is the true essence of the Koran."[37]

The Mojahedin of the People not only reinterpreted the holy texts in a radically new way but also injected new meanings into old religious concepts. In the writings of the Mojahedin, the *ommat*, the community of believers, was transformed into a dynamic society in the dialectic movement toward perfection; *towhid*, monotheism, became egalitarianism; *jihad*, holy war, became revolution for liberating oppressed peoples; *shahid*, the religious martyr, became the revolutionary hero; *mojahed*, the holy war soldier, became the revolutionary; *tafsir*, the gnosis or the knowledge of holy texts became the process of revealing the revolutionary content of these texts; *ejtehad*, the traditional practice of using reason to interpret religious law—a practice monopolized by the higher clergy—was transformed into a radical operation of extracting revolutionary teachings from that same law; *mo'men*, the pious believer, became a real fighter for social justice; *kâfar*, the infidel, became the indifferent one; the imam or charismatic religious leader was transformed into a revolutionary leader; *bot-parast*, the idol worshipper, became the worshipper of private property; and the *mostazafin*, the weak, became the oppressed masses. This last metamorphosis was the most remarkable of all, and the Mojahedin obviously used this expression in its new sense long before Khomeini and today's Islamists took it over.

Furthermore, the Mojahedin gave a new dimension to the symbols, ceremonies and essential personages of Shiite liturgy. In their view, Ashura and Karbala were not only the annual rituals that recalled the Imam Hosseyn's sufferings but also an opportunity to renew his commitment to fight all forms of oppression. Finally, the "society of the Imam of Time" (*Jame'eye emame Zaman*) or the Twelfth Shiite Imam, not only signified the return of the Hidden Imam, but rather the creation of a perfect society, classless, in which everybody will be protected from need, from oppression, and from alienation.

---

[37] *Ibid.*, vol. 2, p. 60.

The clergy did not accept these modifications of Shiite theology, which was hardly astonishing. How dared the Mojahedin interpret otherwise than the *olama*? How dared they question religious authority? For the clergy, it was the acme of desolation and abomination for a handful of young people who knew nothing of religious law, theology, or the holy texts to allow themselves to invent a new interpretation without any respect for what had been said before. The clergy was indignant to see the Mojahedin take over the historic theory of materialism, to quote Lenin and to borrow certain of Marx's famous expressions. It could not allow the Koran to be handled as a historic document instead of as the word of God and of eternal truth. It was unacceptable to say that sexual inequality, private property, or slavery were historical phenomena that must disappear with the development of human societies.

These "interpretive innovations" were no more pleasing to leftist activists, even less to antireligious intellectuals. For them, religion was synonymous with obscurantism, and therefore any attempt to rehabilitate Islam was doomed to failure. The antireligious camp remained totally hostile to the Mojahedin's initiatives. For a large part of Iranian intellectuals, this "return to Islam" was nothing but a huge leap backwards.

Conflict with the Olama

One of the Mojahedin's originalities was contesting the clergy's monopoly on Koranic interpretation. By asserting that anyone capable of reflection could proceed to criticize and comprehend the holy texts, they dared the more-than-thousand-year-old prohibitions concerning Islamic thought. Since the "dogmatic closure of Islam" set up throughout the Muslim world by the Abbasid caliphs of the thirteenth century, nobody had the right to interpret the word of God save those who were religiously qualified to do so—the "professionals of faith." The Shiite clergy applied this prohibition to the very idea of comprehension and declared that, aside from the clergy, who mastered Islamic gnosis, believers were completely incapable of understanding the meaning of the divine word.

This availability of the holy texts to all and sundry, a highly subversive concept, was developed in the Mojahedin's *How to Learn the Koran*:

> After all, whoever feels ready to make an effort can read and understand the Koran. This text is not as complicated and mysterious as

some want us to believe. It is not only a few privileged people who have the right to understand it. It is absurd to say that everybody must remain in ignorance, waiting to be enlightened by the olama.[38]

The practice of *ejtehad*, that is, deducing rules from religious sources, relies on the ability to understand the concept of koranic social change and dynamics. The true essence of *ejtehad* is to accept the fact that human beings constantly transform their social environments. Unfortunately, *ejtehad* has not been correctly practiced since the death of the twelve Shiite Imams. If, theoretically, Shiite beliefs, (contrary to Sunni) have left open the doors of *ejtehad*, the Shiites, like the Sunnis, have not succeeded in understanding the true essence of koranic dynamics.[39]

Believing themselves the sole guardians of the holy message, the great ayatollah categorically rejected these doubts cast on their authority, until then never questioned. In the Mojahedin's innovations, they found traces of Marxism and of materialism which to them totally lacked any Shiite spirituality. With their impertinent declaration that the traditional *olama* falsely interpreted Islam and collaborated with political power, the Mojahedin had overstepped the limits of the acceptable, limits determined by the Shiite clergy for centuries. In the entire history of Islam, very few thinkers had dared to question the notion of authority and to demonstrate the weakness of its legitimacy on a theological level.[40] The Mojahedin approached the issue squarely and asserted with great audacity that the clergy should not have the monopoly of interpreting scripture or the right to claim blind obedience from believers.

For lack of the necessary theological knowledge, the Mojahedin were unable to prove the frailty of the clergy's role in the Muslim religion and to proceed in due form to the theological disqualification of the *olama's* authority over the community of believers. Their position was intuitive; no historic or theological argument enabled them to support their innovative discourse against those who had invented all sorts of religious justifications to legitimate their power. The Mojahedin were content to reject religious authority without proving the correctness of

---

[38] Mojahedin Organization, *op. cit.*, vol. 1, 1980, p. 20.

[39] *Ibid.*, vol. 2, p. 65.

[40] There was always a good deal of controversy on the issue of *ejtehad* or on the interpretation of scripture among the different groups of Shiite Muslims, such as the Akhbari and the Usuli. To know more, see: Morteza Motahhari, *Fundamentals of Islamic Thought*, Berkeley, Mizan Press, 1985; see also: Allamah Majlesi, *Bihar al-Anwar*, 25 vols., Tehran, Amir Kabir, 1943.

169

their thesis by the laws of reason and of religion. The clergy felt threatened and rose up against "a handful of arrogant and ignorant young people." From then on, the latter were accused of all possible evils and condemned to all possible misfortunes. If the Mojahedin had called for armed combat against the shah's police, they were empty-handed when they faced a clergy "armed to the teeth" with the most sophisticated theological, historical, and political arguments.

The anti-clerical position of the Mojahedin clashed head on with the clergy. Khomeini rejected all their theological pretensions and considered them as enemies of Islam since, according to him, "the *olama* were Islam's only authentic representatives. Whoever is against them is necessarily the enemy of Islam."[41] Only the Ayatollah Taleqani established close relations with the Mojahedin in prison. After his liberation he related what he remembered: "The Savak's torturers were afraid of the name of Rajavi. They were afraid of the name of Khyabani."[42] These sentences, engraved in Iranian collective memory, gave great credibility to Rajavi, then the Mojahedin leader who escaped the death penalty in the shah's prisons.[43]

Yet, the Mojahedin's main enemy was not the clergy but the shah's regime, the agent of capitalism and of American imperialism who, they said, dominated Iran to exploit its natural resources, especially oil. Under the Pahlavis, capitalism succeeded in supplanting feudalism, integrating the country into the international economic system, and dominating society through its important repressive institutions, such as the army, the secret police, and the bureaucracy. In denouncing imperialism and capitalism, the Mojahedin of the People hurled countless accusations against the regime. They criticized the court's extravagance and the corruption of high officials, the waste of scarce resources, and the enriching of a tiny elite to the detriment of the impoverished masses. They pointed to the regime's failure

---

[41] Ruhollah Khomeini, "Hypocrites (*Monafeqin*) Are Worse than Infidels (*Koffar*)," *Ettela'at*, Tehran, June 26, 1980. According to Abrahamian, the Ayatollah Khomeini could not stand to see the Mojahedin attack the non-political attitude of the pro-governmental *Olama*. He insisted that the criticisms be removed from their publications and, in particular, from the book *Nehzat-e Hosseyni* (Hosseyn's Movement). *Cf.* Abrahamian, *op. cit.*, 1989, 105–145.

[42] Taleqani implies that the resistance of these two men in prison impressed their torturers.

[43] Some years after the revolution, in the winter of 1981, Khyabani, the emblematic figure of the Mojahedin after Rajavi, and twenty-three important OMPI leaders, including Rajavi's first wife, lost their lives in a bloody assault on their headquarters by the Islamic Republic's police (the Pasdaran). After that massacre, several high-ranking members left the OMPI. Rumors abounded of a settling of accounts between Rajavi and Khyabani. To this day, no light has been shed on that murky affair.

to abolish poverty, illiteracy, housing problems, and the absence of medical equipment. They denounced the gap between the rich and the poor. Finally, the Mojahedin reproached the shah with having abused Islam and attempting to undermine Shiite values by propagating a culture of consumerism, individualism, imperialism, and racism.[44] According to them, the Pahlavi regime remained in power by using terrorism as the foundation of its internal policies and using fear to paralyze Iranians and to reduce them to passivity and submission.

To break this atmosphere of terror, the Mojahedin called for armed combat. Such a fight could prove the weakness of the regime and of its foreign "patrons." It would keep alive the Shiite tradition of martyrdom, resistance, and revolution. It would show the entire world that Muslims, like communist militants, were ready to die in the fight against capitalism and imperialism. Since martyrdom was the ultimate proof of Mojahedin sincerity, each "hero" could inspire other Iranians to take up arms. When all the people took part in the armed struggle, the entire regime would founder in the face of popular protest. Thus, for the Mojahedin, the armed struggle became both the foundation of their thought and the ultimate aim of their action.

In a letter addressed to his parents shortly before his death, Mehdi Rezai (1952–1972), scarcely nineteen years old, wrote:

> No social advancement, no luxury or prestige, will turn us from armed combat. Because we have tried all these things, and they seemed insufficient to us. Our concern is not with ourselves or with our families, even if they are dear to us; it is the "heroic Iranian people." (*Khalq-e ghahraman-e Iran*) who are our first concern. When one of our citizens, whether in Tehran, Balouchistan or Sistan, suffers from poverty, hunger and oppression, we suffer with him. . . That is why we have chosen armed combat. This path alone can lead us to our ideal: a classless society, free and productive.[45]

With their famous slogan, "Each day should be transformed into Ashura and each place into Karbala," the Mojahedin claimed that history had taught them a clear lesson: there was no other road

---

[44] A book published in English attributes most of Iran's contemporary problems to capitalism and imperialism. *Cf.* Mojahedin Organization, *Cities in the Clutches of Imperialism*, Tehran, 1981, pp. 5–7, quoted in Abrahamian, *op. cit.*, 1989, p. 98.

[45] Mojahedin Organization, *Vassiyat namehy-e Mojahede shahid Mehdi Rezaï* (Mehdi Rezaï's Will), Tehran, 1973.

171

toward liberation than armed combat. They claimed to have drawn this conclusion not only from the example of the Imam Hosseyn but also from the history of other countries—Algeria, China, Vietnam, and Cuba—as well as from the events of 1963, when unarmed demonstrators were shot down like sheep. The choice of armed combat was the second major disagreement between the Mojahedin and the *olama*. For the Ayatollah Khomeini, "Only the clergy will be capable of overthrowing the Pahlavi dynasty, and that when the entire clerical corps will join the opposition."[46]

Between 1970 and 1973, the Mojahedin met the Ayatollah Khomeini several times to ask for his support. He refused, categorically opposing armed combat. Years later, he explained that he had quickly realized that, despite their great pretension of being the "champions of Islam," systematically quoting Koranic verses, the Mojahedin were real hypocrites (*monafeq*).[47] Like many others, the Mojahedin did not realize the infinite subversive potential of Khomeini. They only saw in him a "political simpleton," obsessed with theological details, in solidarity with "filthy reactionary *mollah*," "an ignoramus who saw in Marxism a Jewish conspiracy." His concept of revolutionary strategy was limited to publishing, every six months, a proclamation against imperialism, Zionism, and Pahlavism. They disdained him because he was satisfied to live safely in passive exile, while real revolutionaries were being tortured to death.[48] Khomeini, for his part, asserted he could detect the particular odor of Marxism and anti-clericalism of the Mojahedin.

In an interview, Rajavi said that the Mojahedin had few illusions about the apolitical and antigovernmental *olama* but that they had expected the Ayatollah Khomeini, that vehement opponent of the regime, to back

---

[46] Abrahamian, *op. cit.*, 1989, pp. 150–151.

[47] *Ibid*. The two Muslim Mojahedin members sent to the Ayatollah Khomeini in Nadjaf, Ruhani and Haqshenas—both from ecclesiastical families, and having received a thorough theological training—later changed their ideologies to become leaders of the Marxist Mojahedin. *Cf.,* "Interview with Hosseyn Ruhani and Torab Haqshenas," *Peykar*, Tehran, September 1979.

[48] They also left with the clear impression that the Ayatollah Khomeini and his partisans had tried to "exploit" them, both to establish links with the Palestinian movement and to show the whole world that Muslims, like Marxists, could die fighting for a cause. "Since the clerics had few martyrs, they tried to use ours," asserted Haqshenas. Furthermore, according to Afrasiyabe et Dehqan, the Mojahedin's disillusionment with the clergy was exacerbated by the behavior of other anti-regime clerics, some of whom—but this was not the case with Taleqani—signed a denunciation of the Muslim Marxists drawn up by the Savak, in order to be freed from prison. *Cf.* Bahram Afrassiyabi and Saeed Dehqan, *Taleqani va tarikh* (Taleqani and History), Tehran, Nashre Nilufar, 1981, pp. 325–335.

them.[49] This disillusionment occurred at a time when many of them began to feel that the OMPI, despite its apparent success, had reached a serious stalemate. It seemed that in 1974 many of its members realized that no real progress had been made "in preparing the foundations of a revolution."[50] That same year, a part of the Mojahedin left the Organization because they refused to work in close collaboration with the anti-regime clergy and to follow its instructions.[51]

Internal Dichotomy

The regime's brutal repression against opposition groups at the start of the 1970s, led to the execution of nearly all of the OMPI's leadership, including its founders. Most of the OMPI's members were in prison.[52] The group had at that point a very weak organizational structure, and its ideological frailty undermined cohesion among its members. The Mojahedin's heroic resistance under torture in the shah's medieval prisons was the final element that could maintain solidarity among them. From then on, each Mojahed had to live up to his imprisoned comrades and to follow their example in defense of their ideas, which nonetheless remained hypothetical and doubtful.

"The attack that does not kill us strengthens us." That sentence returned like a leitmotiv in the Mojahedin's discourse. Strengthened perhaps but certainly not in greater solidarity. Nothing thenceforth guaranteed the internal cohesion of the OMPI, and the disappearance of their founding members divided the Mojahedin. Many of them turned definitively to Marxism and abandoned their Islamic leanings. Massoud Rajavi—one of the group's rare leaders to have escaped death in prison—and a few of his comrades, remained faithful to the ideals of their departed heroes and denounced the treason of the factionalists. From behind his prison walls, Rajavi proclaimed himself the true heir of the Mojahedin and condemned

---

[49] *Cf.* "Interview with Massoud Rajavi," *Mojahed,* no. 31, Tehran, March 1982.

[50] *Cf.* "Mojahedin Organization," *Tahlile amouzeshie bayaniyehy-e oportunisthay-e chap nama* (Analysis of the Declaration of Ideological Positions of the Pseudo-leftist Opportunists), Tehran, pp. 172–177.

[51] On this point, see: "The Proclamation of the Group of Revolutionary Muslims," *Payam mojahed,* no. 51, Tehran, October 1977.

[52] In 1971, the Mojahedin went into action. Exploding the high-voltage lines that distributed electricity to the big cities, they tried to prevent the festivities of Persepolis marking the twenty-five-hundredth anniversary of the Persian Empire. Denounced to the police, sixty-nine of the most important members were jailed and judged in 1972. Eleven were condemned to death and sixteen to life imprisonment. In reprisal, Mojahedin terrorist acts against the shah's regime multiplied: on all occasions, they exploded bombs in strategic places. As of 1973, the Mojahedin restored active cells in Tehran, profiting from the discreet financial aid of the MLI.

the radicalization of his comrades in Marxism. He called them "pseudo leftist opportunists" (*opportunisthay-e chap-namâ*).

Yet, this radicalization was the direct result of the ideological amalgamation on which the group was founded from the beginning. Most of the Mojahedin came from religious backgrounds. Their attachment to Islam was rooted in the family ties that were very important to them. Their traditionally religious education prevented them from openly declaring their Marxist tendencies, although these led them toward new horizons.

The appearance of a Marxist branch within the OMPI posed real problems for believing Muslims like the Mojahedin. It forced them to see the basic contradiction characteristic of their organization and inherent in the way they thought. To this day, Muslim Mojahedin cannot present a rational analysis on the question. Calling systematically upon emotional arguments—respect for martyrs' blood, desire to be their worthy heirs—they seek at all costs to efface the reasons that provoked the division within their group. In fact, the explanation of Rajavi and his team for this split was stained with denial.

On the other hand, real attempts to explain have come from those who chose Marxism. One of the leaders of this tendency, Torab Haqshenash,[53] after long years in exile, judged that the shah was not wrong in saying the Mojahedin were "Islamist Marxists." That expression clearly highlighted the internal dichotomy that had always characterized the group:

> We were neither real communists, nor were we real Muslims either," wrote Haqshenash. Our objective was the revolution, and we found our references both in the writings of the world's great revolutionaries and in Shiism. Had the case arisen, we could just as well have found them in the Bible or in Buddhism. Religion, for us, was a tool with which to attract the popular classes. But we had to choose between Islam and Marxism and, obviously, the Cuban or Chinese revolutionaries had far more to teach us than the Karbala martyrs.

Divided within and threatened from without, the Mojahedin went through a difficult time during the years preceding the revolution. The myth of their dead heroes pushed theoretical debates into the background, and the emotional quickly replaced the rational. Their strenuous efforts to conciliate Shiism and Marxism, Islam and modernity,

---

[53] Former seminary student Torab Haqshenas was one of the first Mojahedin members when they were founded in 1965.

174

gave way to the glorification of their martyrs. The recitation of their heroic resistance defied belief. As much as the Mojahedin had serious problems in defending their political and ideological views with any coherence or rationality, so much were they at home in the emotional sphere. Gradually, the emotional took a leading part in all the group's activities, to the extent that even the structure of the movement was affected. The militarist conception of political action affected the relations between OMPI militants, and ordinary members faded into the shadow of their hierarchical superiors. With the help of a whole series of heroic discourses, the leaders insisted on "revolutionary obedience" from their members. Total submission was required of all.

From then on, the Mojahedin's political and ideological thought became deadly: from hunger strikes to suicide missions, including the elimination of "traitors," violence and death dominated the OMPI's spirit. They were omnipresent in all the written instructions given to members who had to prepare to become true fighters on the road to "God and the heroic Iranian people." They had to learn that it was only by going beyond life and death that each of them could attain the most far-reaching revolutionary objectives. "So long as a fighter has not eliminated his love of life, he can never surmount the fear of death and will, therefore, never be considered a true Mojahed." And indeed, the Mojahedin required their members to always be prepared to sacrifice themselves in the interests of the OMPI and on the orders of their leader. Sacrificial logic reigned, and each member waited for the opportunity to prove his perfect submission to orders from on high. Ideological discipline had an immense psychological hold on members and functioned so well that doubt did not influence their choices although these were, by definition, deadly.

The Bloody Purge

The disappearance of the OMPI's leaders in 1971 created a vacuum in the organization that necessitated an immediate restructuring, and this proved truly bloodthirsty. To the regime's repression—with its waves of arrests and summary executions—was added the ideological dichotomy between Islam and Marxism on which the OMPI had been based since its inception. The emotional tension that reigned among the Mojahedin grew stronger and aroused such violent reactions that most of the internal conflicts ended by the liquidation of experienced members by their comrades.

The purging of embarrassing members began from the moment when Aram, Shahram, and Sharif-Vaqefi, three high-ranking members of the Mojahedin, replaced those members who had disappeared at the heads of the OMPI's different branches.[54] Between 1972 and 1975, while the Mojahedin intensified their attacks against the regime, the branch directed by Shahram began to reexamine the OMPI's doctrine, calling Islam into question to the advantage of Marxism. Shahram converted Aram and, through him, the entire branch. However, Sharif-Vaqefi and his assistant refused to become Marxists. In May, 1975, Aram and Shahram eliminated him, burning his body and abandoning it outside of Tehran. His assistant, Samadi-Labbaf, was denounced to the Savak and executed in prison shortly thereafter.[55] Needless to say, these assassinations intensified the conflict between the Marxists and the Muslims to a great extent. After that, a majority of the OMPI members joined the Marxists. They included many of the intellectuals who had survived from among the first Mojahedin.[56]

Soon after, when the OMPI was at the height of its popularity, an anti-Islamic manifesto, entitled *The Declaration of the OMPI's Ideological Positions* was published, upsetting both the entire opposition of the country and public opinion.

> Our organization henceforth rejects Islam in favor of Marxist-Leninism because Islam is the opium of the people. It is the utopian ideology of the petite bourgeoisie; while Marxist-Leninism is the true scientific philosophy of the working class and the true path for the liberation of humanity.[57]

The Marxists succeeded in taking control of most of the OMPI, while the majority of the Muslim Mojahedin were in prison and would

---

[54] Bahram Aram (1944–1976), Taqi Shahram (1948–1980) and Morteza Sharif-Vaqefi (1949–1975).

[55] To know more about the purge and the death of Sharif-Vaqefi and Samadi-Labbaf, see: *Ettela'at*, Tehran, May 5, 1979 and January 11, 1982.

[56] Ruhani and Haqshenas, who played a crucial role in the Marxist Mojahedin organization, were members of the first ideological committee of the OMPI. As we have said, they represented the Mojahedin to Khomeini. Haqshenas was one of the rare seminary students in the group, and he had helped write its first booklets. Puran Bazargan, widow of Hanifnejad, came from a fervent religious middle-class family and was the first woman member of the Mojahedin of the People. Sadiqeh Rezai, who became one of the first woman martyrs of the Marxist Mojahedin, was the youngest sister of the famous Rezai brothers. In 1974, she joined the Marxist Mojahedins. Shortly thereafter, when Savak agents tried to arrest her, she committed suicide by swallowing a cyanide tablet.

[57] Mojahedin Organization, *Manifesto on the Ideological Position of the People's Mojahedin Organisation of Iran*, Tehran, Spring, 1975.

therefore remain in a minority position. At that time, Aram and Shahram controlled the organization and kept silent about the purge. In another manifesto, the OMPI wrote:

> In the beginning, we thought it would be possible to combine Marxism and Islam and to accept historic determinism without dialectic materialism. We now realize this is impossible. We have chosen Marxism because it is the true road to the emancipation of the working class.[58]

The Mojahedin's new ideological line was clearly shown in this text that declared that, after ten years of secret existence, four years of armed combat, and two years of ideological reflection, the Mojahedin had reached the conclusion that Marxism and Stalinism—and not Islam—constituted the true path for liberating the Iranian working class. The manifesto then enumerated the main reasons that had led them to that conclusion:

> Marxism is scientific, like physics and the movement of the atoms, and it explains the evolution of human society, while Islam is far from scientific. It is idealistic and incapable of understanding historical change. Marxism, by definition, signifies struggle, revolution and social transformation, while Islam is a sedative used by the dominating classes to pacify the masses. The essence of Marxism is to bring about a classless society, while the term *towhidi* signifies only a metaphysical belief in the oneness of God. Finally, Marxism is necessary to fight injustice, while Islam cannot respond to the elementary question: why should one fight against oppression?
>
> In fact, a Muslim can be pious and practicing while yet remaining passive. If you examine attentively the Koran and the other Islamic texts, you will see that they are somewhat ambiguous about combating oppressors and that they only recommend resistance in the most disastrous situations . . . while Marxism has no difficulty in responding, since combat is the very essence of dialectical materialism.[59]

The process of the Mojahedin's principal leaders adhering to Marxism seems to have lasted scarcely two years, and the ordinary members were converted in an even shorter period, so that in 1975 the conversion

---

[58] *Ibid.*, Summer 1975.
[59] *Ibid.*, Spring 1976.

had been "consummated," to use their own expression. In one of their booklets, the Marxist Mojahedin announced that "the conversion went from top to bottom, and that those who had refused to 'correct themselves' had been purged."[60] Furthermore, Ruhani, one of the principal members of the Organization, explained the sudden ideological change in an interview: "The leadership ordered us to criticize and to reject our past metaphysical and ideological thought, to analyze the errors committed, with the help of Marxist methodology."[61]

By the spring of 1975, the majority of the OMPI's members had gone over to Marxism. Generally called the Marxist Mojahedin, they took official control of most of the OMPI. It was not until the 1979 revolution that they gave themselves the name of *Sazman-e Peykar* (The Organization Fighting for the Freedom of the Workers), in order to definitively distinguish themselves from the Muslim Mojahedin.[62] Negotiations then began afresh with the Fadaiyan to form a united front, but these ended quickly with mutual recriminations. The Fadaiyan accused the Mojahedin of Marxist/Maoist dogmatism, of uselessly polarizing conflicts between Muslims and Marxists, and of falsely pretending to represent the Iranian working class.[63] The Marxist Mojahedin's retort was so brutal that it lastingly affected relations between the two groups.

The Mojahedin's activism redoubled after their conversion to Marxism. They organized several military attacks against the regime.[64] But in 1976, after the death of Aram and the arrest of a number of militants, the OMPI's activities considerably diminished. The Mojahedin had indeed shaken up the Savak by the number of their martyrs and by their spectacular actions, but they had not succeeded in destabilizing the regime or in launching a mass movement. As for coordination with other communist militants, that was a crushing failure. Between 1971 and 1975, the other movements had far surpassed the Mojahedin in their recruitment, political propaganda, and university strikes. Different

---

[60] Abrahamian, *op. cit.*, 1989, p. 146.

[61] Masali, *op. cit.*, 1985, p. 59.

[62] Peykar proclaims Marxism as his ideology and claims to be both Maoist and Stalinist. To know more about the schism according to the Marxist Mojahedin, see: Pykar Organization, *Taghiir va tahavolat daroon sazman-e mojahedin-e khalq-e Iran* (Changing Positions within the OMPI), Tehran, 1979, pp. 1–10.

[63] Bijan Jazani, *Who Betrayed Marxist-Leninism?* Tehran, 19th Bahman Publication, 1979, pp. 43–45.

[64] The most notable actions of the Marxist Mojahedin were the assassinations of a Savak general, of two American military advisers, and a failed attempt against an American diplomat, all in 1975.

Marxist groups mastered the armed struggle better than the Mojahedin, assassinating a number of leading figures of the regime and blowing up several banks and government buildings. After the appearance of the revolutionary wave, and perhaps under pressure from other groups, the Marxist Mojahedin began to call themselves the group that left the Mojahedin. They participated in revolutionary acts that ended in the regime's overthrow, but by their own admission, their role was marginal compared to that of the Fadaiyan.[65]

An Iranian left wing historian, Mazyar Behrooz, judged that the Marxist Mojahedin had been "late comers" among Iranian communists and that their vision of Marxism was, at best, infantile, superficial, and shallow in comparison with the Fadaiyan and the Tudeh. In the same way, their understanding of Iranian society and history was very limited. "Despite their conversion to Marxism, religious dogmatism never left them and characterized their whole Organization from the beginning and until its transformation into the Peykar."[66] Behrooz noted that their dogmatic mentality so frightened the Fadaiyan that they kept silent about the bloodthirsty purges and avoided any reconciliation with the OMPI.

The appearance of the Marxist group within the Mojahedin strongly tainted the OMPI image, especially among Iranian believers; it seriously damaged the popularity of the Mojahedin in general. It renewed the population's old fear of communism and reinstated the desire to reform Islamic thought in the wake of Marxism—from then on, any attempt of reform of Islam becomes synonymous with its transformation to Marxism. This perspective was all the more dangerous in that it seemed strongly confirmed by the division of the OMPI in the beginning of 1975. The return to "pure Islam" under the banner of the *olama*, with the Ayatollah Khomeini at their head, was then on the agenda. The clergy alone succeeded in taking advantage of the situation to bring forth a structured political movement.

The OMPI After the Revolution

When the prisons were opened the day after the revolution, the surviving leaders of the Mojahedin—Massoud Rajavi, Moussa Khiabani—were freed and gathered those who had refused conversion to Marxism. They declared that "pseudo leftist opportunists" had carefully infiltrated the OMPI, gradually taking over key positions. They had succeeded in

---

[65] Peykar, no. 93, Tehran, February, 1981, p. 17.
[66] Behrooz, *op. cit.*, 2000, pp. 72–75.

misguiding the young and ideologically weak recruits and had eliminated those who disagreed with them. It was therefore an "internal coup d'état, worked underhandedly in a Machiavellian way" and a "usurpation of the heroic name of the Mojahedin of the People."

However, contrary to this simplistic version of events, the Marxist members were neither raw recruits nor ideologically naïve members. Their faction was the result of an internal contradiction that had divided the OMPI from the start. By recourse to the "conspiracy theory," in what had become a national tradition among Iranians, the Mojahedin avoided any analytical effort that might have elucidated what had really happened in their movement.

After the revolution, a brief opening in the political sphere enabled the myth of the Mojahedin to beguile large numbers of Iranian adolescents and to attract them to their organization. The Mojahedin called them "militia" (*milishia*) or young combatants. They taught them the ABC of *tashkilati* life. This word, which can be approximately translated as "organizational" has, in fact, no more meaning in Persian than in English, but it fascinated the young recruits, who were filled with admiration for the unbelievable tales told by the Mojahedin of the heroic resistance of the dead comrades who had disappeared in the shah's prisons. The young sympathizers yearned to follow their example and adhered body and soul to the OMPI's purely emotional slogans. Massoud Rajavi, survivor of the shah's medieval prisons, became their leader, without anyone questioning the circumstances that had enabled him to escape the death penalty. Young and handsome, readily using a dramatic, theatrical style, scattering his speech with now Marxist, now Shiite expressions, Rajavi easily won the hearts of the Mojahedin apprentices, who were for the most part still in secondary school.

In the summer of 1981, after the radicalization of the Islamic regime, when a harsh repression fell on the Mojahedin as on other opposition groups, it was those young and naïve adolescents who paid the heaviest price. Several tens of thousands of them were raped, tortured, and summarily executed in Khomeini's prisons, while the "Great Mojahed," Massoud Rajavi, promised them a "very rapid victory" (*piroozi bassi nazdik ast*), inviting them to give their lives for God and for the "heroic Iranian people." While the poor adolescents threw themselves blindly into the claws of the Islamic regime, filling the corridors of death by the thousands, Massoud Rajavi changed wives ceaselessly, collecting "ideological weddings" and "revolutionary divorces" or vice versa.

Henceforth, the OMPI was based on the person of Rajavi. The cult of the charismatic leader crystallized all the attention. His will was the only political strategy of the Mojahedin, justifying the most unjustifiable acts. On his orders, designated members had to go on hunger strikes, immolate themselves, liquidate "traitors," and carry out many other such violent acts to prove their total devotion. Effacing the individual in the interest of the organization prevented any member from expressing his personality. Each was closely examined, even as to the details of his intimate life. According to the leaders' orders, members were married or separated, and this held true both for senior leaders and for those of inferior rank. This was called "revolutionary marriage" in which any affection or tenderness was considered contrary to the Mojahedin's historic struggle.

Such relationships were totally incomprehensible in Iranian eyes and did great harm to the OMPI's popularity. Nobody understood the rapid remarriage of Rajavi in 1981, only a few months after the death of his wife, assassinated before the eyes of their seven-year-old son. This second union did not last long either. Shortly thereafter, Rajavi married the wife of one of his longstanding brothers in arms. She divorced her husband on order of the OMPI to become Mrs. Rajavi, the "First Lady" of the Mojahedin, and was rapidly given the prestigious title "President of the Heroic Iranian People."

The Mojahedin pretended to have a "revolutionary vision" of women's place in society. In principle, they considered them equal to men. Indeed, in the commandos, women and men fought side by side, and in the training camps, all received the same instructions. Yet, in the symbolic case of the rise of Maryam Rajavi to the level of Head of the Mojahedin, and, afterwards, her title of president, it was Massoud Rajavi who decided. She was established in office by her husband's will. Her ascension depended in no way on any collective decision by the group. It was thanks to the man that the woman rose in the hierarchy. Here, as elsewhere, women and men were equal, but only if men wanted it so.

It was also in the name of Islam that the Mojahedin preached wearing the headscarf, or the *hijab*, for women. Some of the movement's bulletins tried hastily to present a "revolutionary purpose." The *hijab*, called Islamic, was supposed to represent an obstacle to women's bodies being seen as objects, said to be common in capitalist societies. The tacit obligation to wear the headscarf for female members had, in fact, no justification other than a respect for popular beliefs.

Exploiting religion to attract the popular masses is fundamental to understand many Mojahedin decisions that might otherwise seem obscure. "It is because our people are Muslim that we must respect religious precepts and that you must wear the headscarf," they told those of their female members who did not understand why they should submit to something that had so little meaning in their eyes.

The Invention of a "Secular Religion"

All the supporters of ideological Islam, from Bazargan and Shariati to the Mojahedin of the People, shared the same deep conviction that interpreting religion must not be left to the clergy. From the moment one gives oneself the right to understand and to interpret religion, independently of the criteria determined by the *olama*, nothing is as it was before. Another world is born, in which the monopoly of interpretation no longer belongs to those who thought themselves the exclusive owners of the sacred meaning.

Ideologizing Islam, which had begun modestly with Bazargan, who limited it to a simple hierarchy of Shiism's political ideas, really took off with the subversive ideas of Shariati. Without ever recognizing it explicitly, he presented a compromise between Islam and Marxism, quite original in the Iranian context. He removed religion from its customary spheres and stripped it of the paralyzing expressions given to it by the Shiite clergy throughout the centuries. He defined a revolutionary religion whose ancient forms were filled with new meaning, borrowed from Marxism. Shariati's Shiism was an invitation to collective action, a call for change, an opening toward the new horizons of the future. Shariati tore religion from the past and gave it a revolutionary dimension, entirely linked to the will of the believers. By insisting on the Koranic verse that says, in substance, that it is not up to God to change men's fate but to themselves alone, Shariati used Holy Scripture to break with transcendence, to empower believers toward action. By so doing, he led them out of the religious universe.

The first fruits of this new mixture were harvested by the Mojahedin. It was they who applied, word for word, Shariati's ideas and faced— without any of the requisite theoretical preparation—the camp of the conservative clergy. While they thought they were fighting the imperial regime, they were committed, body and soul, to a war against the sclerotic thought of official Shiism. For the first time in the Muslim world since the "dogmatic closure," a handful of young people dared to brave the prohibitions, defied the clergy's authority over the sacred texts, and presented "interpretative innovations" on history, dogma, and Islamic symbols. It was in this area that they later marked the collective conscience for a long time and gained the victory.

Indeed, they totally upset religious concepts, without realizing that they themselves would not be spared by the shocks of this quake. Their organization was caught in the destabilizing movement that they had launched. They committed themselves to an undertaking that quickly outstripped them and ended by destroying them. After the Marxists left, the Mojahedin were no more than a pale shadow of what they had been. Yet, whether one recognizes it or not, they—as well as Shariati—had the merit of being the first in the entire Muslim world to defy the clergy and replace traditional and orthodox concepts by new ideas. They tried to "democratize" religious thought by tearing it from the claws of the clergy and opening it up to all. They flouted the supremacy of the Shiite clergy and wanted to dispossess it of its authority. If important theoretical blanks prevented them from continuing their work to the end, they nonetheless succeeded in implanting in the collective conscience the idea of not leaving the key to interpretation to the clergy alone.

All the "new Muslim thinkers" who later appeared among Iranian intellectuals and who resolutely gave themselves the right to seek new horizons of meaning within religion were the direct heirs of the Mojahedin of the People. Antidemocratic, violent, and dogmatic as they were, those young people nevertheless set up a revolutionary religion that broke with the past and was open to the future. They created out of nothing an ideological Islam, close to a "secular religion."

7

Khomeinism

Khomeini's ardent magnetism added a religious facet to the popular discontent that had, until then, remained under the influence of the communist and nationalist militants backed by the liberal elite. Shiite Islam appeared as the majority of Iranians' common language, and the opposition movement fell entirely under Khomeini's control. He succeeded in rallying all the clergy, for the most part conservative. The revolutionary actors were primarily young city dwellers, well educated and ambitious, who wanted to take advantage of their country's wealth and to enjoy democratic freedom. They would later become the revolution's main victims, losing their illusions and often their lives. The juxtaposition of Khomeini's exceptional personality and the powerful ideological movement he created gave the wave of popular contention against the imperial regime a surprising momentum that succeeded in overthrowing the regime and setting up a new political system to which the strange name of "Islamic Republic" was given.

Khomeini was a highly charismatic person, but ambiguous. Nobody really knew his ideas or his intentions, save for what he tirelessly repeated: "Islam can solve all the world's problems." The liberals and the communists thought nothing would be simpler than to exploit Khomeini's Shiism, of whose practices they disapproved but that enabled them to reach the people's hearts. Khomeini's ambition, however, was unlimited; he wanted to turn Islam into both a religious and a political force. Shiism's influence over the popular movement was, for him, more than an expedient. It allowed him to control the movement and to set in motion the political program he had carefully worked out for decades.

Blinded by his fear of communism, the shah underestimated the strength of the popular opposition movement led by Khomeini. The imperial regime's conviction that the Shiite clergy was incapable of any political initiative gave rise to a series of grave errors that were, in the end, fatal to the shah. The Savak thought it sufficient to discredit the image of the retrograde clergy in order to stifle the movement. It is an understatement to say that nobody expected Khomeini to take a leading role in overturning the imperial regime and to then lead the movement of popular revolt to victory.

A So-Called Islamic Revolution

If the 1979 national revolution found no other language than that of religion, if it ended up by thinking in terms of Shiism, it was because no other opposition group knew how to speak to the masses. The communist activists, divided by countless factions and ideological quarrels, were unable to coherently comprehend the ideologies they claimed as their own. The armed struggle of both Marxist and Muslim activists sensitized public opinion; it prepared the way for a collective mobilization but did not succeed in creating a popular uprising.

Both Shariati and the Mojahedin brought Marxism into a religious framework and opened the way to a new interpretation of Islam. Thus redefined, religion left its traditional spheres and entered the world of ideological thought. Turned toward the future and open to change, it hardly resembled clerical Islam, which became an affair of the past. Ideological Islam put awareness of change at its very heart and drew from it a plan of action for society. It became the discourse that served first to conquer power by seducing people, then to justify the exercise of power, once established, by the clergy. It was a discourse able to convince people by offering them a simple and understandable analysis of history based on an appealing vision of the future and of its possibilities. Its specificity was to combine an explanation of the past, a decision on the need for present action, and a belief in future potentialities.

This interpretation of Islam was rejected by the Shiite clergy, who saw in it only an attack against religion and a heretical attempt to benefit the communists. The Ayatollah Khomeini was the only religious dignitary to understand the tremendous mobilizing capacity of the ideological discourse of Muslim activists and intellectuals. He took it over but replaced those ideas borrowed from Marxism with their "Islamic equivalents." Like the Marxists, he called upon the masses to take their fate into their own hands and to act on their destiny, but, unlike them, he placed them under the clergy's guidance, guaranteeing neither their rights nor their liberty. The revolutionary idea of Muslim intellectuals, in Khomeini's writings, was one that allowed the clergy to conquer power with the help of the faithful. Very quickly, he fomented an unprecedented massive mobilization that became the 1979 revolution.

Knowing precisely how to take advantage of the clergy's marginalization under the shah's regime to give it oppositional expression, Khomeini presented himself on the Iranian political stage in a new light and from then on became the leader of the opposition. The ayatollah distanced himself from the traditional clergy without ever breaking his ties with them. It was a decisive shift. However, the element of continuity was equally strong. The result was a kind of compromise that rendered Khomeini's thought and action particularly effective. His religious and political innovations, despite their radical appearance and the resistance they provoked from the orthodox clergy, perpetuated the Shiite tradition of seeking power. His speech, dynamic and mobilizing, swept away the Marxism that had seemed the reference ideology of those in the forefront of the revolutionary process. All other lines of thought seemed failures when compared to Khomeini's Islam—that we might call "Khomeinism."[1] It was an extreme religious ideology that embodied itself in the political regime and represented a specific case of transition between *the world of religion* and *the world of ideology.*

"Khomeinism" or Islamizing Politics

Islam needs blood.
Ayatollah Khomeini

The enigma of Khomeini cannot be understood without taking into account his personal charisma and the emotion he was able to arouse. They were the tools with which he propagated his ideas, giving them the power to mobilize several thousand city dwellers, to overthrow the shah's regime and then to install the clergy to govern the country.

The 1979 revolution and Khomeini's takeover radically changed the relationship between politics and religion. Whereas previously religion had been the auxiliary of politics and was needed to justify it in the eyes of the people, as soon as the Islamic regime came to power, it was religion that took over secular power. This reversal gave rise to a major transformation of religion. The event constituted a

---

[1] I have borrowed this word from historian Ervand Abrahamian's *Khomeinism, Essays on the Islamic Republic,* Berkeley, University of California Press, 1993.

highlight, sharply struck people's minds at that moment in time and even convinced its ideological enemies. Today in Iran, the clergy no longer seeks to take over part of secular power. They dominate politics entirely.

The concept of "political Islam"[2] captures neither that novelty nor its specificity. The more than millennium-long overlapping of religion and politics does not clarify how new and therefore disconcerting this idea was as compared with the past. It does not account for the specific current situation when religion aspires to seize political power throughout the Muslim world and, more especially, the case of Iran where religion has already taken complete control of politics.

Khomeinism, on the other hand, is the ideology that initiated the transition from the world of religion to that of ideology, favoring the takeover of politics by religion. It is true that the origins of *walayat-e faqih* (the absolute power of the doctor of Islamic law) go far back, but it was the Ayatollah Khomeini who gave it its current credentials. By basing his political project on the *walayat-e faqih* thesis, he gave the clergy the keys to secular power. Khomeinism or the "Islamization of politics" was an operation that transformed the clergy to enable them to govern.

Examining the Islamic regime's ideology is the royal road that allows us to comprehend the place and the meaning, in the historic course of the Muslim religion in Iran, of the episode that began with the 1979 revolution. More than thirty years of an Islamic Republic has brought about a deep disillusionment with—or a secularization of—the Muslim religion. If Iranian politics were largely Islamized, the regime's Islam, for its part, has completely left its traditional world to enter the world of ideology and exercise political power. That Islam is primarily a political religion, an *ideology of power*, put into place by clerics who became "politicians."

---

[2] "Political Islam" or "Islamism" designates those religious trends that aim to establish a state founded on the principles of Islam and of the shariat. Those two concepts appeared at the end of the 1970s, defining a political interpretation of Islam. The term "Islamism" tries therefore to designate the new trends of Muslim political thought, to distinguish it from Islam per se. The implication of politics in religious affairs is not recent, and the immense complicity of religion and politics throughout the Muslim world goes back to the tenth century. It is not that the two ideas of Islamism and political Islam are false; it is that they do not include the very new event that comprises the ideologization of Islam and that, for several decades now, has been transforming the relations between religion and politics.

The Weakness of the Shiite Clergy

The olama are Islam's fortress
Ayatollah Khomeini

It was in the 1960s that Khomeini began to develop a new concept of social and political organization.[3] He entrusted the whole of secular power to the clergy, insisting—like his predecessors—on the idea that he possessed the same "authority" as the Prophet and his Holy Imams. To this end, he broadened the notion of the *walayat-e faqih,* until then defined as the clergy's custody over widows, orphans, and the mentally deficient. According to his writings, the *walayat-e faqih* became the clergy's complete domination over all human and social organization. He went so far as to say that to disobey the clergy was to disobey God.

That great expert of the *fiqh* knew perfectly well that his arguments lacked legitimacy and were upheld by no necessity or theological proof. He was also aware of the weakness of the Shiite clergy's status. In fact, it was only in the sixteenth century, on the initiative of the Safavides[4] that clerical functions were institutionalized. Created and institutionalized by the regime, the clergy had power; it had its designated sanctifiers, the guardians of the text, the initiating experts of the divine. This, however, did not grant any direct power over the minds of the faithful. It took abnormal conditions to shape a spiritual power that yet was not constituted without extreme tensions.

The internal structure of Islam, based on the individual autonomy of the believer in his relationship with God, required no ecclesiastical hierarchy such as that of Catholicism. In Sunni Islam, the situation is simple. With no such hierarchy, the *olama*[5] could not, throughout the centuries, extend their spiritual authority to include any effective economic or political power. They did not even work out a coherent and critical theory of relations between political power and the spiritual authority that they were supposed to exercise. They rapidly became mere auxiliaries of politics.

In Shiite Islam, the clergy, in principle, must remain in the incognito of an *Ecclesia spiritualis,* and the esoteric hierarchy cannot enter the

---

[3] Because he never quoted his sources of inspiration, nor admitted the least change in his ideas, it is well-nigh impossible to determine his intellectual influences.
[4] The Safavides dynasty reigned over Iran from 1501 to 1736.
[5] *See note 19 in chapter 1.*

189

profane world because the spiritual world and the world here below are incompatible. Members of the clergy are supposed to possess a spiritual charisma, and their role consists in gradually initiating the faithful into the true meaning of God's message; that is, the spiritual significance of the divine revelations.[6]

Creating the Shiite clerical body in the sixteenth century under the Safavides opened a new page in Islamic religious history. In 1501, Iran was converted to Twelver Shiism under the sword of the dynastic founder, Shah Ismail. True, that conversion was not due solely to the shah's initiative. There was also the people's predisposition for Shiism that, since it was rooted in Zoroastrianism, gave birth to an Iranian religion, different from that of the Arabs and able to reassert a national identity.[7] However, the Safavides' reason for creating a Shiite political/religious pole went far beyond national feelings.

Opposed to the Ottoman Sunni Empire, the Safavides needed to affirm the religious legitimacy of their monarchy. That legitimacy found its official consecration in institutionalizing clerical functions. All possible means were mobilized to strengthen the Shiite *olama*, thus contributing to the creation of a truly official clergy, despite all the theological obstacles, the accusations of heresy by the Sunni *olama*, and the protests of the Ottoman sovereigns.

Very quickly, an important part of property taxes (*kharâj*), originally destined for the shah, was transferred to the *olama*. Henceforth, those taxes provided them with unprecedented economic power and great independence. Under the reign of Shah Abbas (1588–1629), the creation of a ministry of religious affairs, with a *faqih* (specialist of Islamic law) as minister, enabled the clergy to officially establish its authority in politics and in society. The Safavides determination to consolidate the clergy's position incited the *olama* to extend their power to areas previously reserved for the holy imams. Shah Abbas authorized them to exercise essential functions, such as religious jurisdiction, imposing penalties and mandating religious practices such as collective Friday prayers, which had not been observed since the disappearance of the Twelfth Imam, that is, for seven centuries (from the tenth to the seventeenth century).[8]

---

[6] *Cf.* Corbin, *op. cit.,* 1971, pp. 34–35.

[7] On this subject, see, Henry Corbin, *In Iranian Islam, Twelver Shiism: Spiritual and Philosophical Aspects*, 5 vols., Paris, Gallimard, 1971.

[8] The *olama* presided over the courts and applied legal sanctions since the seventeenth century. *Cf.* Mohammad Amir-Moezzi and Christian Jambet, 2004, *op. cit.,* p. 211

Under the Safavides, the *olama's* power grew, and the clergy became an influential institution that perfected the art of covering all clerical initiatives with an Islamic mantle, cloaking political interests under the Prophet's message. The *olama* presented the Koran as a reference and a guide, applying to it their own criteria and preferences that depended on the context in which they lived. In reality, they projected their own interests onto the text, making it say what it had never said. It became the customary practice of Shiite clergy to justify the pursuit of worldly interests in the name of transcendental objectives, a practice that did not await the arrival of Khomeini and his successors.

After the fall of the Safavides and the arrival of the Qajar dynasty, the *olama* became even more powerful. The Qajars' incompetence, the absence of any army or central administrative system, and the country's growing impoverishment enabled the *olama* to strengthen their position in relation to the temporal power. The weaker the monarchy became, the more the *olama* extended their authority over all areas, multiplying their political and social interventions. They also proceeded to clarify concepts that had remained obscure under the Safavides—such as *walayat, marja'iyat, ijtehad, jihad* (holy war), and so on.

The *Mollah* Ahmad Naraqi (1778–1836), the famous *mojtahed* of the *Qajar* period, gave a new definition of the *faqih's* (specialist of Islamic law) place and role in the Shiite community.[9] While it had been admitted that, in the absence of a legal authority, the *faqih* could assume custody over widows, orphans, or the mentally handicapped (*mahjours*), Naraqi went much further and decreed that, beyond those categories, everybody had to obey the *foqaha* (plural of *faqih*). He deemed that the lives of all Muslims in this earthly world was the political and religious responsibility of the ayatollah who seized all the prerogatives of the Twelve Holy Imams. In fact, the power given the *clergy* went far beyond that of the Twelve Imams. Naraqi thus founded the first steps of what would later become, under the Ayatollah Khomeini, the thesis of the *walayat-e faqih* (the absolute power of the doctor of Islamic law).

In the second half of the nineteenth century, the *olama* tried to determine the function of the *marja'iyat* (the highest rank of the clerical hierarchy) and the believers' duty as *moqaled* (imitators). As difficult as it was for them to precisely define the steps that a cleric had to go

---

[9] See: *Mollah* Ahmad Naraqi, *'Ava'ed ol-Ayam: Walayat al- faqih,* Tehran, Sazman-e tablighat eslami, 1980.

through to reach the rank of *marj'a* (*mojtahed* or source of imitation), just so easily did they specify all the moral and legal obligations of the faithful toward the religious authority and the terms of their relationships. Each *marj'a* had to write a practical handbook (*ressaleh*) to determine and codify the daily lives of his faithful. Nothing escaped this codification, from religious ceremonies to the most private areas of daily life. The *olama* established a scale of values, of acts and behavioral norms to grade believers according to their level of devotion, or in other terms their level of obedience. In doing this, they pretended to know God's judgment and will, to be his representatives on earth, and the keepers of divine legitimacy. Religious authority was thereby on a level with divine authority. The *olama* decreed that those who did not follow literally the religious and legal commands of a *marj'a* would be excommunicated from among the believers.

Despite such arbitrary assertions, any theological proof could justify those innovations. Actually, the internal structure of Shiism does not provide any guiding theory for the whole of the Muslim world, and it was therefore difficult to really institutionalize religious authority. Yet the Shiite clergy knew how to skirt such obstacles, and nothing opposed their thirst for power.

Thus, throughout the nineteenth century, while in Egypt and the Ottoman Empire the Sunni *olama* were the subjects of their respective governments, the Iranian *olama* had a financial and social foundation that allowed them not only to escape any political influence but also to exercise decisive control over politicians as well as over the entire believing community. That takeover of power gave rise to a new ambition in the minds of the Shiite clergy, whose dream of ruling over the Muslim world no longer recognized any limits, going beyond the borders of Iran and ignoring even the Shiite/Sunni cleavage.

Despite the countless theological difficulties, Khomeini based his political plan on the clergy's exercise of political power. Adopting his predecessors' ambition, he propelled the clergy to the forefront of the political stage and put it in a governing position with the idea of creating an international Islamic empire. Faithful to the Shiite clerical tradition, which had always managed to read anything at all into the texts and to justify whatever it wanted, Khomeini managed tensions, justified each of his initiatives, and faced down his detractors. If the important ayatollah, who were masters of the art of religious cloaking, did not openly oppose his innovations or the

192

thesis of the *walayat-e faqih* (the absolute power of the doctor of Islamic law), if they remained silent, it was because they could do nothing else without contesting a tradition that was already several centuries old.

Khomeini's Political Plan

Islam is in danger.
Ayatollah Khomeini

Khomeini began on his political path with Shiism's typical ambiguities. His first political essay, *Kashf al-Asrar* ("Revealed Secrets," 1943), accused Reza Shah of numerous "unpardonable sins." He reproached him with closing religious seminaries, confiscating believers' gifts, propagating anticlerical feelings, and replacing religious tribunals with a state judicial system. He added the legalization of drinking alcohol and of listening to "sensual music," creating co-ed schools and prohibiting the long veil (*tchador*)—"thus forcing women to go naked in the street,"[10] wrote Khomeini.

In those early works, however, he explicitly denied any desire to overthrow the Pahlavi regime, and he very often reasserted his allegiance to monarchy in general and to "good monarchs" in particular. He stressed that the Shiite clergy had never opposed any political regime in Iran, even when governments had issued anti-Islamic orders. According to him: "Poor order is better than no order at all."[11] He reiterated the fact that no cleric had ever claimed the right to rule and that many, including Majlesi, had supported political leaders, participated in governments, and encouraged the faithful to pay their taxes and to cooperate with political authorities. Even if, on rare occasions, they had criticized some leaders, it was always personal, and none had ever attacked the monarchy itself. He did not hesitate to recall that the Imam Ali had accepted the worst of the first caliphs.[12]

The demands made in *Kashf al-Asrar* were limited to respect for religion, the presence of a greater number of clergy in Parliament (*Majlis*) and the conformity of laws adopted by Parliament with *shariat.* Khomeini stated that *shariat* could remedy social problems and must be enforced by the clergy, in particular by the *foqaha,* the doctors of

---

[10] Ruhollah Khomeini, *Kashf al-Asrar* (Unveiled Secrets), Tehran, 1943, pp.1–66.
[11] *Ibid.,* pp. 185–188.
[12] *Ibid.,* p. 226.

Islamic law whom he compared to medical doctors—highly qualified people, well versed in curing social illnesses.[13]

The demands of *Kashf al-Asrar* thus remained very limited. At that period, Khomeini made no allusion to the key concepts he would use later on, such as revolution, republic, martyrdom, oppressed masses (*mostazafin*), or even to the *walayat-e faqih* (the absolute power of the doctor of Islamic law). Until the 1970s, he maintained the *olama's* traditional positions toward the shah. Even in 1963, when he showed himself to be the most virulent anti-regime cleric, he did not call for revolution or for the overturn of the monarchy. He castigated the shah for "anti-religious transgressions," and for the decisive role he had played in the imperialist and Zionist conspiracy. He opposed women's right to vote and the possibility given to those of religious minorities to take an oath on holy books other than the Koran. He accused the shah of having plotted with Israel against Arab countries, thus leading "our Sunni brothers to think that we Shiites are in collusion with the Jews." Above all, Khomeini reproached the shah with having exempted American military personnel from obeying Iranian laws, not hesitating to appeal to popular emotion: "Today, if an American cook assassinated our religious leaders or made an attempt against the shah's life, he would not need to worry about our country's laws."[14] He claimed deep indignation at the humiliation that the shah constantly inflicted on the *olama*—"the true guardians of Islam,"[15] according to him. Those accusations were formulated as warnings rather than as a revolutionary threat. Even in 1965, after having been expelled from the country, Khomeini did not question the Pahlavi monarchy's legitimacy.[16]

It was only in the 1960s that he began to develop a new concept of social and political organization. Since Khomeini never quoted his sources of inspiration, nor admitted the least change in his ideas,[17] it is almost impossible to determine which intellectual influences contributed to this transformation. Furthermore, during the crucial period from

---

[13] Khomeini, *op. cit.*, 1943, p. 195.

[14] *Cf.* Hamid Ruhani, *Nehzat-e* Imam *Khomeini* (The Imam Khomeini's Movement), Tehran, Imam Khomeini Foundation, 1994.

[15] *Ibid.*, p. 198.

[16] In one of his proclamations published in the 1960s, he exhorted the monarchs of Islamic countries to work hand in hand against Israel. *Ibid.*

[17] He did not usually use footnotes in his writings or provide references to his sources when they were necessary, in particular if those sources were foreign or secular.

1965 to 1970, while he was developing his new ideas in exile in Nadjaf, Khomeini remained unusually silent, refusing all interviews, sermons, or public declarations. It is therefore difficult to pinpoint the origins of the change. Of course, one thinks of the Shiite theologians of Nadjaf, who were at that time led to forge a new concept of religion in order to resist the influence of communism. Those theologians then had many followers among Iraqi Shiites. The Ayatollah Mohammad-Baqer Sadre was the most famous of all. He defended tooth and nail the superiority of Islam's radical economic theory over all other systems of thought, including socialism. Even if the two ayatollah were not on good terms, the latter's works circulated widely among the Nadjaf clerics; they could not therefore have been unknown to Khomeini.[18] Moreover, on the only occasion when he praised Iranian radical intellectuals, it was to criticize apolitical clerics. He said he was ashamed to see the clergy still asleep: "We cannot remain silent," he stated, "until students force us to do our duty."[19]

Khomeini broke his long silence at the beginning of the 1970s with his famous lectures on the *walayat-e faqih* thesis. It was then that he clearly declared that Islam was intrinsically incompatible with any form of monarchy. He claimed that Muslims had the sacred duty to oppose unjust regimes, and they must neither collaborate with them nor make use of their institutions. Khomeini announced very vehemently that it was the "sacred duty" of all Muslims to rebel against politicians because most of them were dictators, oppressors, and mass murderers.[20] He denounced the shah and advanced the divine legitimacy of the clergy to govern in his stead.[21] Of the famous Koranic commandment "Obey those among you who hold authority," he gave an interpretation whose clear objective was to force Muslims to obey the clergy. Highly contested by other Shiite dignitaries, Khomeini did not renounce his political plan, although it was founded on highly simplistic reasoning. To justify clerical power, he invoked the Imams and referred to other

---

[18] *Cf.* Abrahamian, *op. cit.*, 1993, pp.111–113.

[19] *Cf.* Ruhollah Khomeini, *walayat-e faqih,* Tehran, Imam Khomeini Foundation, 1989, pp. 177–179. Bazargan, in his turn, admitted later that the student movement had greatly impressed the Iranian people and invited Khomeini to correspond with the Confederation in order to limit the influence of Marxism.

[20] Many years later, Khomeini maintained that Iranian kings, without a single exception, and including Shah Abbas, the famous Safavide sovereign, and Anooshirvan, whom Iranians recognized as the "incarnation of justice," were all criminals. *Cf.* Abrahamian, *op. cit.*, 1993, pp. 17–26.

[21] *Cf.* Khomeini, *op. cit.*, 1969, pp. 76–127.

Shiite sources. He tried, at all costs, to invent a theological proof to support his statement and affirmed:

> Did not the twelve Imams qualify the clergy as the fortress of Islam? Did not the Twelfth Imam instruct future generations to obey those who knew his teaching? In truth, the clergy are his representatives among believers, as they are God's representatives. Did not the Prophet himself declare that knowledge led to paradise and that "men of knowledge" were superior to ordinary mortals? Did not God create holy Law to guide the community? Did he not create the clergy to understand and apply holy Law?[22]

All his efforts consisted in entrusting the clergy with total political power, stressing the hypothesis that they had the same "authority" as the Prophet and the Holy Imams.[23] To this end, Khomeini adopted the definition of *walayat-e faqih* as propounded by the *Mollah* Ahmad Naraqi, the famous *mojtahed* of the Qajar era, transforming it into total domination of the clergy over all social and human organization. He was well aware that his innovation might shock many: "True Islam may seem strange," he warned his listeners. Indeed, nothing could have been stranger than to affirm the clergy's domination over society, while the very existence of the clergy remained difficult to justify.

Among the *olama,* strong disagreement existed on the *walayat-e faqih* concept. One of the clergy's most important responsibilities, the function of *waly-e faqih* (doctor of Islamic law) was considered fundamentally apolitical. Thus, for the majority of the clergy, that concept was limited to the legal custody the important clerics exercised over people judged incapable of attending to their own interests—minors and the insane. For some, this meant that the high-ranking clergy could intervene in politics—but only temporarily, if politicians were clearly endangering the whole community. As we saw, in 1891, the Ayatollah Mirza Shirazi was one of the first *marja'e taqlid* (sources of imitation) to pronounce a *fatwa* against the government that had decided to sell the tobacco concession to a foreign contractor. Shirazi opposed only the shah's faulty legal advisers and left politics as soon as the tobacco concession had been annulled. Similarly, in 1906, when part of the

---

[22] *Ibid.*

[23] It must be specified that the idea of "authority" remains one of the most debatable issues in Shiism. Many theologians have said that the authority of the imams concerns no effective power and involves only the spiritual. For a detailed analysis, see: Corbin, op. cit., 1971; see also: Mohammed Arkoun, *Islam, hier, demain,* Paris, Buchet-Chastel, 1982.

clergy participated in the constitutional revolution, it was neither to overthrow the monarchy nor to establish a theocracy, but to set up a watchdog committee to ensure that parliamentary legislation would conform to the *shariat.*

None of the high-ranking clerical dignitaries ever approved Khomeini's thesis of *walayat-e faqih,* but their legendary conservatism did not allow them to oppose it openly. They systematically said that the clergy should remain within the limits of their functions and not intervene in politics. Master of manipulation, Khomeini appealed to national feelings to skirt the obstacle. He recalled that the clergy had always protected Islam and Iran from foreign imperialism and from royal despotism, during the 1891 tobacco crisis, the 1906 constitutional revolution, the dark days of Reza Shah and of course, during the June 1963 uprising under Mohammad-Reza Shah. "The whole of the clergy had kept alive social conscience. It remained the strong fortress of independence against imperialism, secularism, and other 'isms' imported from the West,"[24] he wrote. Once again, thanks to the redoubtable weapon of emotional provocation, the most hypothetical religious theories appeared legitimate to all.

If Khomeini had not convinced the *olama,* at least he had silenced them. Nobody dared to denounce his plan's lack of religious legitimacy. Even the most strongly opposed among them, of whom the Ayatollah Shariatmadari was one, were silenced. Whereas theologically nothing justified the clergy's emerging from its "divine incognito," the spiritual world in which it had to remain, Khomeini propelled it to the height of the country's political functions, turning the "men of God" into "statesmen." A transformation that would change the very nature of the Shiite clergy and would cost Islam dearly.

Ideas in Evolution

The Khomeinist conception of social and human organization was strongly influenced by his political plans. Before the year 1970, his writings highlighted the traditional ideas of social organization inspired by the Imam Ali's Nahjol-balaqeh and by Shiite clerical teachings. Those writings were in harmony with the immense traditional religious literature produced throughout the centuries, in both Arabic and Persian. Khomeini repeated a whole series of conventional and paternalistic hypotheses according to which God created human

---

[24] "Khomeini's Speeches," *Ettela'at,* Tehran, June 16, 1981.

beings, private property, and social organization; this last consisted of mutually dependent hierarchical layers; the poor had to accept their fate and not envy the rich. The latter must give thanks to God, avoid conspicuous consumption, and give generously to the poor. If that vision of the world seemed simple, it was far from clear. "Holy Law," he wrote, "protects wealth as a 'divine gift' and it is the sacred duty of an Islamic government to maintain the necessary balance for the different social layers to live together."[25] However, he was silent as to what he understood by "necessary balance," as well as the means the Islamic government should employ to ensure that balance.

In his first writings, Khomeini remained faithful to the classical conception of Islam, rooted for several centuries in the Muslim world. At that time, he rarely used the word *class*, to avoid that term's strong Marxist connotation; he also tended to avoid the word *revolution*, even if he occasionally called for an uprising (*qiyam*). In the eyes of the traditional clergy, revolution was synonymous with chaos, anarchy, and class hatred. Later, toward the end of the 1970s, he diverged from traditional clerical speech. He portrayed a society strongly divided into two classes, a prey to permanent conflict between the poor and the rich. He used strong images to describe the pitiless struggle of the "oppressed nation" against "Satan's government," that of the "slum dwellers" against the "palace dwellers." In the past, such images would have been used by communist militants rather than by the clergy. Khomeini crassly exploited social antagonisms, without however falling into the theoretical and incomprehensible details that sprinkled communist militant analyses. The leftist militants, attracted by communist activism, had never succeeded in forging a coherent view of social organization. Khomeini, on the other hand, had the gift of presenting a simple, understandable and very coherent explanation of social conflict that mobilized all those who felt inferior in one way or another. The highly emotional images he gave of the gap in living standards between the different social strata spoke to the vast majority of the population and aroused its desire to obtain social justice so as to live in harmony with each other.

The change in Khomeini's thought was shown by his use of the words *oppressed* (*mostazafin*) and *martyr* (*shahid*). Those two words rarely appeared in his early writings, where the first was used only in the

---

[25] *Ibid.*

Koranic sense to designate the passivity and weakness of believers, in particular, orphans, widows, and the mentally handicapped. It was not until the 1970s that the word *mostazafin* appeared systematically to evoke the anger of the poor, the exploited, and the oppressed masses. After the revolution, Khomeini gradually extended the use of this term to the middle classes who actively supported him. The word *shahid* was similarly transformed. In his first works, Khomeini rarely used it, save in the conventional sense, when speaking of the Holy Imams who had given their lives in obedience to God's will. He hardly ever used it to refer to those who died in the shah's prisons or during confrontations with the Savak. In his proclamations from 1963 to 1964, for example, he described those who died in the June insurrection not as martyrs (*shohada*) but as unfortunates (*bichareha*). During the revolution, however, he constantly paid homage to all those killed during demonstrations as glorious and revolutionary martyrs.

Here as elsewhere, Khomeini followed others, without ever alluding to them or crediting them. In 1964, Tudeh published a memorial to the communist martyrs killed by the Pahlavi regime."[26] Toward the end of the 1960s, the book *Nehzat-e Hosseyni* (*Hosseyn's Movement*) appeared, in which the Mojahedin highlighted the first Shiite martyrs who had taken arms to overthrow the authoritarianism of the caliphs. At the start of the 1970s, Shariati glorified martyrdom by popularizing a nineteenth-century saying: "Each place must be transformed into Karbala and each day into Ashura."[27] Khomeini adopted this slogan after the Mojahedin who had made it one of the leitmotivs of the revolution.

He did indeed copy others, but this did not lessen the originality of his action. Contrary to Shariati, who introduced Marxism into religious discourse to build a religious ideology of revolution, and contrary to the Mojahedin, who remained on the edge of Marxism and Islam without daring to assert their true preferences, Khomeini's language was understandable to all, for it referred to "local" elements. Religious forms were omnipresent but emptied of their spiritual meaning and filled with a political and social content.

Like all ideological speech, that of Khomeini contained two distinct levels. The first was essentially based on the very controversial thesis of the *walayat-e faqih* (the absolute power of the doctor of Islamic law),

---

[26] Rahim Namvar, *Yadnameh Sahidan* (Memorial of the Martyrs), Tehran, Tudeh Editions, 1954.
[27] Ali Shariati, *Shahadat* (Martyr), Tehran, Hosseyniy-e Ershad, 1972.

a true political plan to submit the country to clerical domination. That part of Khomeini's thought remained in the background, and it was only after the 1979 revolution that it began to emerge in political debates to end by becoming one of the clauses of the regime's constitution. The second level was directed toward public opinion and sought to arouse emotions against injustice to mobilize it for specific ends known to him alone. In the 1970s, this great expert of religious law rarely mentioned doctrinal questions and in particular said nothing at all of the *walayat-e faqih*. It seemed that even his closest disciples ignored his true political objectives and that they were completely disoriented when Khomeini evoked the *walayat-e faqih,* for the first time several months after the revolution.[28] Judiciously avoiding any revelation of his real thought, he was content, like other opponents, to criticize the shah for a myriad of socioeconomic issues.[29]

"Islam is in danger," he repeated constantly. "It is threatened from without by imperialism and from within by those monarchists, leftists and secularists." If that rhetoric, inherently populist, seemed very simple and understandable on the surface, it was in reality remarkably ambiguous:

> Islam belongs to the oppressed, not to the oppressors.
> Islam is equality and social justice.
> Islam represents the slum dwellers and not the palace dwellers.
> Islam will eliminate class distinctions.
> The clergy's duty is to free the hungry from the hold of the wealthy.
> The poor were for the Prophet; the rich were against him.
> The poor die for the Islamic Revolution; the rich plot against it.
> The martyrs of the Islamic Revolution all came from the lower classes: peasants, factory workers and *Bazaar* shopkeepers.
> Oppressed of the world, unite.
> The problems of the East come from the West, particularly from American imperialism and Zionism.
> Neither East nor West, but Islam.

Khomeini felt it unnecessary to present any theological justification to legitimate what he said. He never explained, for instance, in what

---

[28] Abrahamian, *op. cit.,* 1993, p. 46.

[29] Khomeini accused the shah of having widened the gap between rich and poor, wasting oil resources, condemning the working class to a life of poverty and misery, creating huge slums, ruining the *Bazaar*s by refusing to protect them against foreign competition and aggravating social problems by not combating the rise of criminality, alcoholism, prostitution, and drugs.

200

way equality and social justice were synonymous with Islam, and nobody knew what he meant by that "Islam in danger" to which he constantly alluded.

Like all ideologues, Khomeini reinterpreted the past deliberately, all the better to use it in the present. Yet, when Shariati and the Mojahedin did the same thing, he did not hesitate to shout "blasphemy." Khomeini exploited "Islam's golden age" and all its holy figures in a specific interpretation in support of his populist ideas. He asserted that, contrary to what historians said, the Prophet had been a simple worker and not a prosperous merchant, and that many prophets that had preceded him were also simple workers waiting impatiently for the day when "the oppressed would become oppressors and the oppressors oppressed." He also claimed that most of the Shiite clergy, including the important ayatollah, were of simple origin, that they had lived humbly and died in poverty.

That populist rhetoric reached its paroxysm in 1979. After the fall of the old regime, Khomeini incorporated two words, carefully avoided until then, into his vocabulary: *revolution* and *republic*. The revolution opened the way to a true Islamic society, he declared. That society, the complete opposite of the Pahlavi regime's Iran, would know no misery, hunger, unemployment, drugs, nepotism, corruption, exploitation, foreign intervention, and so on. It would be a society founded on equality, fraternity, and social justice.[30]

Khomeini eliminated several of Shiism's traditional features, promising to achieve utopia. Whereas for centuries Shiites had glorified the past, viewing with nostalgia Islam's golden age, Khomeini proclaimed that revolutionary Iran had already gone beyond those societies of early Islam and had solved their "insoluble" problems. Whereas Shiite beliefs were based on the reappearance of the Twelfth Imam, the Mahdi, in a world in which injustice and tyranny had reached an apex, to unveil the hidden meaning of the truth to all those who had lost it,[31] Khomeini minimized the significance of the Twelfth Imam and his spiritual meaning, to give him a new role. He became the instrument for explaining and justifying the social and political order already established by Khomeini's Islamic Republic. He announced that henceforth, the Mahdi would return when Muslims created a just society and exported the revolution to other countries. A reinterpretation that was light years from

---

[30] For Khomeini's speeches, before and after the Islamic Revolution, see: Ruhani, *op. cit.*, 1944.
[31] Corbin, *op. cit.*, 1971, pp. 4–5.

the Twelfth Imam's role in Shiite spirituality. This political-theological usurpation violated Shiite tradition, in which the imam was to remain "hidden" (*ghaybat*) until the end of time. It aroused forms of devotion directed to Khomeini's person and strengthened the religious roots of his regime while opening it to a purely political future.

The Shiite belief in the Twelfth Imam came from far back indeed.[32] It had its origin in the Zoroastrian beliefs of ancient Persia with their idea of a savior. For five centuries, Twelver Shiism had been the Iranian nation's official religion, but since the implantation of Islam in Iran, many proofs confirm that Iranians have always had a bond on loyalty to Shiite Islam. Furthermore, the Shiite idea of the Twelfth Imam, "the Hidden Imam," "the Long-Awaited Imam," presented a remarkable affinity with that of the Savior of ancient Zoroastrian Persia. By emptying the Twelfth Imam's spiritual significance as "guide of consciences" and revealer of the hidden truth, Khomeini brought him down into this world, making him more a political than a religious personality. In fact, the Twelfth Imam was reduced to handing over his responsibilities to his collaborators, of whom Khomeini was the principal one. The Imam became a superfluous character whose only vocation was to appreciate what Khomeini had accomplished in his absence.

In Khomeini's language, it was not only the Twelfth Imam whose nature was changed but all the "Fourteen Immaculates" of the pleroma (the Prophet, his daughter Fatima, the Twelve Imams), as well as the entire Shiite liturgy. They were all reorganized to explain and justify the order established by the Islamic Republic's clergy. Of course, it was in the name of the past that Khomeini and his partisans opened up to the future, but it was a totally transformed and different past.

Contrary to the left-wing intellectuals and the communist militants who erased the past to turn toward new perspectives, Khomeini glorified the past but interpreted it according to his own wishes, to justify his present political orientations. He removed Shiism from its spiritual universe to bring it down into a world in which religion became a tool to legitimize a secular power he himself had instigated. Khomeini's Shiism was a specific mixture, composed of an explanation of the past, a justification of the need for present action, and, above all, a promise for the future. He "secularized" Shiism and subjected it to his political ends.

---

[32] *Ibid.*

Nonetheless, it must be noted that, far from being reduced to Khomeinism, Shiism goes far beyond its contemporary ideological interpretation. Its roots are plunged in Iranian religious thought[33] that was, from its origins, guided by the eschatological conscience of the outcome of the cosmic drama, inaugurated by the invasion of the Ahrimanic powers.[34] Shiism is above all a spiritual universe that has still to be understood.[35] It is therefore not monolithic, and its concept can in no way be identified with the political interpretation made of it by Khomeini.[36]

Ideologization of Shiism

Khomeini's ideological discourse transformed Shiism's more than thousand-year-old beliefs to conform to his own political aims. In order to set up a clerical government, or the *waly-e faqih's* domination over the whole country, he gave body to a new, highly politicized version of Shiism. He usurped not only the divine role of the savior, attributed to the Twelfth Imam, but the entire religion.

Thus, Khomeinism rapidly imposed itself as the only force able to mobilize a mob and to control it. The ideologization of Shiism and of its powerful mythology—that of Hassan and Hosseyn and of the other martyred Imam, that had begun with Shariati and the Mojahedin, reached its apotheosis with Khomeini. It was nourished by Shiite traditions, popular meetings, processions, and mourning celebrations that took over its meeting and discussion places, its mosques and hosseyniyehs. The clergy, undoubtedly divided, but independent of the state and hierachized, provided him with the means.

---

[33] This part is largely based on Henry Corbin's book, *En Islam iranien: aspects spirituals et philosophiques*, 5 vols., Paris, Gallimard, 1971.

[34] The Mazdian, followed by Zoroastrian thought, divided the world between the forces of good (*Ahoura-Mazda*) and the forces of evil (*Ahriman*).

[35] Islamic Iran was the preeminent country of Islam's great philosophers and mystics—from Molla Sadra Shirazi to Sohravadi, including Mohammad Kharaqani, Heydar Amoli, Abdollah Ansari, etc., the list is long. For mystic theologians, religious thought can no longer isolate itself from the spiritual universes that are the site of its fructification. Thus, the royal road for understanding religion must include understanding the concrete totality that man nourishes of his own substance beyond the limits of this life and that comprises his spiritual world. Corbin, *op. cit.*, 1971, pp. 4–5.

[36] According to Norbert Elias, religion and belief in an all-powerful God who punishes and rewards never, in themselves, had a civilizing or moderating effect on emotional life. On the contrary, religion is precisely as civilized as the society and the social class that practice it. "Religions reflect societies in which they are practiced; they are neither modern nor backward; they are the image of the men who believe in them." Norbert Elias, *La civilisation des mœurs*, Paris, Calmann-Lévy, 2973, p. 290.

The political and religious structure of Khomeini's thought was gradually differentiated from the traditional religious discourse; little by little, he affirmed his authority with regard to religion. Distancing himself from the religious universe was in no way a complete or rapid break. He swung back and forth constantly, for a long time insisting on a religion well beyond its official forms, so that there was a lengthy period of hesitation while Khomeini's thought shifted between religion and ideology.

The Power of an Ideological Discourse

Khomeini's discourse was by its very nature plural and composite, whence the difficulty in understanding him precisely. He was a mixture of several ideologies. At times he was influenced by nationalism when he spoke of the nation's interest, at times by communism when he exploited class antagonism. But despite all these tendencies from different ideological horizons—easily detected in his writings—Khomeini was perfectly capable of erasing those references and presenting his ideas in a unified and coherent way, accessible to all. Three distinct themes were combined:

- First, a *theoretical* component that gave a religious explanation of the historic movement as to what influenced society and where it was headed. In his idea, everything referred to God, who gave the clergy his authority to govern the world. In other words, it is divine will, expressed and carried out by the clergy, that moves human societies.
- Next, a *pragmatic* component centered on action. This was a political discourse on what should be done in the present, given the world's direction and the perspectives engendered by it. Khomeini aimed at change while yet maintaining the status quo as far as possible. He could be described as a conservative revolutionary.
- Lastly, a *prophetic* component focused on the future that made him easily comprehensible to the people by addressing what they expected or feared from the future. On one side, he described a utopian society where God's justice reigned supreme and, on the other, he enumerated all the dangers threatening it from different directions.

With this polyvalent language, Khomeini seduced the vast majority of Iranians. If the intellectuals had been unable to reconcile the subjective with reality, if their speech seemed strangely abstract, Khomeini knew how to integrate the people's hopes in the concrete future of the society he painted. Thus it was that so many Iranians recognized their aspirations in his words and in his action. They succumbed easily to the attraction of his discourse and responded positively to his sacrificial demands during the revolution and the Iran-Iraq war. After the revolution, when Khomeini asked them to give their lives to consolidate the foundations of Islam, because "Islam is in danger," the poor and the excluded, as well as the less poor and better established, the popular classes and the middle classes both engaged in the war against Iraq, trusting in his extravagant promises. Khomeini incarnated their aspirations and gave them the sense of participating in a movement to change the world and to build a better one. He manipulated them and made them believe, temporarily but efficiently, that they were at the heart of his young regime's concerns: "The government is yours, and its ministers are but your servants," he repeated in the early days of the Islamic Republic. That charismatic guide who lived so austerely became the idol of the poorest, the most marginalized, and those who most yearned to climb socially. They identified all the more easily with his speech in that he promised them a better life, whether in this world or in the next. He also aroused the admiration of the upper classes who saw in him the prestige of an exceptional revolutionary leader, detached from this earthly world.

Khomeini never ceased reminding people that the revolution had succeeded thanks to the active participation of the needy, that without them the Islamic regime had no future. At the same time, he did not fail to insist on Islam's respect for private property: "Contrary to communism, Islam respects private property to ensure social justice and to grease the wheels of a healthy economy." In speaking to the *Bazaar* merchants, in particular, he stressed that Islam guaranteed private property. He encouraged private investments in agriculture and industry and announced a balanced economy in which the private sector would be recognized. This in no way prevented him from asking the Muslims and all the world's disadvantaged not to passively await a better life. He urged them to rise up to overthrow imperialists and tyrants.

With this language, he seduced the *Bazaar* merchants. The political and financial support they brought him was most useful to strengthen his movement. The *mostazafin* were thus not the only ones to be captivated by his ideological language. The *Bazaaris*, private investors, the rich and the less rich were just as enthralled. Paradoxically, that austere and not very eloquent man, with his countrified accent and his dull face, knew how to communicate with everybody, beguiling both the people and the elite, the poor and the rich. At least, for a while.

The Institutionalization of Khomeinism

All the features of Khomeini's rhetoric were found in turn in the Islamic Republic's constitution.[37] That text, with its 175 articles, read like a summary of Khomeini's thought. It began by establishing that the Islamic Republic was a system based on the faith in one God—"There is no god but God"—affirming the exclusivity of its sovereignty, its exclusive power to legislate, and the necessity of submitting to its commandments.[38]

Superficially, the Islamic Republic's constitution bore certain resemblances to most democratic constitutions, particularly with regard to the separation of the executive, judiciary, and legislative powers. The legislative power was entrusted to Parliament, the *Majles*, elected by universal suffrage;[39] the executive power belonged to a government composed of ministers with a head of state at the top; the judiciary power belonged to judges, most of whom were clerics. Ten years later, in 1989, two new articles, founded on the *walayat-e faqih* were added to the constitution. They changed everything. The new constitution gave absolute power to the person of the *waly-e faqih,* described as the doctor of Islamic law—during his lifetime this person was Khomeini. That absolute power interfered with the functioning of the three powers and removed all political autonomy. The *waly-e faqih* had the right to retire the president, to name the principal military commanders, to declare war and peace, and to decide in the place of all the country's leaders (political and/or religious), as well as in the place of the people. He even had the right to impose his veto, should the results of universal suffrage not suit him, by judging them, for instance, not in conformity with the *shariat.* Finally, implementing the constitution was theoretically under the supervision of an assembly of experts, Shoray-e Négahban[40]

---

[37] On April 1, 1979, Khomeini installed the Islamic Republic, after having insisted on that name and opposing those who wanted to add the term "democratic." Taking advantage of his charisma and exploiting the popular religious fervor and enthusiasm, Khomeini had ordered: "Not one word more or less."

[38] *Cf.* http://www.jurispolis.com/dt/mat/dr_ir_constit1979/dt_ir_constit1979_index.htm, for a complete version, in French, of the Islamic Republic's constitution.

[39] For years, Khomeini had claimed that the vote for women was anti-Islamic. After founding the Islamic Republic, he changed his mind, asserting that to deprive women of the vote was contrary to Islam.

[40] The Shoray-e Négahban was composed of six faqih (specialists of Islamic Law) chosen by the guide and of six jurists named by Parliament and by the head of the judiciary. Like all the Republic's institutions that had their counterparts, there was yet another body, Majels Tashkhis Maslahat Nezam (Council for Discerning the Regime's Interests) that was to decide in case of a dispute between Parliament and the Shoray-e Négahban.

(the equivalent of the Supreme Court in the United States), whose principal function was to organize the succession of the revolution's guide and to guarantee the coherence of parliamentary laws with the Islamic Republic's constitution.

That first version of the constitution was a concentration of all the ingredients of Khomeinism. The first paragraph of its preamble contains two terms strongly contested by the orthodox clergy: *revolution* (*enqelab*) and *republic* (*jomhuri*). It glorified Khomeini but not simply as the leader of the revolution, the founder of the Islamic Republic, and the most respected of the religious dignitaries, but also as an imam, thus giving him a Shiite title traditionally reserved for the twelve venerated Imams. That innovation was judged blasphemous by part of the Shiite clergy.

Faithful to Khomeini, his successors showed their pragmatism, deeply modifying the constitution on several occasions. The succession of the guide was one remarkable example. The text specified that if no *marja'e taqlid* (source of imitation) appeared apt to exercise that function after Khomeini's disappearance, the leadership would go to a committee composed of three or five high-ranking religious dignitaries, chosen by the assembly of experts. When the time came, that provision was not applied. The assembly of experts, mistrusting the *foqaha* and their view of Islam, modified the constitution, abandoning the clause that the guide could only be chosen among the sources of imitation. It was thus that the succession could be given to the *hojatol-eslam* Ali Khameney—a middle-ranking cleric who was neither *faqih* nor ayatollah. That modification unconsciously sapped the theoretical bases of the *walayat-e faqih* thesis in which Khomeini said that only high-ranking religious dignitaries had the necessary qualifications to understand the subtleties of Islamic law.

At the end of his life, anticipating the problem of his succession, Khomeini himself began to modify his concept of *walayat-e faqih*. In March, 1989, three months before his death, he made an important declaration, dividing the clergy into two separate categories. He mentioned first those who best knew Islamic law (the *fiqh*), including holy law (the *shariat*), then those who best knew the contemporary world, especially its economic, social, and political aspects. For Khomeini, it was the latter who would decide on political affairs, because they were the only ones abreast of current problems. After having insisted for over two decades on the rule of the doctors of Islamic law, he suddenly decided that the political clergy were most capable of assuming total authority. Those changes were more indicative of the mind of a pragmatic politician than of a traditional cleric.

The institutionalization of Khomeini's ideas was also shown by the ambiguity of the place of women in the Islamic Republic's constitution, whose twentieth principle, known as the "equality principle," asserts: "All members of the Nation, women and men, are under the protection of the law and enjoy all human, political, economic, social and cultural rights, contingent on the respect of Islamic precepts."[41] We note that the text does not stipulate that men and women are equal before the law. Moreover, respect for Islamic precepts is a restrictive measure referring directly to Islamic law, the *shariat,* according to which a woman's life is worth half that of a man's. By submitting the penal code of the Islamic Republic, family rights and everything that in any way concerns women's place in society and in private life, to the observance of Islamic precepts, the law attributes a secondary status to women. Furthermore, in those areas of penal justice concerning masculine mores, a woman's testimony is never accepted. On this subject, Shirin Ebadi, lawyer and Nobel Peace Prize recipient, recalled that the seventy-sixth article of the Islamic Republic's penal code foresaw a penalty of eighty whiplashes for women who dared to bear witness against a man.[42] She also showed that the Islamic Republic's labor laws gave women so many privileges (in cases of marriage, pregnancy, et al.) that, paradoxically, it is in the interest of no employer to hire them.

Completely steeped in Khomeinism, the regime's constitution promoted a highly prophetic rhetoric. It promised all citizens various state protections—social security, unemployment benefits, disability pensions, free medical services, and education. It promised to eradicate hoarding, usury, unemployment, poverty, and social misery. It also promised to make Iran totally independent and guaranteed that the state would repay foreign debts, cancel foreign concessions, fight for total unity of all Muslims worldwide, and come to the aid of all the oppressed engaged in the international combat against oppressors.

---

[41] *Cf.* The Constitution of the Islamic Republic, *op. cit.*

[42] "Since the legal person of a woman, as a human being in her own right, is not recognized by law in many cases, her testimony has no value. If ten adult women, respectable and respected by all, saw a man forcibly enter a house and rape the woman and her children, their testimony would not be legal. If they insisted to be heard as witnesses against the man who had committed those acts, the Iranian penal code would punish them." Shirin Ebadi, *Hoquq zan dar qavanin jomhouri eslami* (Women's Rights According to the Laws of the Islamic Republic), Tehran, Ganj-e Danesh, 2004, pp. 77–79.

This exceptional rhetoric repelled as much as it attracted. If at first it bewitched people by seeming to give substance to the noblest aspirations, it rapidly sowed fear by its weakness when the facts opposed it. After the first enthusiasm, reality asserted itself cruelly and invalidated the worldview of an ideology that found no concrete factual support.

The economy was rebellious against the promises of a guide who, confronted with daily reality, was unable to save his face and, even less, that of his revolution. Gradually, the pendulum swung back; the population had less and less confidence in its political leaders and turned its back on the revolution and the regime, while maintaining its respect for the guide yet awhile.

From the Religious to the Political

As much as Khomeini's ideological discourse could mobilize the masses and overthrow royal power, just so much did it lack the theological bases that would have made it possible to found an Islamic regime. All his life, Khomeini manipulated power, but he could never make it religious nor invent a legitimate Islamic power. There is, in fact, nothing in Islam to justify establishing a political authority that would also be a religious authority, and the holders of power have never had any religious legitimacy. They governed in the name of God, but the legitimacy was God's alone, and the power principle was linked to his presence. Thus, all worldly legitimacy is irremediably weak, since both those in power and their opponents can call upon the same source for justification. "For this reason the religion of the divine All Powerful contains a strong ferment of anarchy. Islam tends to unstable and contentious political societies. The subjection that the powers deem themselves justified in demanding does not stop them from being permanently exposed to an opposition equally based on religion."[43]

In such a framework, ruling by force is the only way to compensate for the weakness of a power that wants to be religious but that has no legitimacy to be so. If Khomeini's ideological speech was turned toward the future, his Islam was based on a traditional and extremely authoritarian conception of power. He functioned according to the ruling primacy of politics; power was there to relay a transcendent principle, divine will, in accordance with which it imposed its order on the collectivity, from without and from on high. Thus, power comes

---

[43] Marcel Gauchet, *La condition historique,* Paris, Gallimard, 2003, p. 161.

first; it creates society and determines its order. It becomes the cause of a society that depends on it to such an extent that the two can no longer be separated, just as a torso could not live without the head. It recognizes no autonomy for society and seeks only to dominate it.

Beyond its intrinsic contradictions, this traditional conception of power was at odds with political and social reality in Iran. Misunderstanding that fact added to the clergy's weakness, and their task of governing the country became particularly difficult.

Since the shah had strictly excluded them from Iranian politics, the Shiite clergy had not fully understood the changes that ensued during the imperial regime's period of modernization. It did not understand that more than fifty years of Pahlavi rule had modified the very essence of politics and the way it was presented. Nor did it realize the very important role politics played in society. It still believed that religion alone still ruled society, whereas it would have to confront politics and dispute its sovereignty.

Busy with the visible aspects of politics, the ayatollah did not seize the significance of the changes, and the situation cruelly escaped them. Taking over state functions, they wanted to dominate politics and submit it to transcendence. This could not work, however. The Iranian political system under the shah had been given first-class political institutions: Parliament, the Senate, the judiciary power founded on its own appeals systems—Court of Appeal, Supreme Court of Appeal, Supreme Court. Politics thus had the tools required to function efficiently, while religion continued to rely on its ancient structures that indeed still worked but were less and less compatible with the new society's requirements.

The clergy thus often mistook the meaning of political events since the constitutional revolution (1907). First of all, they had opposed the constitution and defended the priority of the *shariat*. Then they paid no attention to the oil industry's nationalization that, under Mossadeq, gave rise to the Iranian nation in its new sense. Obsessed by the dream of expanding an Islamic empire throughout the world, they had always rejected the nationalist movements that overturned the country's politics from the start of the twentieth century to the end of the 1960s. Their universalist ambition, colored by a refractory antinationalism, prevented them from realizing all that nationalization had brought to the Iranians.

Blind to the transformed role of politics in society, and ignorant of the state's role in the international community, the Shiite dignitaries erred completely on the most basic facts of the process in which they became involved after the 1979 revolution, both nationally and internationally. That process transformed them, all unwittingly, into political actors at the very time when their ignorance of the system constantly led them into error. They ignored the fact that the function of politics was intimately linked to its structuring dimension. They did not see to what extent the infrastructural role of politics gave it the force and above all the possibility to change things, beginning with the clergy itself.

While the ayatollah thought they held the keys to power, politics continued to work in depth. It blinded them and, by so doing, forced them to adopt its laws, its requirements, and its rules, defined by the principles of autonomy. Those men who thought to subordinate politics to religion, could only obey politics whose workings were hidden from them. Politics continued to dig its own path and to destabilize the heteronymous structure. That destabilization was the starting point of the clergy's collapse, a collapse that progressed slowly but inevitably. The clergy allowed themselves to be invaded by politics, and politics obliged them to play according to its logic. By so doing, it destroyed them. The phenomenon took place silently without any spectacular display. It did not install—at least not at first—a democratic power. It worked within a state that relied comfortably on oil revenues with no accountability to anybody.

The shock and the stimulus came from outside the clergy. Under the weight of politics, the Shiite dignitaries politicized religion, exposing it to immanence and manipulating transcendence. In the end, they accelerated the collapse of heteronymous structure and the installing of autonomous principles in the social order. Thus, unwillingly and unconsciously, they became the actors of a society in the process of inventing itself and open to the future.

Khomeini and Power

As soon as he returned to Iran, in conformity with Shiite tradition, Khomeini took drastic measures to submit Iranian postrevolutionary society to transcendence. Denying individual autonomy, destroying human rights, and dismantling the country's judicial and educational systems that had been in place for fifty years, became his priorities.

The day after the revolution, he decreed the compulsion for women to wear the veil in accordance with the *shariat*. The crystallization of religious constraints around women's bodies—wearing the veil, forbidding them to enter public spaces or to enter a whole series of professions, ousting women who had occupied key positions under the shah—was not mere misogyny on the part of the ayatollah toward the female population. It was part of the process of strengthening the patriarchal principles that had lost their automatism under the Pahlavi regime's modernization. The clergy directly placed women's bodies into the power struggle; they stigmatized them, broke them, tortured them, and exacted from them signs of subjection. Women's veiled bodies were the first object on which the *shariat* displayed its full power, the supreme object of the clergy's emphatic assertion and its "intrinsic superiority." That superiority took possession of the female body to prove it was marked, vanquished, broken. If the Muslim man must *be* and *appear* simultaneously, the Muslim woman must be veiled to show her submission toward God and men.

Khomeini made veil wearing a daily spectacle that staged a politics of power: he made the body a sensitive issue for all. His new regime was exhibited on women's bodies. The veiled body became the point at which the Shiite clergy's power began, a power that began with women to spread to all of society. It was inscribed in a system of domination where the *olama* demanded, decided and executed their will, first on women and then on men.[44] The veil was compulsory because it represented the force and will of religion: first on bodies and then on minds. Numerous punishments were decreed for those who dared, no matter how slightly, to defy the law. For Khomeini, the least disobedience was an act of hostility. He did not need to justify his decisions, merely to point out his enemies and eliminate them.

Khomeini's second decisive measure to ensure his regime's survival was to introduce the thesis of *walayat-e faqih* (the absolute power of the doctor of Islamic law) into the constitution. That thesis institutionalized religious power and became afterwards the keystone of the Islamic Republic. The 1979 constitution stipulated that "the only legitimate holders of authority were the *olama* as the Prophet's heirs; the law could come only from on high, and the most worthy of the erudite clergy must exercise authority while awaiting the return of the Imam of time."[45] Contrary to the 1907 Iranian constitution and the fundamental rights it gave to members of the nation, the

---

[44] Later, a whole series of clothing obligations was established for men, such as the prohibition against wearing a tie, short sleeves, colored shirts, etc.

[45] *Cf.* The Constitution of the Islamic Republic, *op. cit.*

walayat-e faqih trampled on individual freedom.[46] Inscribed in the continuity of nineteenth-century *olama* thinking, Khomeini's thesis divided men into two distinct categories: the clergy and the others. It went still further, however, and dug a real abyss between the two. On the one side were the strong and devout, humanly superior men, on the other, the weak and impious, in whom no capacity for thought was recognized. Ordinary citizens thus had a social status identical to that of the mentally handicapped (*mahjour*), placed under the clergy's custody in all aspects of their private and public lives. At the expense of civil, political, and social rights, the *walayat-e faqih* principle recognized only moral and religious obligations.

Dismantling the judicial system was continued by giving total authority to the *foqaha* to judge litigations according to the *shariat*. In choosing an ayatollah as minister of justice, Khomeini placed the judiciary under religious power and denied it any independence. The clergy's power, no longer limited to the judiciary alone, extended to the executive and the legislative. The new constitution justified the omnipotence of the *waly-e faqih* (doctor of Islamic law) and ended by implicitly nullifying the separation of powers. Usurping the independence of the three powers went side by side with contempt for the equality of individuals before the law. The twentieth principle of the constitution, the "equality principle," stated that all members of the nation, women and men, were under the protection of the law, subject to respect for Islamic precepts"[47] without ever stipulating that they were equal before the law. Indeed, as soon as people are defined by their submission to a religious order, equality before the law loses its meaning: in the absence of freedom of thought or of action, nobody needs rights.

Finally, the death stroke to individual rights came from a radical cleric, the *hodjatol-eslam* Khalkhali, named by Khomeini to head the revolutionary tribunals the day after the victory of the 1979 revolution. That cleric had invented the concept of "obvious guilt," according to which the accused was presumed guilty if his crimes seemed clear even before the trial opened. Khalkhali applied the *shariat* literally and proceeded with a series of executions. Without trial or judgment, he established his "revolutionary courts" and executed the "presumed guilty" wherever he wanted: in the street, in cellars, or in the desert.

---

[46] As we already saw, the origins of the *walayat-e faqih* go back to the Ayatollah Naraqi in the nineteenth century, but it was the Ayatollah Khomeini who gave it its "credentials."
[47] *Cf.* The Constitution of the Islamic Republic, *op. cit.*

During an interview he asserted that he must have executed more than a thousand people between 1979 and 1980. Expeditious in his judgments, he was nicknamed "the Republic's butcher."[48] His disrespect for judicial and administrative procedures, his ignorance of the penal code, and, above all, his contempt for human life, gave the final blow to the image of justice and, with that, the citizens' trust. Khalkhali alone pushed the Iranian judicial system several centuries back.

For that regime—which claimed to be religious but manipulated religion and transformed it completely to suit the requirements of its ambitions—the *shariat,* which could establish a hierarchy in the population and anchor it to its founding past, served as the cornerstone. Thus the Islamic Republic deprived Iranians of their fundamental rights and reduced them to silence. That deprivation of rights, institutionalized in the constitution under the name of *walayat-e faqih,* ended by eliminating the "subject of right" in Iran.

Manipulating Religion

Khomeinism or the "Islamization of politics" introduced religion into the world of power. It favored exercising politics in the name of religion. That did not only modify relations between politics and religion; it led to consecrating the first and deconsecrating the second. Khomeini's Islam was a religious ideology, bearing a powerful political message that could mobilize populations and give them hope for a better future.

Under the domination of ideological Islam, the clergy became political. That change gave the ayatollah (the men of God) an unprecedented effective power, completely taking over the country's secular affairs. On the other hand, based on no intrinsic religious legitimacy, that power destroyed the spiritual authority that the clergy had held over believers. When "the man of God" became the "statesman," he lost the kingdom of heaven in exchange for much more real power but now lacked charisma.

The evolution of the clergy's role did not stop there. This was no longer the time when the ayatollah depended on the approval of the

---

[48] In February 1979, Khalkhali ordered the execution of former leaders of the Pahlavi regime, sometimes carrying out the sentence himself, as he did for Hoveida, the shah's prime minister, into whose head he emptied his pistol. After Khomeini's death in 1989, he lost his support in the regime. He then retired to Qom to teach in religious seminaries until his death in November, 2003.

214

faithful and lived thanks to their donations. In the postrevolutionary regime, the clergy who had conquered power governed the people and, far from being at its service, took the whole of society hostage. The exclusive privilege that political power gave them placed them effectively in a dominant position above the people.

Yet, the facts must be faced. That new situation, promising as it seemed, brought the clergy onto a new playing field to which they were not accustomed. Khomeini's ideological Islam allowed them to take power without having taught them how to govern. Their archaic conception of power and of society led them only to terror and violence to maintain their dominion over the people. They were obliged to justify a domination that no longer had anything spiritual about it. Without the slightest theological proof and the disappearance of their former charisma, they had a huge problem: how could they justify being in power? How explain that the clergy had taken over the economic and financial networks, that they had become middle class bourgeois and that, far from concerning themselves with the souls of the believers, they were concerned with their own interests?

Faced with this dilemma, Khomeini could only manipulate transcendence. Considering himself the supreme "voice of Islam," he pretended that his word was that of God and his choices those of the Prophet. That was a double-edged sword, because it could be used just as well to justify as to discredit the clergy. Calls on transcendence passed the limits of what could be imagined or believed. They opened the way to a world of make-believe where Khomeini thought he could do anything at all. When he crossed that threshold of fiction, nothing could prevent his successors from doing the same. From then on, the Republic's leaders rivaled with each other to boast publicly of their special relations with this spirits of the Holy Imams or with heaven.

The implicit hypocrisy that characterized that practice came close to ridicule, was so much written about that its extreme functional efficiency remained invisible. With the specific aim of conquering power, it ended in doubly transforming the clergy. First in its capacity to subject society. Since the regime's leaders pretended to be in direct contact with the hereafter and to receive their orders from Heaven, their political choices could not be questioned. Then too, the clergy was freed from the need for any external legitimacy. Their privileged link with the hereafter was, in itself, irrefutable proof of what separated them from the other members of society, by definition, mediocre. It showed that they were intrinsically different and therefore superior to others. As soon as the clergy, who had taken over the state to lead it, identified themselves with transcendence, they fell into the illusion of self-sufficiency. That illusion was so strong that they felt they no longer needed to hide behind theological precepts and justifications. Paradoxically, by identifying with transcendence, the clergy freed themselves from it.

Toward the end of the war, that illusion reached a height. Khomeini referred less and less to religion to justify his political choices, sometimes authoritarian, sometimes contrary to national interests. Some doubted his faith, and rumors circulated about his origins: Indian, Buddhist or some other. Some said he was neither Iranian nor Muslim. Yet, if he no longer spoke of the Koran or of the Prophet, even less of other religious sources, it was because he saw himself as personifying the religion. The effect of that illusion meant that whatever came from him was automatically legitimate, since he believed he could find the source of all religious legitimacy in his own words. The mere fact that words came from his mouth sufficed for them to be considered as words of Islam. Without differentiating Shiites from Sunnis, Khomeini spoke of a united Islam that was, moreover, threatened. He no longer saw himself as a *representative of God* but as the *Savior of Islam,* the *incarnation of God himself.* For instance, when he announced that "Islam is politics and politics is Islam,"[49] he felt no need for a reference to support that statement. The words were legitimate because they were his. Some of his speeches toward the end of his life, made it seem that he saw himself even beyond religion; he thought he was God and announced: "Khomeini's word is that of God."[50]

Far from being limited to the person of Khomeini, the manipulation of religion was gradually practiced by all those who, in one way or another, identified with him. By becoming commonplace, this lost its usefulness. Khomeini thus reduced transcendence to immanent objectives, emptied of all spirituality and devoted to political calculations and bargaining. Devaluing religion thus, the direct consequence of manipulating it, weakened the heteronymous structure and will end, sooner or later, by its collapse. Yet, that inevitable collapse will be, first

---

[49] *Cf. Sahiféy-e nour* (Anthology of Khomeini's Speeches), Tehran, vol. 21.

[50] *Ibid.* Khomeini always spoke of himself in the third person. The twenty-first volume of this anthology includes his speeches made from September 1988 to June 1989, i.e., several days before his death.

of all, the result of the ayatollah's blindness as to the role and function of politics in the country's social organization. It is all the more surprising in that the clergy themselves will have orchestrated it, but unbeknownst to them and contrary to their expectations.

International Misunderstanding

The clergy's illusion concerning the nature of power gave rise to scarcely credible ambitions that overflowed Iranian borders. Their blindness as to how a political system functioned led them to believe they could bring their dearest dream to life: to go beyond the Shiite/Sunni cleavage and rule the entire Muslim world.

As we have seen, the Shiite clergy had always dreamed of influencing the Sunnis. Later on, they tried to reconcile Shiism and Sunnism to create a united Muslim world, independent of any cultural or national bonds. The political changes at the beginning of the twentieth century, the two world wars and the coming to power of the Pahlavi dynasty, greatly marginalized the clergy, preventing any such conquest of the Muslim world. For their part, the ayatollah, distanced themselves completely from whatever was in any way linked to Iranian patriotism.

With the inception of the Islamic Republic, a great wind of hope fanned this dream once again. Disdaining national interests, and thanks to Iranian oil revenues, the Islamic regime was generous toward Islamist movements and invested funds in Muslim countries to captivate their populations. After Khomeini, a deep crisis of legitimacy exposed the regime to internal conflicts. It was saved by a headlong rush forward and a wild quest for international power. The men of the regime allied themselves with underdeveloped countries, often in economic difficulty or at war, to make common cause against the world's great powers, considered as the "enemies of Islam." While the Iranian standard of living fell day by day,[51] the regime continued its search for international power and poured Iranian petrodollars into the accounts of the regime's foreign allies—among others the Hamas and the Lebanese Hezbollah.

However, it was not until they claimed to possess atomic technology that they really succeeded in seducing international Muslim opinion. As much as the Iranians, weary of wars, conflicts, and endless embargos, were hostile to this project, just so much did public opinion in Arab

---

[51] Between 2012 and 2013, Iran's rial lost more than three quarters of its value against the American dollar.

countries admire the courage of Islamic leaders who stood up to the masters of the world. Never mind if Iran had lived under an embargo since 1980, or if it had been classified among the "rogue states" that might be subject to a preventive military attack. What counted was the granting of the ayatollah's dearest wish: to dominate world Islam. Henceforth, "the entire world would have to submit to Islam," as Khomeini had wished. In that Islamic Republic, foreign policy and domestic policy were interdependent, and both were operational levers of an ideology of power that wanted to conquer the world.

Beyond any doubt, Islamic Iran was a danger, both for Iranians and for the rest of the world. This was all the more true in that the Islamist leaders were far from naïve Muslims. They knew how to thwart the principles on which the modern world was based and they opposed them while yet pretending to observe them. The nuclear crisis allowed the present regime to assume a false air of power that particularly attracted the oppressed peoples of the world. And it is perhaps in that way that Iranian nuclear power will prove most dangerous.

The strength of the Islamic regime lies in its ideology. It renders it unpredictable and elusive, giving it the possibility of extending its hold on the region and, at times, of exporting its "revolution." The three decades of the Islamic Republic's existence show that as soon as the fictional world of Iranian leaders does not correspond to reality, they do everything required to disguise it. They believe they can solve everything by force. The reliance on terror, declarations of war, atomic threats, and other methods of intimidation, all seem legitimate to bend the world to the ayatollah's demands. Their supreme contempt for immediate consequences, their neglect of national interests, their disdain for utilitarian considerations, their attachment to an illusory ideological world, all give them a highly unpredictable character, more worrying than would have been overt aggression.

It would perhaps be less difficult for the international community to manage if the Islamic regime openly declared atomic war on its enemies, like North Korea. However, nobody knows how to raise the curtain on the secret intentions of the Iranian leaders who constantly claim their "inalienable right" to a peaceful use of nuclear energy, like all the world's states.

However, the Islamic Republic is not like other states. The greater its power, the more its true objectives become enigmatic. The decisive element is that the regime conducts its foreign policy on the hypothesis that the world belongs to it. Faced with a logic so different from their own, the democratic nations do not have the means needed to manage that crisis. Their surprise at the Islamic Republic comes from their total ignorance of the religious modes of thought that frame the regime's strategies, founded as they are on principles irreconcilable with the modern world. The Western countries forget that they face a state that ignores all considerations of economic, national, human, and military interest, to promote an Islamic movement for world conquest, a state that has no objective but to change the world order according to the laws of Islam in some unknown, far-off, and undefined future.

The Islamic regime succeeded in creating a powerful movement of thought that today has fired the entire Muslim world. Khomeini's political plan to base the constitution on the *shariat* and to restore traditional social strata is today followed by all the Islamist movements. Although these refuse to recognize the bonds that link them to the Iranian ayatollah, their imprint is too flagrant to be denied. It is as visible in the claims of the Egyptian Muslim Brotherhood and the Libyan leaders as in the language of young suburbanites in France and England. They all dream of an Islamic regime based on the Koran, of founding religious tribunals, and of applying the *shariat* literally.

Recourse to the *shariat*

The importance given to the *shariat* by Khomeini and other Islamist leaders, and the efforts they deployed to introduce it into the judicial system as soon as they came to power, seem enigmatic until one realizes the system of subjugation they wanted to set up. Everything was linked to their authoritarian conception of power, whose aim was to strengthen the axes of religious structuring: domination, hierarchy, belonging, and tradition.

The *shariat* or Islamic law subjects human relations to norms, objectives, models. In a legal system turned toward God and centered on him, faith was reduced to a law, took on a legal dimension, and gave rise to a *legal conception of religion* that saw the Koran as a constitution and/or a civil code. All the Koran's features extended over the law and gave it a sacred aspect, eternal and unchangeable. The law would thus be detached from all temporality, since the Koran was not linked to any particular region or to any specific period. By rejecting the rule of historical and social evolution, the Shiite clergy claimed the unchangeable nature of the *shariat.* Thus, according to them, Islamic law is not supposed to adapt itself to society but to transform it.

Far from being the source of law, the *shariat* was a set of immutable norms that formed a moral system unaffected by time, in a nearly indissoluble union with the dogma. It divided men into different categories, inferior and superior, ensured the supremacy of the latter and required the submission of the former. It determined the place and the role of everyone according to the rules of an omnipresent past, and it applied as much to public as to private life, including the most intimate areas. Men could do nothing but obey the law literally. By definition, it is not human but of divine origin. What counted was its continuity in time. It came from the past and is perpetuated in the present to shape the future in the image of the past.

The *shariat* saw the Muslim as a subjugated being with duties to accomplish. The Muslim was distinguished by his concrete and visible subjection to religious laws. He was all obedience and showed that obedience in public. The moral duties demanded by the *shariat* aimed at ensuring transcendent order and men's obedience to that order. Rather than defining human rights, it concerns, for the most part, men's legal and religious obligations. Nothing distinguishes sin from misdemeanor, moral from political infractions; all are similarly punished. Most laws are formulated negatively and, without the least reference to respecting the rights of others, they are justified by divine will, by definition unfathomable. For example, if it is formally forbidden (*haram*) to kill or to violate one's neighbor, it is not because the latter has a right to life or to dignity, but because God's law must not be transgressed.

The *shariat* classifies human actions into five distinct categories and decrees for each of these a different status: obligatory or licit (*wajeb*), meritorious or desirable (*mostahab*), neutral or indifferent (*mobah*), blameworthy or reprehensible (*makrouh*) and, finally, forbidden or illicit (*haram*). Punishments and rewards are planned to discourage transgression and to impose obedience to the laws. Those five categories form a codified set of rules of conduct that serve to grade Muslims among themselves; a rigorous hierarchy whose function is also to separate and to reconnect clergy and believers, new and old generations, men and women. It ends up by subjugating all believers to the exclusive control of the clergy.[52]

---

[52] To this were added two of the ten pillars of Shiism that encouraged good (*amre be ma'ruf*) and prevented evil (*nahie az munkar*). In fact, they encouraged a close surveillance among believers, so that each watched to see that his neighbor correctly observed his religious obligations.

As for the clergy, it is spanned from top to bottom by a rigid classification. That hierarchical whole made it possible to weld it and to guarantee its authority over politics and society. The *olama* assumed the right to speak in God's name and thought they had the exclusive power to dictate the law and to say what it approved, what it detested, and what it forbade. Inequality between men and women was unanimously agreed upon by the *foqaha:* the testimony of a woman, like that of children and slaves, was not accepted in court,[53] and her life was worth half that of a man's.

Everything was thus designed to register bodily inequalities, to introduce these into the popular mentality, and to install a "discriminatory view"[54] of people to the *nth* degree. To question unalterable truths or to criticize, however slightly, the *olama's* decision was labeled apostasy. To say that each generation could adapt its understanding to its historic situation was the act of a disbeliever. To historicize the norms was not to believe.[55] Thus, the Koran's prescriptions were applied literally, regardless of the circumstances or of the period. That arbitrary whole that the Muslim must believe had no other function than to validate the solutions chosen by the *olama*, and to prevent any attempt at rebellion, to guarantee the perennial power of the clergy.

The Deprivation of Rights

The *shariat* preaches a traditional view of the human and social world, according to which not the human individual but only society really counts. The order to which each person must submit precedes and preexists him; he must only perpetuate it. Nothing allows believers to consider themselves as independent, free, and equal beings. The community thus maintains a unilateral relationship with its members, recognizing no existence but its own. This leads to the massification of society and guarantees the undivided rule of the clergy.

Therefore, shortly after its inception, and thanks to the *shariat,* the Islamic Republic was able to rule according to its traditional concept

---

[53] Because women, although human beings in their own right, are not recognized by law, in many cases, their testimony has no value. Islamic law provides a punishment of eighty whiplashes for women who dare to bear witness against a man. *Cf.* Shirin Ebadi, *Hoquq zan dar qavanin jomhouri eslami* (Women's Rights According to the Laws of the Islamic Republic), Tehran, Ganje Danesh, 2004, pp. 220–221.

[54] According to Fakhr-al-Din Razi, a twelfth-century Iranian theosophist, "This inequality in subordination to obligations reflects a discriminatory view that nearly denies the status of a human being to those who differ by sex, by color, etc." Al-Râzi, *al-Mahsul*, III, pp. 220–221.

[55] Ali Mezghani, *L'État inachevé*, Paris, Gallimard, 2011, p. 102.

of power. A real regression took place: the three separate powers were no longer independent; state institutions were deprived of their power, since they were duplicated by religious organizations;[56] individual rights were pitilessly flouted, and the least resistance was called "counterrevolutionary."

The crucial event of the Iraqi attack on Iran, one year after the 1979 revolution, led to the radicalization of the new regime: where persuasion strategies no longer sufficed, violence was commonly used. Eight years of war enabled the Islamic Republic to silence dissident voices and to exert its authority unrestrainedly. The call for solidarity and national cohesion stifled any hope for freedom. The public sphere became the battlefield for agents of order who imposed laws and "Islamic measures" (*mavazin-e eslami*) by force. Whatever opposed carrying out the autocratic view of power was banished in the name of Islam. No opposition group was in a position to effectively object, and those who dared to criticize the regime were considered "enemies of God and of Islam," against whom violence could be unleashed. Countless verbal and physical aggressions were inflicted on those who did not literally respect the rules of "good behavior" or the prohibitions of the *shariat.* Whipping "poorly veiled" women in public became commonplace.

The use of terror enabled the regime to neutralize the reforms that had been carried out in Iran since the beginning of the twentieth century. Contrary to the Pahlavi regime that recognized fundamental rights, Khomeini announced that "human rights" did not correspond to the *shariat.* He eradicated fundamental rights from the positive legal machinery of the country by introducing the *shariat,* and thereby created a new dynamics that gave rise to very new problems, with a strong "dejuridification" of the country. It did not only change society's structure; it altered the psychological structure of the people. The attack on basic individual rights wounded their dignity. It was what Hegel and Mead precisely called "contempt," the consequence of which was the collapse of personal identity.[57]

The crystallization of taboos on the body, and the physical violence of the regime's agents against individuals who transgressed, however

---

[56] Just like the army by *Sépah,* the police by the *Bassij,* and the judicial system by Islamic justice, the universities were destroyed from within and had as counterpart the Islamic University, where nothing conformed to universal standards. For an in-depth analysis of this destructive operation, see Mahnaz Shirali, *"La jeunesse iranienne, une génération en crise,"* Paris, PUF/Le Monde, 2001.
[57] Axel Honneth, *La lutte pour la reconnaissance,* Paris, Cerf, 2000, p. 161.

slightly, those taboos, prevented Iranians from disposing of their own bodies freely. Physical violence is the most elementary form of personal abasement: it creates a loss of self-confidence and of confidence in the world. By depriving individuals of their rights and humiliating them in public, Khomeini's regime succeeded in suppressing the spirit of rebellion and dissident voices. When the judicial, social, educational and cultural structures of the country are dismantled by the use of intimidation and terror, it is not difficult to neutralize society.

In this way Khomeini's regime was set up. In its favor were simplicity, clarity, and the apparent radicalism of its ideological language, justified by the timely event of the war. The regime used the need for national solidarity against the foreign enemy to legitimate the suppression of individual freedom and to authorize the brutal repression that shattered opposition groups. Terror and the *shariat* thus became the basic pillars of a regime that drew its strength from its ideology.

The War (1980–1988)

The development of the Islamic Republic and, following that, its radicalization by terror, were directly linked to the crucial event of the war launched by Iraq one year after the 1979 revolution. During that eight-year-long war, Iranians were in solidarity against the common enemy, and national cohesion became a stake, enabling the new regime to silence all dissident voices and to exercise unlimited authority. In the name of unity Khomeini and his disciples claimed total power. That unity, already at the core of revolutionary discourse, was applied to the specific wartime conditions and rendered illegitimate any political conception that distanced itself from Khomeinism. It became a constraint imposed on society, forbidding citizens to think differently. The need for wartime solidarity violently excluded all who refused to align themselves with Khomeinism, whose two basic pillars were closure and exclusion. From then on, whatever opposed the implementation of the state's autocratic vision was banished in the name of Islam. No opposition group managed to counter this effectively for lack of a qualified intelligentsia with democratic experience.

The longer the war lasted, the more the need to preserve Islamic unity was used to justify the repression that spread over all social and human organization, enabling the Islamic Republic to implement its authoritarian concept of politics founded on Khomeini's ideological Islam. He never ceased repeating that the Islamic state was the incarnation of Islam and the voice of society. He proclaimed that the state and society were one, and that there was no longer any gap between them. The facts were quite different. For the regime, unity meant society's submission to the new order, with no room for individual freedoms.

For Khomeini, unanimity (*vahdat-e kaléma,* as it is called in Persian) was the only remedy for the dangers threatening his new regime. It was only by unanimity that the Islamic Republic could resist, particularly against those who contested Khomeini's views.

The process was summed up in one sentence: war destroys freedom. It did so in more than one way. Under the pretext of war, the regime gave itself the right to liquidate tens of thousands of young people and adolescents in its prisons,[58] after having tortured and raped them, while other young Iranians were dying as martyrs on the battlefields. The pitiless repression thus blurred the borders between a defensive war against a foreign enemy and an offensive war against the opponents of the Islamic regime within the country.

Ideologically, war destroyed freedom by exacting the devotion of citizens to a common cause and forcing them to obey orders from above. It made them all equal in obedience and before death. In the name of solidarity, the war contributed decisively to justify the installation of the regime's repressive apparatus and for a very long time. In fact, the repression against the regime's opponents seemed all the more justified and justifiable because Iraqi troops were advancing on Iranian territory and slaying Khomeini's very young and completely inexperienced soldiers—those called the *Bassiji.*

The war destroyed freedom daily by the repression of the bodies and minds of citizens, beginning with women, under the pretext of respect for the martyrs. This efficiently legitimated the countless prohibitions imposed by the regime on people's daily lives. Women became the focal point of a domination that aimed at neutralizing the whole of society. From one straying lock of hair to wearing blue jeans, thousands of similar details were considered disrespectful toward the war victims. With a whole series of practical and legal provisions, the regime invented numerous forms of punishment to prevent women from freely using their bodies and their minds. By imposing the Islamic veil, the regime stigmatized women's bodies and branded them

---

[58] In 1988, for example, Khomeini did not hesitate to sign the authorization of the collective execution of the imprisoned political opponents of the regime. Some seven thousand youths and adolescents were buried under the ruins of their cells, after one of the wings of the Evin prison was dynamited. For more information, see: http://rahekargar.wordpress.com/2011/09/03/nawi-5631/.

with the red iron of its domination. Through the systematic aggressions and humiliations they were made to suffer publicly, the regime humiliated half of society, the better to rule the rest. Through women, the entire population was targeted. People systematically suffered physical and psychological aggression by regime agents who did not hesitate to attack their freedom and to flout their most basic rights. Without laws recognizing that the individual had legal rights and was respected by other members of society, Iranians had no solid foundation on which to base their fundamental human rights.

If the war magnified the dead by exalting their resolution, courage, heroism, and self-sacrifice, it was contemptuous of the living and left an ineradicable imprint on the bodies and minds of those it did not devour. The generalized experience of disdain so invaded the emotional lives of Iranians that the positive image a great majority had acquired of themselves, particularly the young, was henceforth gravely wounded, even destroyed.[59] From then on, rejection of morality and contempt for common sense became the favorite weapon of those who had suffered humiliation and social wounds throughout their lives in the name of Islamic values. The war began the vicious cycle of humiliation and contempt, and Iranian society will bear those stigmata for a long time to come.

This regime lives by mobilizing the masses. It must convince the population of the necessity for its choices. Far from being able to do whatever it wants, despite its absolute power, it must be able to rely on a society that functions more or less well, and it also needs a minimal consent without which the cost of violence would become unbearable. Its work of justification and legitimacy is all the more important because it must link the will at the top to that at the bottom.[60] The regime's repression cannot be understood as a simple burst of violence from above. The regime depends on the most strongly rooted beliefs and the deepest fears of Iranians to make a portion of them its accomplices. In the name of the martyrs' blood and by awakening the obsolete mores of the old patriarchate, strongly destabilized by the shah's modernization, the regime's clergy justifies its violence against women, after that, against the young, and, finally, against all.

---

[59] The destruction of the personality and the collapse of mores are more visible in those young who were born and grew up after the revolution. For an in-depth analysis of the life of young people in Iran, see: Shirali, *op. cit.*, 2001.

[60] This is particularly the case for those revolutionary regimes that live by mobilizing the masses.

Politically, the war accelerated the need to call upon religious legitimacy. As time passed, victory receded. The more the losses in human life mounted and internal repression increased, the more the regime was obliged to justify its political choices in the people's eyes. Rapidly, its terror was aimed not only at its declared opponents; it targeted a large part of the population. All those who defended even their most elementary individual rights, were a danger for a regime that needed amorphous masses in order to rule. Despite the tremendous violence directed against the elite and the intellectuals, the real enemy was the man in the street who refused to become a "true Muslim"—that is, a docile and obedient person. According to the clergy's sermons, a "true Muslim" was a being sheltered from sin who entrusted his life to spiritual guides, the men of the regime.

The war did a prodigious job of de-sanctification, both on the individual and on the social level, in the name of constraint and legitimacy. In the Islamic Republic at war, everything was justified religiously. The whole of the pleroma of the "Fourteen Immaculates" became the privileged instrument for legitimizing violence against external enemies and even more against the country's internal opponents. "The Prophet conquered the world by the force of his sword," recalled Khomeini, who also added: "The twelve Imams had no pity for the enemies of Islam." Many examples, anecdotes, and tales were evoked or completely invented to draw a parallel between the regime's repression and events at the birth of Islam during the Prophet's lifetime. If opponents were tortured and summarily executed, if women were humiliated, if the regime's agents used violence to force respect for order, it was because the regime's "holy duty" was to implement the will of God Almighty.

Toward the end of the war, the Islamic Republic had so used and abused religious and historical references that a great wave of black humor flooded the public sphere, revealing the collective dejection that resulted from the ridiculous character of politicized religion. Day after day, the strongest religious beliefs collapsed under the process of de-sanctification. Yet nothing made the leaders draw back. "The Imam Ali, in person, assassinated four hundred infidels (*koffar*) in a single day," explained Khomeini, to trivialize the violence that reigned both behind the closed doors of his prisons and in full public view. And when young soldiers were cut down massively on the front, by lack of organization and experience, he referred to the Golden age of Islam to assure the people that these dead were now far happier in paradise than they had been when alive. "Islam needs blood [to survive]," he asserted in a sentence that will forever remain engraved in Iranian collective memory.

We must now speak of a change in religious speech. The clergy's traditional scaffolding that asked simultaneously for divine clemency and the believers' patience before life's misfortunes was no longer on the agenda. It shattered before the immanent demands of politics, based on violence, terror, and repression in earthly society. Contrary to the old religious language, supremely passive, which called on transcendence and referred to the world to come, the new language magnified action and the dynamics of violence to enact repressive policies and enjoy full power. The war thus became the tomb of traditional religion; it introduced a political content into the ancient religious form: it emptied it of its meaning by using it for its immanent objectives; it ended by causing the incarnation of heaven on earth to wane.

War and history thus came together to accredit violence in the name of Khomeini's ideological Islam. That solution had both legitimacy and the authority of religious experience. However, that aspiration to incarnate power was very different from what had been promised by the orthodox clergy. Khomeini set up his regime to a great degree thanks to the war and consolidated it with violence that he justified religiously. But his justifications abandoned the traditional framework, and the movement they set in motion was not clear. They sanctified politics while deconsecrating religion and exposing it to immanence. By so doing, religion itself was undoubtedly "disenchanted," even "secularized." That multidimensional transformation of religion and politics created strong doubts about the institutional heteronomy or politics according to transcendence.

Khomeini refused to end the war that had paradoxically strengthened his regime. When Iran was in a position of force, he rejected the peace-fire, sacrificing both national interests and revolutionary objectives. His aim was not only to consolidate internal unanimity, strengthened by the war, but to export the Islamic Revolution: "War must continue until the downfall of Saddam Hussein and the installation of an Islamic Republic in Iraq." And that was not all: "After Iraq, it will be Lebanon's turn."

The Islamic regime was finally obliged to give up the war from sheer exhaustion and frustration.[61] In 1988, Khomeini accepted the cease-fire demanded by Resolution 598 of the UN Security Council. The loss of human life was estimated at over a million dead for the Iranians and more than two hundred thousand for the Iraqis.

Loss of Credibility

> *The Islamic Republic was a cassock*
> *Sewn for Khomeini alone.*
> Mehdi Bazargan[62]

Khomeini's charismatic personality was so fascinating, and the timing of the war so perfect that the Islamic Republic could justify everything to strengthen its power, even the worst. After Khomeini's death in 1989, his successors had trouble ensuring the regime's survival, because of its continual loss of credibility. Lacking the manipulative talent of their guide, they were constantly ridiculed in Iranian eyes by their continued attempts to appropriate the divine.

Yet, they dared everything in pursuit of their ends. Most Iranians had trouble accepting a regime that thus manipulated religion, and the most devout believers were indignant to see how religion was treated. Some of the traditionalists and the disadvantaged consented to the commercialization of the divine and adopted similar behavior. Superstition was particularly rampant in working-class environments and spread more and more widely throughout society. In that post-Khomeini period, more than ever, religious practices were mixed with magic and witchcraft. Manipulating transcendence gradually led to the vulgar degradation of religion. To compensate for their dizzying loss of legitimacy, the Khomeinists led the entire society into the irrational.

After Khomeini's death, the regime's internal tensions erupted into the open. They were primarily linked to the dichotomy of the Islamic Republic

---

[61] In a letter dated August 14, 1990, Saddam Hussein accepted a return to the Algiers Agreement of 1975. He freed a number of prisoners of war (the others were only freed more than ten years after the end of the hostilities) and he left the occupied territories. In fact, this was a return to the *status quo ante*. Nonetheless, no peace treaty formalized this return.

[62] The Islamic Republic is a political system that only suits the person of the Ayatollah Khomeini (i.e., without Khomeini, the system will not last). Although history has contradicted this famous sentence of Mehdi Bazargan, Khomeini's first prime minister, it does contain something significant concerning the central place held by Khomeini. *Cf.* Saïd Barzin, *Biography of Mehdi Bazargan*, (Zendegi-nameh-ye siasi-ye mohandes Mehdi Bazargan), Tehran, Nashre Markaz, 2010.

whose legitimacy came from two sources, not only different but diametrically opposed: one was "transcendence" and the other popular. The first relied on the principle of heteronomy, while the second, essentially populist, retained some components of the autonomy principle of the postrevolutionary regimes. The supreme guide represented transcendence (principle of heteronomy), and the president of the republic was elected by universal suffrage (principle of autonomy). All the regime's difficulties came from the impossibility of reconciling those two modes of thought.

It was only by desperate efforts that this double and contradictory structure managed to give an appearance of stability. Khomeini's successor, the Ayatollah Khameney, the new supreme guide, got along very badly with the successive presidents of the republic. Despite the filtering system set up by the regime to block access of independent elites to the presidency, presidents considered themselves as having been elected by the people and were proud of that; whence the growing embarrassment of the supreme guide with regard to their authority. He did everything he could to limit their scope of action, to the point where the populist façade of the regime, with its electoral institutions, could no longer stand up to the selective structures and to the *waly-e faqih* (doctor of Islamic law), the guide's unlimited power. Still, no matter how weak, the electoral façade remained necessary for a regime that pretended to "govern by the people's hearts."

Thirty years after the start of the Islamic Republic, the paradoxical situation was at its height. On the one hand, the clergy's omnipotence allowed them to impose a political and a military domination over the whole country and, on the other, they had no credibility at all with the people. Despite the total supremacy given the guide by the regime's constitution—in accordance with the *walayat-e faqih* principle—the guide was unable to use his power without grave popular disapproval, as was shown by the events of 2009, the day after the presidential electoral results were announced.

The voters' infatuation for one of the candidates and their rejection of the official results, judged fraudulent, saw an explosion of anti-regime demonstrations during the summer of 2009. While the street demanded that President Ahmadinejad resign, the Ayatollah Khameney, the *waly-e faqi, or* guide, refused to annul the elections and openly defended the outgoing president. Instead of appeasing the people, this provoked real anger, so much so that the protesters targeted the person of the *waly-e faqih* himself and his unbounded power. A large number of Iranians went into the streets peacefully to denounce the constitution and the principle of the *walayat-e faqih* (the absolute power of the doctor of Islamic law) that flouted the people's right to dispose of themselves. Military repression was the regime's only response.

Iranians were indignant that the Ayatollah Khameney—albeit within his constitutional rights—returned the outgoing president to his functions, disregarding the protests provoked by electoral fraud. For the first time since the Islamic Republic had begun, its founding principle, the *walayat-e faqih,* was openly questioned. Through that, it was the principle of heteronymous public and social order that was contested. If nobody dared criticize "divine Law" theoretically, in fact and openly, its legitimacy was defied. Just when the fullness of his power had become a fact, the supreme guide was questioned. This unprecedented event was far more important than the denunciation of electoral fraud. It showed above all Iranian disapproval of the transcendent legitimacy of the Islamic regime in a country considered by its leaders as the very land of Islam.

Three decades of the Islamic Republic had passed and much blood had flowed before such an event could take place. The movement of June, 2009, announced the entry of Iranian society into a new phase that revealed a vision of collectivity that admitted of no intervention from on high, neither God nor master. This was affirmed through a social movement in a double rupture with the past. On the one hand, for the first time in the country's history, Iranians were united against the clergy. On the other, they organized and opposed a ferocious regime without any real leader or any charismatic figure at their head. True, the absence of a strong personality with a solid political program and a clear, coherent idea, capable of taking the head of this movement, was flagrant. Yet how could a movement that wanted to free itself from any outside intervention, that refused all authority from on high, place itself under the aegis of a leader?

If the protest movement of 2009 had no convincing follow-up, it was in no way meaningless. On the contrary, from then on, the demand for society's autonomy by political means has remained at the heart of Iranian collective conscience.

A Paradoxical Modernity

Beyond the more-than-thousand-year-old complicity between the clergy and politics, the founding of the Islamic Republic marked a new, determining phase. The seizure of temporal power by the Shiite clergy characterized the period that began with the fall of the *Pahlavi* dynasty and the inception of the Islamist regime; it continues to the present day. It is an original configuration that swung politics into religion and that was to redefine the balance of power between the two. This shift of the structure of religious form into politics characterized the enigmatic nature of present Iranian history. It was the result of a long period of preparation of an ideological Islam that installed the clergy in the world of power.

We have seen how Khomeini's ideological language was able to mobilize Iranians, to catapult the clergy to center stage and enable them to take political power. Yet, despite its immense mobilizing capacity, ideological Islam gave the clergy no tools with which to govern a country like Iran. Lacking the necessary knowledge to exercise state functions, they understood neither the role nor the functioning of politics in human/social organization. The meaning of the operation they themselves had set in motion, escaped them.

Khomeini and his successors, in promoting the *shariat,* strengthened the axes of religious structures—in order to subordinate society to heteronymous order. They used religion for the short-term interests of their regime and to justify their initiatives. The clergy thus left their usual role and, instead of concerning themselves with religious beliefs and practices, they governed the country by force. Religion was then used for secular ends, emptied of its spiritual meaning and filled with political content. Even transcendence did not escape that manipulation.

Contrary to the clergy's expectations, all this took a different turn, and an important part of its development was unseen by them. Everything took place without their knowledge and completely blinded them as to the result of their action. They did not see to what extent the exercise of politics that transformed them into "statesmen" took away their charisma and harmed their religion. Nor did they see that their Islamization of politics, through their manipulation of religion, changed the nature of the latter, exposed it to immanence and ended inevitably in its desacralization.

Khomeini's ideological Islam, by Islamizing politics, politicized religion and accelerated its change. It was a double operation that destabilized the religious structures on which society was based. This reflected back on society and demolished the features that bound it to its religion, its past, its tradition. It finally weakened the clergy's hold and contributed to opening society toward the future. Thus, in spite of themselves, and without meaning to, the clergy distanced society from its Islamic heritage and favored its modernization. It was one more step, a decisive one, in the process of emerging from religion: structural modernity *by* the clergy, but *in spite of* them.

It was indeed not Shiism that modernized itself. Politicizing religion did not lead to its modernization, but the result was to modernize society: a modernization carried out through politics, imposed from outside the clerical body. It took place in spite of the clergy's will but because of their ignorance of how a state system functions. We must bow to the evidence: the Shiite clergy did not modernize itself; nor did it modernize Iranian society, but by its politicization, it led to its own destruction and thereby freed society from its more-than-millennium-long hold.

It would be a grave error to speak of the Shiite clergy's modernity or of any clerical ability to modernize itself. The important ayatollah never showed the least sympathy for modernity and never hesitated to loudly proclaim their categorical rejection of its principles. They affirmed, over and over again, that Islam was "basically incompatible" with democracy.

Today, as yesterday, the Shiite clergy opposed the very idea of change and rose up against the slightest attempt to free social structure from heteronymous order. It was true that many reforms took place among them throughout the twentieth century to adapt them to the new needs of believers, but nothing shows any religious modernity in Shiism. If Khomeini's ideas were different from those of the traditional clergy, and if his innovations met with their resistance, he never denied the foundations of Shiite tradition. On the contrary, his ambition was to strengthen the clergy—in his way—and to put the *shariat* on the agenda so as to set up a society stratified by the determinism of that legacy. He wanted to establish a society where the a priori designation of the roles and places of human beings would cause the disappearance of equal freedom of individuals before the law.

His relentlessness in dismantling the Iranian legal system and introducing the *shariat* into the constitution, which led to the elimination of fundamental individual rights, only contributed to consolidating clerical power. The holistic nature of the *walayat-e faqih* thesis, that doctrine that crushed the individual in the most intimate areas of his life, was at the antipode of "individual rights" as practiced in modern democracies.

Khomeini did indeed go far beyond official forms, so that there was a long period of hesitation during which he swung between religion and ideology, before ending with that ideological Islam that is now at work throughout the entire Muslim world. Yet he never broke his ties with the past. Despite the reactions they provoked, his innovations remained faithful to Shiite tradition.

It would then be absurd to speak of religious modernity or to interpret Khomeini's or other ayatollah's authoritarian initiatives as an opening toward political modernity. The de-sanctification of Islam, which accelerated the process of leaving religion in Iran since the 1979 revolution, took place in spite of them and because of their monumental illusion as to the outcome of their operation. Because of their blindness and contempt, all those who were always opposed to history, in the name of defending the legacy of the past, became history's actors. Ironically, Khomeini—that supremely retrograde cleric, that fervent opponent of modernity, that sworn enemy of democracy and of individual freedom and fundamental rights—unwillingly and even unknowingly became one of the powerful actors of the modernization of Iranian society.

8

The Political-Religious Debate

Under the domination of theological Islam, Iran today lives a real ideocratic moment of intellectual thought. This moment corresponds to a specific phase of religion when the ideologization of Islam has greatly weakened the old religious forms. The results of that weakening are remarkable. The hierarchic, traditional, and community wheels of religious structure gradually leave the social sphere, and politics takes over, imposing its laws and requirements. Yet, the ancient religious forms retain enough presence in the collective function to slow the progressive march of society toward democracy.

Since the 1905 constitutional revolution, the Iranian intellectual sphere was divided between two tendencies: on one side, the conservative clergy who opposed democracy and modernity to protect Islam and, on the other, the antireligious, persuaded that religion was the enemy of progress and had no place in the modern world. While the defenders of political Islam believed in the incompatibility between religion and democracy, the "antireligion" adepts categorically rejected the former to achieve the latter.

The political-religious debate was specific to the polemic phase of leaving religion, and it marked the entry of Iranian society into that phase. This debate was pursued with unprecedented intensity, and the sudden appearance of the "new religious thinkers" who wanted to conciliate Islam and democracy gave it a previously unsuspected content. On the conservative side, the clergy, the theoreticians of orthodox Islam and the regime's allies, defended the idea that political order must necessarily depend on religion and that religion itself must be continued in politics. On the opposite side, the "antireligious" thinkers wanted to construct a society completely freed from any religious reference, that is, an autonomous political order.

Between the two appeared thinkers whose ambition was to find the role of religion in the modern world. That tendency was not as new as some claimed, for since the constitutional revolution many of the elite hoped to "Islamize" democratic principles. It was only after the 1979 revolution, however, that the new Muslim thinkers became particularly prolific, at times even original. Their object was to reconsider the relationship between Islam and democracy. They felt that nothing opposed the two and, like their predecessors, hoped either to "democratize Islam" or to "Islamize democracy." The undertaking turned out to be at the least ambiguous because, as in other camps, the great enigma of that debate was religion itself. Everybody thought he knew what religion was, but nobody presented a clear explanation of it. Most of the time, religion was taken as a set of beliefs and practices, personal or collective. It was then difficult to understand why it was in danger or how it could be dangerous. In fact, the question was to know what it was: what was to be understood by that religion that some wanted to protect and others to eliminate?

The Religion of Leaving Religion

Since the constitutional revolution, Iran had entered a process of leaving religion, but it was not until the appearance of the Islamic regime that the political-religious debate crystallized around the issue of separating politics and religion. Iranians became aware of the problematic role of religion in society and politics from the moment they found themselves under the yoke of Khomeinism and after the confiscation of all individual and political freedoms in the name of Islam. From then on, it became imperative, as never before, to define the precise terms of the relationship between religion and politics. The thinkers, militants, and politicians were then confronted with a new alternative between the need to separate religion from power and the will to strengthen their symbiosis. Yet, as long as the idea of religion remained opaque and undefined, both options brought the same amount of ambiguity to the debate.

Religion could only be understood in the perspective of modernity, itself the result of a process of leaving religion. If one abides by, confines oneself to, the definition of modernity given by Marcel Gauchet—the result of a movement consisting of replacing the old heteronymous structure of human/social establishment by a mode of autonomous structure—in that process, religion must be understood as a *complete system of organization of human communities* and not as a more or less organized whole of religious beliefs and practices. It is a *method of structuring* that can be called heteronymous, insofar as it determines the form of social relations in accordance with a subjugation of the

236

Other, an order of external and superior reality as compared with the visible reality. In that perspective, religion can be understood as a temporal organization of collective existence where the transcendence of the founding law establishes the priority of tradition and the prevalence of past models. In other words, heteronymous structure subordinates the community to divine law to ensure its cohesion and constitutes the religious form of societies.

Modernity is the historic process that overturns that religious form; it replaces obedience to tradition and submission to the past with the freedom to invent the future. It can then be defined as the substitution of an autonomous structure of human communities for their ancient heteronymous structure, in favor of the process of leaving religion.

Leaving the religious or heteronymous structure to build an autonomous world, independent of beliefs that link men to transcendence, does not impose the death of religion. Leaving religion means leaving a world where religion is the principle that structures society. In the autonomous world, whose structure is free of any transcendent reference, religion is the perfect link uniting man to the world to come. It constitutes all the beliefs and practices that give meaning to the lives of believers. It is not dangerous because it only acts on an individual level, and, so long as there are people who believe in it, it will be in no danger.

Political Religion against Antireligious Politics

The prominence of the political-religious stake gradually led the debate to the realm of the unconscious, preventing both sides from seeing what they had in common. The party of radical autonomy was unaware of what it had borrowed from heteronomy; the party of heteronomy did not see the nonreligious features that characterized its approach. Caught between confusion and blindness, both camps were the systematic victims of their own contradictions. The first did not see the religious roots of the autonomy they called for; the others ignored what heteronomy owed to the autonomous world they fought.

That debate created tumult, amalgamations, and overlapping speech. It was the result of a transient situation representing a final compromise between persistence of heteronymous structure and assertion of autonomous structure. It did not always divide the protagonists into two opposing camps with clear claims and well-defined positions on each side. Very often, it created personal tensions and confusion, so that the thinkers themselves did not clearly perceive the exact nature of their claims. It even happened that authors who thought they were defending democratic principles remained attached to the old religious order. As much as it is important to understand the actors' approach to leaving religion, just so much must one bear in mind the aspects that link them to the old hierarchical and traditional order.

It is true that boundaries separated the antireligious thinkers from the conservatives. Yet, despite appearances, there were not strong democrats on one side and hardcore fundamentalists on the other. Indeed, despite the hatred the latter aroused among the vast majority of Iranians and, reciprocally, despite a certain sympathy that favored the antireligious thinkers, the present political sphere does not lend itself to a Manichean interpretation. All the complexity of the situation is rooted in the entanglement of democratic and religious tendencies at work within each camp.

The defenders of political religion, the regime's leaders, the clergy, and religious conservatives fear less the antireligion camp than that of the new Muslim thinkers. All the venom of their criticisms is turned against the latter, attempting to discredit them at all costs. Under the immense repression that stifles the Iranian public sphere, a sort of confrontation of ideas has gradually been set up between the religious conservatives and these new thinkers. The latter communicate their ideas through prison walls or from abroad, so that controversies ceaselessly inflame the debate on relations between religion and democracy in Iran. Every new repressive measure of the regime incites Muslim thinkers to react, and that reaction still further fans the animosity of their adversaries. The virulent exchanges give rise to many disputes within each camp. Iranians follow this controversy with great interest, hoping that it will open the way to a real change of the political system.

The Antireligious Camp

In this confused and controversial scene, where several religious and political currents of thought confront each other, it is the antireligious camp that has the wind in its sails. Its partisans are secular, republican, democratic, modern, and anti-imperialist, without however defining precisely what they want or what motivates them. The gist of their discourse is the rejection of religion and everything referring to it. They wipe the slate clean of the past and want to build a society rid of its Islamic heritage. More than thirty years of religious despotism has given them great credibility among the young and made them more audible than ever—an all time first in Iranian history.

Under the iron yoke of the regime, the anachronistic reading of Islamic texts in which the antireligious intellectuals engage seems not only extremely courageous but above all heartening. They attack religion with the same vehemence with which their adversaries defend it. In fact, they limit religion to a few holy figures whom they try to discredit at all costs. The Prophet's and the imams' polygamy and the psychological analysis of their behavior are at the core of their reflections. Under the pen of some, the "Muslim" is a weak person who, in the illusory hope of a better life in the world to come, submits to all the tribulations of this earthly world. Others present him as a dissolute man, like his Prophet, whose piety and religious devotion guarantee the entrance to a paradise described as a huge brothel where the nymphs of night await him. The flagrant absence of any critical reflection on religious thought greatly prejudices the credibility of their analyses. Their intellectual process lacks objectivity and suffers from countless methodological errors. It attracts many Iranians because it contains the emotional charge of a society martyred by religious repression. It is the immediate rejection of the current situation.

The place of women in Islamic countries is particularly criticized, and these thinkers have made the defense of women's and minority rights their key issue. The justice of the causes they defend attracts attention but does not suffice to hide the absence of a global view of human status in societies ruled on traditional principles. Where the fundamental rights of all citizens are systematically flouted and where, in the absence of a real rule of law, the individual does not exist legally, minority rights take on a very different meaning.

Often, the antireligious thinkers show an idolatrous admiration for certain currents of Western thought. They endow some emblematic figures—Spinoza, Lenin, Stalin—with features and attributes that believers give to the supreme being. Their devotion toward these figures can reach fanatic extremes and is comparable to the adoration of holy figures by the most zealous believers. Their absolute trust in the words of their "heroes" and the categorical way in which they refer to their doctrines are in every way comparable to the dogmatism of the clergy. Instead of liberating their thought from the hold of transcendence, they raise their idols to the level of gods.

In line with the nationalist intellectuals of the 1950s, those of the antireligious camp are also anti-imperialists. They do not see that modernization has crushed empires and that the de-imperialization of the world has become the global law.[1] Their inveterate anti-imperialism is confused with anticolonialism and prevents them from rationally approaching different currents of modern political thought. Some are satisfied with declaring that democracy is not the best system and that it suffers from faults inherent in its working. They propose that Iran should not imitate Western countries but should create its own political system, in conformity with its culture and its history. However, since they present no other option, their discourse remains ambiguous.

Even if the antireligious thinkers do not update their ideas, nothing blocks their growing popularity or lessens their importance in Iranian politics. Three decades of the Islamic Republic, eight years of war, international sanctions, and the economic crash have not changed their analysis of Iran's political and social situation. They remain faithful to the approximate images they had of society and of the balance of power that existed more than thirty years ago. Their speech can be summed up as propaganda against Islam and the Islamic Republic, inciting the people to overthrow "the *mollah's* totalitarian regime," in order to restore Iran's past glory—as if it would suffice to reject religion *in toto* and announce their will to establish an Iranian political system for things to change of themselves. Most of these intellectuals—mainly those who live abroad—continue to reproach Iranians with their lack of enthusiasm for a new revolution that would enable the exiled to return to Iran and take power.[2] To hear them, one would think that the 1979 revolution was born in a day, on the initiative of a few wise elites, before being confiscated by Khomeini.

Their rejection of the religious system is so strong that they lump together the new Muslim thinkers and the conservative clergy. Denouncing their former complicity, the intellectuals of the antireligion camp judge the differences between the two other camps as more futile than real. It is true that the Muslim thinkers emerged from within the Islamic regime and were, at first, convinced Khomeinists.

---

[1] Jean-Michel Sallmann, *The Grand Désenclavement du monde 1200–1600*, Paris, Payot, 2011.

[2] The financial support these intellectuals receive from Western governments has a unfavorable echo in public opinion, and Iranians mistrust political elites who depend on foreign aid. At times, they call them the new members of the Tudeh Party (*Toudehiy haye jadid*), without any link to the USSR or to communism. The Iranian community in the United States, the richest and strongest of all Iranian diasporas, says it can support dissidents of the regime and disapproves some of them who resort to help from Western countries. This subject calls for detailed inquiry and is not the issue of our book. See: Mohamad Borqe'i, *Toudehiy haye jadid*, http://www.rahesabz. net/story/45474/, December 2011.

But their opposition to the present political leaders, often paid for with their blood, has cost them so dearly that it is difficult to dismiss it as a superficial affair of no importance.

The Camp of Political Religion

On the other side, the conservative clergy see the antireligion camp as stemming from a spirit of anarchy, common to modern societies, against which must be reestablished the authoritarian primacy of political order. However, contrary to what one might imagine, the conservative clergy have a clear conception of democratic thought and argue with precision to say in what way it does not suit them. Ignoring to what extent they are themselves impregnated with principles of autonomy, they reject it in the name of transcendence.

They assert that the regime's legitimacy does not come from the people's will but from the representative of God on earth, that is, the *waly-e faqih*, the guide. For them, it is unthinkable to define the foundation of legitimacy as coming from individuals, for that would be an incredible overthrow of political order that would then be founded on a universal political freedom of the autonomous individual. To go from the legitimacy of transcendence, traditional source of all power, to the individual and his rights, would be to affirm the predominance of the "nation," that is, the totality of individuals, says Dominique Schnapper.[3]

The conservative clergy see the current regime not as a republic but as an "Islamic government" (*hokoomate eslami*). It needs then no constitution, since it is based on the *shariat*. It is indeed true that a constitution is useless in a regime that is not at the service of its people.

The camp of "political religion" is characterized by its contempt for law and freedom that constitute the foundation of democratic systems. Since it expresses the will of the individuals, the law guarantees freedoms. "The people who are submitted to laws must be their authors," stresses Dominique Schnapper. "Only those who form an association can determine the conditions of association. A power is thus legitimate insofar as it is the product of the general Will, the expression of the will of the people that is unlimited, inalienable and indivisible."[4]

Since, for the defenders of the political religion camp, the legitimacy of power is not based on the consent and the will of the people, and

---

[3] Dominique Schnapper, *Qu'est-ce que la citoyenneté ?*, Paris, Gallimard, 2000, p. 24.
[4] *Ibid.*, pp. 45–49.

social order is not founded on a decision by all the people to create a society, to accept its privileges and its obligations, they cannot have a constitution or a rule of law. For them it is unthinkable for social order to be based on individual citizens who determine their own laws and choose their political leaders. How can one admit that the source of political legitimacy comes from the individual or from all the citizens, when these are deemed radically corrupt? How can one accept that such [corrupt] men should be free and equal, and what point is there in guaranteeing the freedom and equality of each citizen?

Since they believe they are chosen by God, the conservative clergy cannot recognize the least right of the people to decide their own destiny, to give themselves laws and to choose the politicians who will lead them. In point of fact, the immense power given the leaders of the Islamic regime by petrodollars frees them from needing the support of the people. They are thus convinced that they have no need to serve society in order to govern it. The illusion of self-sufficiency has enabled the men of the regime, for more than thirty years, to take the country hostage and despoil it with impunity.

The camp of political religion is not, however, homogenous. From the growth of violence to the silence of the important ayatollah, one finds a fairly varied gamut of viewpoints, often in contradiction of each other, yet in fundamental solidarity. The Ayatollah Mesbah-Yazdi, called by Iranians the "theoretician of violence," is one of the most brilliant theoreticians of ideological Islam.[5] For him, slavery and physical aggression are religiously justifiable and should be practiced according to the original concept of Islam. His thesis is based on the sinful nature of man, corrupt by definition. Ordinary people must submit themselves to political leaders to find salvation. "To obey one's leaders" he said, "is to obey God."[6]

---

[5] Born in 1924, member of the Iranian Shiite clergy, the Ayatollah Mesbah-Yazdi is also one of the strong men of the regime. He is clever in finding religious justifications to Islamize whatever relates to violence. However, he is not supported by the majority of the clergy in the Qom seminaries. He is generally considered the ideological mentor of President Mahmoud Ahmadinejad. After completing his elementary and secondary education in Yazd, Mesbah-Yazdi studied the *fiqh* in Qom until his degree in 1960. Among his professors were such important personalities as the Ayatollah Khomeini and Mohammad Taqi Bayat, as well as the *allameh* Tabatabai. Before the Islamic Revolution, he was Editor-in-Chief of a newspaper, *The Revenge*. He was one of the founders of the Haghani school, a very influential religious school in Iran. Author of numerous books on the *fiqh*, the exegesis of the Koran, divinity, and other subjects related to Islam, he is the present Director of the "Imam Khomeini" Institute of Research and Education in Qom and is also a member of the Assembly of Experts.

[6] *Keyhan*, December 12, 2009.

In the name of the *shariat,* Mesbah-Yazdi rejects the right of citizens to freedom and to democracy:

> Against the enemies of the Islamic Republic, there is no room for negotiation. They must die or be amputated of their hands and feet, according to the shariat. Here, there is no question of individual freedom, of democracy or of Human rights; this is not the place to speak of such things. If someone insults the saints or the Muslim political authorities, there is no need for a tribunal. Islam permits us to spill that person's blood immediately.[7]

Seeing no point in universal suffrage, Mesbah-Yazdi believes that the Islamic Republic should rapidly be changed into an "Islamic government" (*hokoomate eslami*), the supreme guide taking the place of the president at the head of the executive. He also calls for "the Islamization of the country's universities," since in his eyes only Islamic teaching is credible. He is against women holding positions of responsibility, saying that those who promote such ideas are trying to exploit them to satisfy their masculine desire. Mesbah-Yazdi has, however, nothing against Western technology, and he sees no contradiction between Islam and technology. In a lecture given on February 15, 2006, he asserted that the use of the nuclear bomb had religious justification.

In general, the important ayatollah are highly conservative. They defend the Islam of the *shariat* and the practice of all its norms and punitive measures—the law of retaliation, lapidation, amputation of hands and feet, whip lashing—presenting them as coming from the will of God. After waiting for centuries, thanks to the present regime they can finally apply Islamic law literally and give free rein to their dreams of power. In the name of the interest of Islam, they remain silent rather than criticize politicians, knowing full well that their fate is linked to that of the regime. To weaken it would be nothing less than collective suicide. They prefer to save their skins, rather than to save religion.

This silence was added to that which they observed with regard to Khomeini's thesis on the *walayat-e faqih* (the absolute power of the doctor of Islamic law). True, they never approved it officially, but no real opposition was ever voiced. The only one who openly contested the theological legitimacy of that thesis, together with the application of the *shariat* in the Iranian judicial system was the Ayatollah Saneï. The result was that the title of *marja'e taqlid* was immediately taken from

---

[7] *Ibid.*

him. The fate of other ayatollah who did not want to play the regime's political games or to accept the *walayat-e faqih* thesis was a good deal more tragic that that of the Ayatollah Saneï.[8]

This silence was significant with regard to immediate policy. It amounted to approval of Khomeini's political plan and to politicizing religion. This approval in turn compensated for the lack of theological legitimacy of, to say the least, that improbable undertaking. It provided the clergy with an immense power with which to take over politics. This was added to all the consequences it entailed for religion itself, beginning with the elimination of its spiritual meaning up to its very destruction.

The importance given by the Islamic Republic, from its inception, to putting the *shariat* in place, set back the Iranian judiciary system by several centuries.[9] For this regime, which wanted to be religious but manipulated religion and completely transformed it to serve its ambitions, the *shariat* was the cornerstone that maintained the last links with the founding past. In this way, not only did the Islamic Republic determine the religious framework of its ideological thought, but it also succeeded in satisfying, even in mastering, the *olama* who had always constituted a dissident force against the previous political regimes. It was what enabled Khomeini to be so bold without encountering any real resistance. He often irritated the clergy, but practically none of the higher ayatollah ever really opposed him.

Nobody has yet forgotten Khomeini's political maneuvers on the issue of the vote for women. Before he headed the regime, he was against women voting, like all the other *olama,* and declared it "unlawful," but when he came to power, he changed his mind and made it "lawful." A clever politician, he justified himself by affirming that the *faqih* had

---

[8] The death of the Ayatollah Shariatmadari is a subject of controversy, the Ayatollah Montazeri was assigned to home arrest for some fifteen years, until his death. Aside from repeated insults proffered by Khomeini against *olama* who did not adhere to his regime, he also discharged a number of "sources of imitation." The Ayatollah Seyed Hassan Tabatabi-Qomi (1911–2007) was one of the great Shiite sources of imitation. He was against the unveiling of women and opposed Reza Shah. The shah expelled him from Iran and exiled him to Iraq. He was one of Khomeini's companions in combat during the 1979 Revolution. Yet, he refused to adhere to the *walayat-e faqih* thesis and was critical of some policies of the Islamic Republic. Khomeini soon considered him an enemy and assigned him to house arrest where he died after twenty years. The Ayatollah Shirazi and Rouhani, two other "sources of imitation," criticized Khomeini and died in isolation.

[9] The discriminatory measures of the *shariat* against women are so numerous that the abolition of Islamic Law has currently become the prime demand of Iranian women. Many Iranians feel that the legal part of religion is obsolete and should not therefore be applied.

the right, if he thought it best, to go so far as to suspend daily prayers or the Ramadan fast—two of the three main pillars of Islam. Most of the *olama* certainly did not appreciate those innovations, but they preferred not to criticize them openly, for fear of weakening the Islamic regime.

One can posit that it was not in the *olama's* interest to criticize the regime's repressive policy, because they did not want to suffer the same fate as that of certain rebellious ayatollah, such as Shariatmadari, Montazeri, Qomi, Rohani, and others. Yet, the principal reason for their nonintervention was that their view of relations between society and power was the same as that of the present regime. They shared the same line of thought as the leaders, feeling that ordinary people must submit to the clergy, both in political and in private affairs. The great common denominator between the *olama* and the regime was that both shared that view. If the *olama* had resisted the shah's regime, it was because they wanted to replace it with an Islamic system. They had felt themselves strong and able to incite Iranians to follow them in rebelling against the Pahlavis. This time, their position with regard to the regime was very different. If they diverged on several points, they remained discreet, because they agreed fundamentally with their colleagues in power.

The deep complicity between the *olama* and the regime, at times implicit, at others explicit, did not protect them against the disgrace brought on the clergy by the ideologization of Islam. The consequences of thus metamorphosing religion reflected first of all on the status of the high Shiite dignitaries and discredited them in the eyes of all. Throughout all Iranian Islamic history, the *olama* were never so rich and powerful but, paradoxically, so little respected by the believing community as under the Islamic Republic. Thanks to the public funds placed at their disposal by the regime, they became very wealthy. Yet, this sudden enrichment cost them the economic independence from the state that they had enjoyed until then. Very often, for example, Khomeini spoke violently and insultingly to the important olama— those who showed themselves even slightly critical of him—whereas nobody had ever dared to speak to them in that way before. Even Reza Shah—the most anti-clerical of all Iran's monarchs—could not do what Khomeini did. Still, this policy of the carrot and the stick did not seem to revolt the clergy. Far from it, they seemed to accept it quite well.

To tell the truth, despite their great conservatism and their high rank in the clerical hierarchy, the *olama* were above all men of their time, clearly more motivated by their personal interests than by those of religion. They were far from understanding that politicizing religion contributed to its destruction. And if, at times, they were conscious of that, it did not seem a sufficient reason to break their silence.

The New Muslim Thinkers

The crux of the political-religious debate is situated outside the two preceding camps, with thinkers who sought conscientiously to conciliate the idea of autonomy with that of heteronomy. But that partial awareness did not make their task easier and did not necessarily dissipate their blindness as to the substantial antinomy between heteronymous order and the autonomy of the human/social world. The crucial problem they had to solve was to find a way to conciliate subjection to tradition, submission to the past, and obedience to transcendent order on the one hand, with freedom to invent the future, power of a representative society, and the possibility of people to determine their own laws on the other. Of course, they did not ignore the incompatibility between these two ways of thinking, but—amazingly—they tried to erase it.

Believing and practicing Muslims, it was difficult for them to imagine life without religion; yet their opening toward the future prevented them from enclosing themselves completely in the ancient way of thinking. Torn between two conceptions of the relationship between religion and politics, they engaged in paradoxical rationalizations to reconcile the irreconcilable and did not discern the scope of the conceptual difficulties they had to face. The difficulty came primarily from the fact that they had no clear definition of the subjects they approached. Mistakenly identifying religion with religious structuring or heteronomy, they thought that leaving a world structured by religion threatened to kill their faith in God.

Enclosed in despotism and violence, religion was undoubtedly the first victim of a political system that turned ideological Islam into the instrument of repression of the social organization. Having become the expression of the will of politicians, the regime's Islam was fearful. Never had Iranians been so detached from religion—even hostile to it—as under this regime. This went so far that the desperate efforts of the "new Muslim thinkers" (*now andishane dini*) to find another interpretation of religion, different from that of the regime, scarcely attracted any attention. Far from it, they were systematically accused of being in collusion with the regime. Yet, the latter made them the scapegoats, and not a day passed without a new repressive measure being taken against them.

Most of them were fervent revolutionary actors who defended the clerical government and the instauration of the Islamic Republic. At the regime's inception, the majority of them held important positions in governmental institutions. Gradually, however, they distanced themselves or were removed from their functions. Very soon, most became dissidents, lashing out at their former colleagues yet without defining themselves as opponents of the regime. Insofar as the regime became more radical, it no longer tolerated former friends who had become critical toward it. Nonetheless, despite the repression they suffered, their ties of family or friendship with the regime's leaders protected them. No ordinary citizen would have dared to openly express his discontent as they did.

One of the noteworthy figures of this current of thought was undoubtedly Abdolkarim Soroush. A revolutionary from the very beginning and a defender of the Islamic Republic,[10] he was a member of the "Cultural Revolution Committee" set up in Iranian universities that played an important part in liquidating professors considered nonrevolutionary, which resulted in his being rejected by the elite and the intellectuals. However, his televised daily lessons on Hafez and Rûmi[11] made him known to the public at large and particularly to the young, until then strongly impressed by Shariati and Khomeini. His speech sounded fair to them and was different from the tendencies made fashionable during those years of revolutionary effervescence. In his programs, the spiritual Islam of Rûmi, the great master of Sufism (*tasawof*), was presented so intelligently that the young television audience was able to discover the existence of Iranian mysticism (*erfân irani*). It constituted a religious way of thinking oriented contrary to Shariati's revolutionarism, rejected by Khomeini, and disdained by the thinkers of ideological Islam who saw in it "the opium of the people."

He rapidly became very popular. His conception of Islam, sharply contrasting with that of the clergy, soon made him *persona non grata*

---

[10] A revolutionary thinker, who became one of the great dissident figures, Soroush is an atypical intellectual. Born in Tehran in 1945, he came to philosophy after studying pharmacology in the United Kingdom. He returned to Iran in 1979. Author of many works on the philosophy of science or Islamic law, his concept of a "modern Islam" makes him one of the important voices of the opposition movement that has shaken Iran for some years now.

[11] Mowlana Jalâloddin Mohammad Balkhi, known in the West under the name of Rûmi, was a great Iranian philosopher, spiritualist, and poet of the seventh century. For an English translation, see: Reynold A. Nicholson (Translator, 1868–1945), *The Mathnawi of Jalâloddin Rûmi*, Cambridge, E. J. W. Memorial, 1971.

with the Islamic regime. His seminars at the University of Tehran were suspended, and he suffered many attacks and humiliations at the hands of the regime's militia. He then retired to his home and began publishing important books on spiritual thought. Some years later, he chose the path of exile, settling first in Germany, then in the United States.

He deeply marked the political-religious debate in Iran; Soroush's presentation of Islamic spiritual figures inaugurated a new approach to that universe until then reserved for the rare initiates and nearly inaccessible to the rest of the people. Over the years, he succeeded in showing that mystical experience was in no way a flight from the bitter reality of life, but consisted essentially in discovering, at all times, the world of inner man in opposition to the world of external man. His unequalled mastery of ancient texts enabled him to see spiritual Islam with new eyes and to make his audience aware of the tension that existed between the *shariat* and the *haqiqat,* or the outer letter of positive religion and its esoteric truth.

To read or listen to him, one would think him a Sufi master of the seventh century who, by mistake or by miracle, lived in our era. Soroush wrote in ancient Persian and reasoned so well with the tools of thought belonging to the seventh century that he was recognized by his distinguished style. Whatever subject he handled, he always embroidered his speech with several verses by Rûmi or by Hafez. That beautiful combination of prose and poetry was at the height of Persian literary tradition and pleased many Iranians. Yet, it was prejudicial to the methodological credibility of his thought. That mystical philosopher who, despite himself, lived in the twenty-first century, saw practically no difference between today's human and social organization and that of his favorite theosophists. He defended the individual and his fundamental rights in the same terms as Rûmi when the latter spoke of freedom of mind and of his capacity to fly in the free heavens of love. Yet, while the reader cannot help being enchanted by Soroush's stylistic finesse, he has trouble establishing the logical link between Rûmi's thought and modern ideas such as that of the individual or of society. In Soroush's works, the beauty of form compensates for the absence of method and sometimes conceals the incorrect content.

He could evoke the problems of past centuries that also characterize today's world and quote from ancient thinkers, far removed from our issues, statements that supported what he wanted to bring out. The polysemy of poetic language and his own personal ambiguity enabled that atypical philosopher to go back and forth constantly between the past and the present without synchronizing his arguments. The ease with which he put side by side quotations from Nietzsche, Marx, Habermas, and others with those of Hafez, Saadi, and Rûmi was, at the least, debatable. Soroush analyzed modern thought with the tools borrowed from the Muslim theosophists of more than ten centuries earlier.

In his book entitled *Bigger than Ideology*, a title as surprising as it was ambiguous, he tried to explain the difference between religion and ideology. He accepted as gospel truth Marx's definition of ideology, without looking to see what other thinkers had said. He then presented the mystical conception of religion and naïvely deduced that it was undoubtedly superior to ideology. This ingenious reasoning leaves the reader perplexed. Even those familiar with mystical thought have trouble understanding the very particular, even personal, interpretation of Soroush. In fact, he was far more credible when he limited himself to the seventh century and revealed the mysteries of that era than when he returned to the twenty-first century.

In 2009, in an open letter, Soroush criticized the silence of the Ayatollah Khameney, the leader of the Islamic Republic, after the fraudulent reelection of President Ahmadinejad. That letter summed up his political thoughts, filled with ambiguity and confusion. Although he began by announcing the imminent downfall of the religious dictatorship of the present regime and the forthcoming arrival of the *farâ-dini* society (beyond religion), the rest of his text was deeply immersed in religious thought. Intending to primarily criticize the repressive policy of the regime, he addressed God to complain of the Islamist leaders. He continued in the same discordant tones. On one side, he defended freedom, justice, the people's participation in its own political destiny and, on the other, he prayed to God to intervene to change his country's fate. Soroush combined two contradictory logics and reasoned at times according to the principles of autonomy, at times according to heteronomy. He wanted a representative regime but hoped that God would lose patience and destroy the unjust government of the Ayatollah Khomeini.

In his many books, Soroush venerated democratic principles and saw himself as a convinced democrat. Yet, he spoke of the "parasites" of modernity and presented certain phenomena of contemporary society as the sequels of democracy—divorce, single parenthood, homosexuality—that Muslims must avoid importing when they fought to democratize their country.

On the issue of legitimate law and social order, his thought was more ambiguous than ever. Deeming the *shariat* a set of laws taken from the *fiqh* and established by men of the early centuries of Islam, he excluded its sanctification. Like those who had compiled the *shariat* at the time, Muslims had every right, and even more the duty, to remake the laws according to the world in which they lived: "They were men; we are men. They defined the *shariat*; we can redefine it in our own way" he wrote. Yet, the *fiqh* was immense, its origin was divine, so that the thought of Shoroush remained deeply anchored in heteronymous thought. Thus he affirmed: "Even if a certain secularization is desired between religion and the state, I do not believe that an anti-Islamic government or one indifferent to religion could win in Iran. That is a fact."

To all appearances, Soroush proposed a different interpretation of Islam from that of the regime. He meant to be open to modernity and democracy, while the regime opposed them resolutely. But fundamentally both believed in the divine legitimacy of political power and of the social order. Both felt that a society that determined its own laws was condemned to decadence. If Soroush defended free elections, a parliamentary system, freedom of the press and other media, he thought that individuals were incapable of finding their salvation without the help of spiritual guides. In fact, his intellectual path was less complicated than it seemed at first. It was not a question of combining the two antagonistic sides of the process of leaving religion. It was not a question of rebuilding the old in the new or of accomplishing modernity with the aid of the ancient. Soroush juxtaposed old and new without attempting to harmonize them or to give them the least unity. This is in fact anachronism.

Another supporter of the Muslim thinkers' camp was Askbar Ganji.[12] The day after the revolution, he joined the newly established Pasdaran[13] army. During the Iran-Iraq war, he had volunteered for the front, but after the border town of Khoramshahr was liberated in 1982, he denounced the useless continuation of a war that no longer had any clear

---

[12] Akbar Ganji, born in 1960 in Qazvin, is an Iranian journalist and intellectual, member of the opposition to the Islamic Republic. He denounced violations of human rights in Iran and reminded Western democracies of their duty to denounce attacks on Iranian rights by the present regime. He received several international prizes for his political activities in defense of human rights.

[13] "The Pasdaran Army of the Islamic Revolution" was the name given by the regime to a parallel military structure, in many points a competitor of the country's national army. After its creation, the Islamic Republic had no confidence in the institutions it had inherited from the previous regime. It particularly mistrusted the shah's generals and sought to be rid of them by liquidating some and retiring others, whence the key role of the Pasdaran.

objective and demanded the immediate resignation of the Pasdaran general staff. He was quickly accused of desertion and condemned to capital punishment. After the intervention of several ayatollah, his sentence was suspended and he was freed. That event began a major crisis within the Pasdaran that lasted until the end of the war. In 1984, he left the Pasdaran and began to work in the Islamic Republic's ministry of information

In the ministry, Ganji was responsible for the cultural purification of the public sphere. He headed a team that evaluated the publications of Iranian dissidents abroad to block their dissemination and to censure the works of writers and thinkers in Iran. That led him to read many books translated or written in Persian and forbidden in Iran. He soon became an ardent reader of political literature and felt great admiration for certain thinkers and writers of various origins, such as Hannah Arendt, Jean-Paul Sartre, Alexandre Soljenitsyn, and so on. Later, he said he had been deeply impressed by the Persian translation of Vitali Chentalinski's book, *Slaves of Freedom*.[14]

The 1990s were marked by the disappearance and assassination of more than ninety intellectuals, writers, poets, translators, editors, political militants, and at times even ordinary citizens. In 1998, one year after the presidency of Mohammad Khatami and following the savage murder of two founding members of the MLI, the Forouhar couple, those assassinations took on a disturbing dimension and provoked a real national crisis. In 2000, in his book, *The Black Room of Ghosts*, whose style was close to that of Chentalinski, Ganji denounced loud and clear the instigating role of the Islamic Republic's leaders—and in particular, that of the supreme guide, the Ayatollah Khameney—in organizing those crimes. The same year, in his second book, *Red and Grey Eminences*, he carried out a remarkable analysis—à la Arendt—of the place of the individual in the Islamic regime. That book was primarily devoted to analyzing the internal organization of the Islamic Republic in which the author reveals the matrix of the balance of power that consolidates the power of the regime's leaders. Based on many true facts, he showed the importance of personalities who remained in the background to influence those who were center stage. He was the first to point out that in Khomeini's *walayat-e faqih* thesis, the

---

[14] This book that explores the KGB files on Soviet writers was translated into Persian the day after its publication in Russia in 1995. Immediately censured by the Ministry of Information, *The Slaves of Freedom* had not yet appeared in Iran.

individual had no legal status, so that the law did not protect ordinary citizens. This led him to compare the regime's structure with those of totalitarian countries and to conclude decisively that the Islamic Republic was fascist.

Those two books, which rapidly became best sellers, and other articles published in the social science magazine *Kyan* made him the target for the lightning bolts of regime leaders. Invited to participate in the famous Berlin Conference,[15] Ganji was arrested upon his return at the Tehran airport. He was condemned to six years imprisonment for insult and propaganda against the Islamic regime. In August, 2005, while he was on a hunger strike, the United Nations General Secretary, Kofi Annan, called upon the Iranian leaders to grant him mercy for humanitarian reasons. After his liberation, he sought refuge in the United States, where he now lives, attempting to assert himself as one of the opposition leaders.

Akbar Ganji believes the Islamic Republic is a totalitarian regime: "The summary executions, based on a penal code that authorizes one citizen to assassinate another if he is judged 'impious,' the absence of freedom of expression or the authoritarian yoke that grants no respect to the private lives of individuals are features that situate the Iranian regime side by side with Stalinism, fascism and Nazism."[16] He is convinced that democracy is the only valid option to save Iran from its present crisis; and this, he says, requires separating "politics" from "religion." In his writing, the definition of democracy is still ambiguous; policy is confused with politics, and there is no distinction between *religion* (the links between man and transcendence) and the *religious* (the links that unite men among themselves in the name of transcendence).[17] Thus, to discredit the divine legitimacy that the leaders of the Islamic Republic attribute to themselves, Ganji proceeds to decompose, even disintegrate

---

[15] In 2000, on the initiative of the German Green Party, some ten Iranian reformers were invited to Berlin to the Heinrich Böll Foundation. The Iranian opponents living in the German capital organized protest demonstrations against the regime and against those reformers who thought they could improve the regime. Most of the reformers were arrested upon their return to Iran, among them Akbar Ganji and the *hojatoleslam* Youssefi-Eshkevari. They were condemned respectively to six and ten years of prison. The last-named was "defrocked" upon his liberation.

[16] Akbar Ganji, "Eslam-e fashisti va Iran-e hitleri" (Islamic Fascism and Iranian Hitlerism), in Radio Zamaneh, November 2007, online: http://zamaaneh.com/analysis/2007/11/post_454.html.

[17] The confusion between Islam as a religion and Islam as a historic framework of a culture and a civilization continues and becomes more and more complex worldwide. It is not a domain reserved to Iranian thinkers.

religion. Heir of Shariati and the Mojahedin and former admirer of Khomeini, he reviews the Shiite beliefs—such as the holiness of the imams, the uncreated Koran, the belief in the Twelfth Imam—at times to give them a new meaning, at times to completely dismantle them.

If his predecessors ideologized Islam to transform it into an ideology of combat, if Khomeini manipulated Shiism to save his regime, Ganji's only objective is to delegitimate the power of the clergy. He deconstructs the religious forms on which Khomeini's manipulation of religion was based. Emptied of their meaning, those forms have no strength to resist Ganji's inquisitorial examination, and they collapse of themselves. In fact, he but completes the movement that the regime's leaders began long before him. If they emptied religious forms of all spirituality to introduce a political content, Ganji gives them the final blow, revealing their eminently political essence. Even if he thinks differently, his analyses of religion are directly inscribed in the continuity of Khomeinism.

In a series of articles entitled "Mohammad's Koran" (*Qor'an-e Mohammadi*) circulated on the Internet, he questions the Shiite dogma and rejects all belief in divine revelation. He concludes that not only Islam but the other monotheistic religious, Christianity and Judaism, are simply instruments of political domination. At the high price of rejecting the three religions, Ganji finally succeeds in discrediting the religious pretensions of the regime. Like those of the antireligion camp, this process prevents him from conceiving the least place for religion in democracy. However, unlike them, he does not decree the immediate death of religion; he condemns it to a slow death through a life without soul, empty, deprived of form and of content. In fact, he fulfills the process of "putting Islam to death" begun by Khomeini.

As it happens, Ganji's political analyses seem far more pertinent than his theoretical (not to say theological) works. This man's strength lies in his extraordinary intuition in understanding the implicit tendencies at play within political systems. Yet, he lacks the theoretical foundation required to follow his ideas through to the end and to provide his hypotheses with solid bases. He was the first to speak of the paradoxical modernization of Iranian society under the Islamic Republic, but, unable to prove his assertions by a logical construction, he soon had to stop. His criticism of religious thought lacks objectivity and suffers from countless theological, historical, and philosophical gaps. In fact, far from being an expert on religion, Ganji is a real politician with intuition, particularly in his efforts for his own interests, or at times, those of others.[18]

His sharp pen does not spare the idols of his youth, like Shariati, Motahari, and many others, yet his adherence to the ideas of certain philosophers like Karl Popper, Michel Foucault, Charles Taylor, and some others, seems unconditional. In his writings, he refers to them with the same determinism as that used by the clergy for the Koran and the Hadith. Self-taught, an engineer by training, Ganji suffers from the same limitations that handicapped other Iranian intellectuals and militants since the 1953 coup d'état. The absence of a clear, coherent understanding of the subjects that are the crux of his reflection—like modernity, democracy, politics, religion—lead him to insuperable errors of which the decomposition of religion is an example. Underestimating the methodology of critical thought, he thinks it suffices to read some modern philosophers or writers to become one. He is clearly neither the first nor the last Iranian intellectual who fails to perceive the need to acquire the tools of modern thought and, in the absence of a global view, falls into illusion and blindness.

In that entanglement of borders between arrogance and ignorance that is the dominant feature of the theological-political debate in Iran today, most of the thinkers and intellectuals approach political and philosophical issues without mastering their meaning. Contrary to that general tendency, Shirin Ebadi, jurist and lawyer, is an exception. She is one of the rare thinkers who is careful not to go beyond the limits of her professional and intellectual competences.[19] A convinced feminist, she opposes the *shariat* according to which the life of a woman is worth half

---

[18] Hardly had he arrived in the United States than Ganji placed himself at the head of the Iranian opposition, spending fantastic sums to develop the movement against the regime. Far from improving his image, this situation aroused a great mistrust by Iranians against the entire foreign opposition movement.

[19] Shirin Ebadi, born in 1947 in Hamadan, Iran, is an Iranian lawyer. In 1974, she became the first Iranian woman judge but had to renounce that position in 1979, after the revolution, when the conservative clergy took over the country and harshly eliminated the role of women. She fought for women to have a more important role in public life. In 2000, she was accused of having disseminated a video cassette in which an extremist cleric admitted that the regime's leaders had fomented a series of murders of intellectuals and writers. She was condemned to prison and forbidden to practice. She was part of the leadership of the *Iranian Organization to Protect the Rights of Children* and of the *Association of Defenders of Human Rights in Iran*. Her action won her the Nobel Peace Prize in 2003. Assadollah Badamchian, an Iranian conservative politician, called that prize "infamous," adding that Shirin Ebadi had been "rewarded for services rendered to Oppression and Western Colonialism."

that of a man. She belongs to a minority of believing Muslim women who dare to question, directly and without the slightest ambiguity, the so-called sacred legitimacy of Islamic law. "The legal part of the Muslim religion has no sacred character and must be completely replaced by laws conforming to the culture, the mores, the norms and the values of present Iranian society,"[20] she says with conviction. She uses the laws promulgated by the Islamic Republic to show what is lacking and what is contradictory in the system. Using the legal framework proposed by the regime to defend citizens' rights, she nevertheless asserts loudly and clearly that the said citizens must determine their own laws. By remaining faithful to the limits of her profession, in a country where technocrats are ideologists, where the clergy practice politics, and where practically nobody is in his or her proper place, Shirin Ebadi succeeds perfectly in being heard.

Her rational language contains no imprint of militancy. Point by point, Ebadi dismantles the changes brought in the penal code and, more generally, in the judicial system. By simply comparing the situation before and after the application of religious laws, she points out to what extent, since the establishment of the Islamic Republic, the fundamental rights of individuals have been trampled down. In a language accessible to all and with a clarity unusual in Iranian authors, the lawyer stresses the fundamental contradictions that characterize the laws in force in the present regime. If, for example, the *shariat* considers that a woman's life is worth no more than half that of a man's and if the regime's entire penal code is based on that discrimination, the labor law, on the other hand, spells out a whole series of situations that benefit women. Thus, in case of pregnancy or breastfeeding, the new Islamic Law allows a far more flexible working time that did the old labor law of the Pahlavi regime. The legislator justifies this "positive discrimination" by the eminently favorable place of mothers in Islam: "Since (according to a well-known *Hadith*) Paradise lies under the feet of mothers, in this life on earth we must facilitate the working conditions of mothers," explains the labor law of the Islamic Republic. According to Shirin Ebadi, this type of privilege is but a ruse of the Islamist lawmaker to block women's access to work.[21]

---

[20] Ebadi, *op. cit.*, 2004, p. 35.

[21] "In a society where the official unemployment rate is around 20%, and where one can estimate that the real rate is far higher, that kind of privilege is in fact discriminatory for women, since heads of industry prefer to employ somebody who will cost them less. Therefore, in Iran, women are less and less employed." *Ibid.*

The lawyer arrives at the indisputable fact that, under the present regime, women are doubly repressed: first by the patriarchy still active in Iran, and then by discriminatory laws. In questioning the status of women in the *shariat,* not only does she reveal the inferiority assigned to Iranian women, but she further points out the practical weakness of laws from another era and another historical context.

It is true that the day after the advent of this regime, women realized the threat that the Islamic Republic represented for them. However, Shirin Ebadi's detailed work drew attention to the importance of Islamic laws and their discriminatory character toward women. Gradually, changing the family code and the penal code, both essentially based on the *shariat,* became a central demand of Iranian women. Although their movement remains embryonic and suffers from all the ills that paralyze the other opposition movements in the country—divisions, rivalries, lack of organization, absence of clearly defined aims—it is nonetheless the first, since the beginning of the 1990s, to focus on defending the fundamental rights of women and, through them, of all citizens. It was not until years later, with the appearance of the opposition to President Ahmadinejad's reelection in 2009, that the attacks on individual rights and the failures of the constitution, particularly with regard to the *walayat-e faqih,* became the principal concern of a large part of Iranians.

Shirin Ebadi's strength also lies in her modesty. She defends her ideas actively without the least philosophical or militant pretension. Yet her work and that of her jurist colleagues to improve the status of women goes far beyond feminism and contributes to arousing the awareness of Iranians to their rights and their duties.

Several decades after the 1953 coup d'état, mistrust of the West has prevented Iranians from mastering, as they should and as they must, the democratic thought at the base of all modern political organization. They also find it difficult to understand the specificities of the political and social establishment of their country. On the one side, Soroush and his disciples reduce democracy to universal suffrage without tackling such thorny issues as the legitimacy of political power from the people and the right of citizens to shape the laws that govern them. On the other side, without any clear understanding of the religious phenomenon, Ganji and his friends think that the movement toward democracy requires the disappearance of all religious beliefs. In fact, the difficulty for Muslim thinkers to conceive the relationship between Islam and democracy questions their knowledge of both concepts. This bitter, but objective, statement does not augur an imminent change in relations between a society that wants to free itself from politics and an authoritarian regime that has taken it hostage.

In this immense cacophony, the most relevant voices are those of the lawyer Shirin Ebadi and of some jurists who plainly say "no" to the *shariat* and to the *Walâyat-é faqih.* They defend the need to change the laws so that citizens can choose their own leaders and decide their own fate. They know that a democratic society can be established only by recognizing the preeminence of the national citizenry, posited as the principle of political organization and the founding value of social order.[22]

---

[22] *Cf.* Dominique Schnapper, *La communauté des citoyens*, Paris, Gallimard, 2002.

Conclusion

Iran in a Changing World

The present state of Iranian intellectual thought and its slow but steady progress toward democracy shows that more than one hundred years after the constitutional revolution the will to bring political modernity to Iran is still present. Yet there are tragedies that leave indelible stamps. The country is scarred by its sufferings during the two world wars and, after them, by the 1953 coup d'état. The scars left by relations with foreign powers are everywhere visible, affecting collective judgment as to what Western political and philosophical thought can offer Iran. The memories of an ill-assumed past obsess the actors and hide from them some of the realities of the road traveled. The collective conscience has difficulty in recognizing the successes obtained since then, or rather it minimizes them, reducing them to a material prosperity of which, it is true, none would have dared to dream under the Qajar reign. Iran did emerge from the abyss of history in which it nearly foundered; it conquered the suicidal forces at work within it, and it strives today to emerge from a restrictive religion, to invent a regime of freedom.

Long years of urbanization and mass education have enabled a large part of the country's population to understand and to explain what happened. Today's youth is so alert that the leaders of the Islamic regime cannot convince it with their deceptive arguments. In a country where more than 70 percent of the population is under thirty-five and where the overwhelming majority of the young want only to live in freedom, nothing remains of those believing masses of the beginning of the twentieth century, pliable and hanging on the sermons of the clergy. Only the regime's allies—diverse and basically divided, motivated more by their political and financial interests than by divine grace—continue to support the clergy in power.

Khomeini and his successors tried systematically to subordinate politics to religion and, to this end, they ceaselessly effected all the necessary transformations of the latter to adapt it to their immediate interests. They took the outer shape of religion and emptied it of all its spiritual meaning to inject a political content. They instrumentalized religion the better to seize power. In doing so, they abandoned their customary role and, instead of concerning themselves with beliefs and religious practices, they began to govern the country. Their aim was to satisfy their thirst for power, to prevent the principles of autonomy from developing, and to preserve the heteronymous structure of human/social organization. By seizing the reins of government, they wanted to dominate politics and submit it to transcendence. There lie the roots of the great religious illusion. This illusion, shared by far more than the conservatives of the Islamic Republic, spreads wherever ideological Islam is at work.[1]

The clergy, held strictly separate from Iranian politics under the shah, did not take the full measure of the changes ensuing during the period of modernization under the imperial regime. They forgot that more than fifty years rule by the Pahlavi modified the very essence of politics and how it was seen. They did not even realize the matrix role of politics in the social establishment. They thought that religion still reigned alone over society and did not see that it must henceforth face politics squarely and combat it for sovereignty.

Busy with the visible aspects of politics, the clergy did not realize the meaning of the changes that had taken place, and they were cruelly uncomprehending of the situation. The principal features of the political evolution remained invisible to them and they were thus led into three errors:

The first was their blindness to the huge change in the country's governmental machinery. The old Iranian governmental system had been replaced by important political institutions, such as Parliament, the Senate, and the central judiciary system based on its own appeal systems (Court of Appeal, Supreme Court of Appeal, Supreme Court). From then on, politics had the necessary tools to exercise its structuring function. Religion, on the other hand, continued based on its ancient

---

[1] This illusion spread throughout the Muslim world, currently in the throes of political and ideological effervescence.

foundations, still functional indeed, but less and less compatible with society's new requirements.

The second was their misunderstanding of Iranian national sentiment. The clergy always underestimated the importance of Mossadeq's nationalizing the oil industry, which gave birth to the Iranian nation in its new sense. Borne by the dream of expanding an Islamic empire throughout the world, they were never favorable to the nationalist movement that completely overthrew the country's political situation, from the start of the twentieth century to the end of the 1960s. Their universalist ambition, tinged with a contumacious antinationalism prevented them from seeing what nationalism had brought Iranians. They refused to recognize that the events occurring between the two revolutions—the 1905 constitutional revolution and the 1979 Iranian Revolution—had completely disrupted the country. The amorphous masses of the beginning of the twentieth century had completely disappeared, giving way to a nation conscious of Iran's historic backwardness and very worried over its future.

The clergy's third error was its incomprehension of the birth of the nation-state and, consequently, the role of politics in society. The nation-state gave politics free reign to deploy fully. It was no longer limited to functions of appearance; it was able to develop deep in the social and human organization of the country. Thus, politics began to found social institutions and, thanks to its mediating dimension, it enabled the State to turn toward the world outside and to become the institution that links a political community to its environment.[2]

Blind to the evolution of the place of politics in Iranian social organization, with no understanding of the state's role in the international community, Khomeini's populist regime was born solely of a will for power and domination.[3] Yet, over the years, it came to experience deep changes both in its form and in the ways in which it worked. Khomeini was power hungry and needed the people's admiration: "The entire world must submit to Islam, and we are ready to sacrifice the last drop of our blood for the victory of Islam."[4] The

---

[2] See chapter 3, "Modernization," p. 71.

[3] The adoration of powers or, still more, the pretension of powers to be adored is the source of all tyranny. *Cf.* Raymond Aron, *Paix et guerre entre les nations,* Paris, Calmann-Lévy, 1962.

[4] "Discours de Khomeini," *Keyhan,* Tehran, October, 25 1979.

words are revealing. What this imperial assertion seeks above all is not the material fact of outward expansion, it implies the interior political form, the corresponding style of power, the mobilization of collective forces, the grouping of all around the unique objective proclaimed: "Islam requires blood and sacrifice." Inner cohesion could then not be achieved without outer projection.

Under the shah, Iran was a country open to the world and with good relations with the international community. It was considered one of the principal actors in Middle East peace negotiations. The advent to power of the Islamic regime's clergy, after the 1979 revolution, completely overturned the balance of these relations. Khomeini even declared war on both West and East. The Islamic regime can undoubtedly constitute a threat, both for Iranians and for the rest of the world. However, neither Khomeini nor his successors succeeded in making the country an autarchic system. Iran today is a marginalized country, but it is not cut off from the rest of the world. Understanding the importance of international relations, the regime's leaders systematically relied on the mediating function of politics, thus transforming themselves into perfect negotiators.

Faced with internal conflicts from day one, the regime forged blindly ahead in a drive for worldwide power. The aim was to transform the Islamic Republic into the most powerful country in the Middle East, able to face up to the Americans, as well as to the Israelis, without forgetting the Arab countries. The regime's leaders allied with poor countries, often in economic difficulties or in war, so as to create a front against the great powers, seen as "enemies of Islam." In so doing, they proved themselves masters in the art of sowing discord in the international community, the better to assert their power. While Iranian petrodollars were poured into the coffers of the regime's allies—among others, the Hamas and the Lebanese Hezbollah—national interests were largely forgotten. The Iranian standard of living grew lower daily and the value of the *rial*, the national coin, weakened regularly.

If the regime's domestic policy was disastrous, Iran did not appear to present a frontal threat for world peace. It must not be forgotten that until then the Islamist leaders had not *officially* transgressed the diplomatic principles of the international community. They systematically rejected all responsibility for terrorist actions that attacked their enemies all over the world and, despite overwhelming proofs, never admitted the least implication in the assassinations of Iranian opponents. At the same time, despite the extent of the potential danger of Iranian nuclear power, its real aim was to defy Western powers. True, it allowed the regime a false appearance of power, yet Iran was very far from exporting the Islamic Revolution to the rest of the world, which was Khomeini 's dearest wish.

Politics founds society as we know, but it also founds all those who enter its arena. Caught up in their relations with the international community and obliged to manage their national community as well, the regime's leaders can only adapt to politics' requirements. The clergy, who are at the head of the state and who hold all the keys of power, are engaged in this process since the 1979 revolution. It transforms them, unwittingly, into political actors, while their ignorance of the system's functioning constantly leads them into error. They ignore that the apparent function of politics is closely linked to its structuring dimension. They do not see to what extent the infrastructural role of politics gives it the strength and above all the possibility to change things, beginning with the clergy themselves. While they believe they hold power, politics continues to act in depth. It encloses them in blindness and, in so doing, makes them adopt its laws, its requirements, and its rules, defined by the principles of autonomy. These men think they are bending politics to religion, when in fact they are only obeying those politics whose functioning they cannot see. Politics continues to plough its furrow and to destabilize heteronymous functioning.

This destabilization becomes the starting point for modernizing the clergy, a modernization that develops slowly but inexorably. No spectacular demonstration is seen and—at least at first—no democratic power is set up. It works within a state resting comfortably on its oil income, with no accounting owed to anyone. The clergy allow themselves to be invaded by politics that ends up by transforming them. Whereas they should remain within the *divine incognito*, politics forces them to go down to earth and to register themselves in immanence and play the game according to the principles of autonomy. Thus, despite themselves, they become actors in a society in the process of inventing itself and open to the future. It is there that the confrontation of two ways of structuring social organization takes a decisive turning point.

It is nonetheless difficult to hope that this evolution will lead to a democratic overthrow. In a country with immense oil wealth, the principal feature of the state is its independence from the nation; it is far from being its tool. Under the shah or under Khomeini, politicians never thought of themselves as being at the service of society. On the contrary, it was at their disposal. This economic independence always gave political institutions, royal or Islamic, a very strong authoritarian dimension. Politicians gives themselves modern institutions and develop in spaces formerly reserved to the clergy; they upset the latter and force them to open up to society's movement. But their economic independence allows them to impose on the population arbitrarily; and from this stems the overall impression that nothing is changing or moving, while, in fact, everything is taking place underground.

The primary event is the metamorphosis of the clergy. They are drawn into a process led by politics: leaving their specific enclosed space, opening up to the world and to the future. Truth be told, it is here that something revolutionary is taking place. By governing the country, the clergy are condemned to betray themselves by denying their own nature. We see then the clergy destroying themselves. This destruction comes from substituting politics for religion as the collective institution. The politician replaces the clergy as the one that controls society, gives it coherence, a visible representation of its order and identity. This substitution naturally deprives the clergy of their prime role in organizing collective beliefs and thereby introduces an entirely different way of being and of functioning for the collectivity. Iranian society is now living in this new configuration, original and problematic. For with the upset of the clergy, the process of constituting the collective life changes in aspect and nature. The clergy have precipitated their self-destruction and are dragging with them a large part of society.

At the head of the Islamic Republic, the clergy have become full-fledged politicians. They defend their own interests and act for their own future. They realized quickly that resisting societal change would—once again—marginalize them. They had, therefore, to reexamine their conservative positions, to change their language and adapt to the new situation. It was no longer the time to invite people to resign themselves. The clergy came to believe that from now on they can best achieve their end and dominate society through political populism. They do not, however, see to what extent, by opening themselves to these changes, they participate in their own destruction, as in that of the founding past and its traditional principles. They do not realize how much this process rids Iranian society of its old traditional and religious features and leaves it open to the future. They are very far from understanding that they have transformed themselves into actors building an autonomous world, actors of history's society.

This clerical metamorphosis has immediate repercussions on Iranian society, freeing it from those features that had linked it to its religion, its past, its tradition. Centuries of the Iranian people's submission to the authority of the clergy are erased before an emerging society of individuals that want neither God nor master. The Iranian rejection of the present regime is so strong that one wonders, amazed, how it can yet hold on.

The current situation's difficulty lies in the fact that the regime's disastrous policies have all but ruined the country. Indeed, in destroying themselves, the clergy also destroyed a large part of the human and social organization. The country's economic and cultural impoverishment results from more than three decades of a regime that undid the religious, cultural, moral, scientific, and educational structures of Iranian society. This dismantling is such that the overwhelming majority of those born under this regime had no access to culture, science, or education, as judged by international standards. Iranian youth is avid for learning and is open to the world, but it is also a victim of the educational and cultural vacuum created in Iran by the Islamic Republic. Steeped in the old patriarchal principles reactivated by the regime, psychologically, humanly, and individually torn, these young people are so absorbed by the daily struggle to claim their most elementary human rights[5] that they cannot manage to broaden their claims to include recognition of their political rights.

While the youth of the Middle East hope to see religion in power, Iranians, deeply scarred by the social wounds inflicted on them in the name of Islam,[6] want only to be rid of that. Such is the abyss separating Iran from the other Muslim countries.

---

[5] We refer to rights as simple as listening to music, wearing the clothes of one's choice, etc.
[6] Hegel defined social wounds as physical wounds, legal wounds, or wounds to the dignity of the individual. *Cf.* Axel Honneth, *La lutte pour la reconnaissance, op. cit.,* 2000.

Under a regime whose agents are masters in the art of handling insult and contempt, to the point of cruelly wounding individual pride, the mechanisms for developing human personality are shaken to the depths. With populations who are impoverished and terrorized by forces of repression, and a youth traumatized by repressive measures imposed by the clergy, the major risk threatening the regime since the death of Khomeini does not come from Iranian society. *A priori*, it does not come either from foreign countries, too democratic to take decisive measures against the Islamic Republic. The only danger lies within itself, in its own forces. Haunted by the fear of a military coup d'état, the leaders of this strange republic have sought the solution in privatizing public services and state institutions (schools, universities, hospitals, postal service, telephone system, natural gas supplies, highways, and soon railroad stations and airports) for the profit of *Pasdaran* army generals. They forget that enriching the military has never protected any authoritarian regime from a rebellion by its army.

Since the constitutional revolution, Iranian progress toward democracy has been marked by the treason of the Shiite clergy. Yet, their accession to power and more than thirty years controlling politics at the head of the Islamic Republic has largely contributed to their destruction. This process buried with it a good part of the foundations of Iranian society, to such an extent that it is difficult at present to count on any opposition forces to bring the country out of its present calamitous situation. On the one hand, the intellectuals, paralyzed by the arrogance of ignorance, seem incapable of supplying the theoretical basis needed to consolidate the democratic movement in Iran. On the other hand, Iranian youth, morally and socially despised, is hostile to the very concept of authority and cannot stand any political organization whatsoever. Under these circumstances, no valid option exists to oppose the regime, and nothing augurs, in the short term, any major transformation in the balance of power. Perhaps the Islamic regime will collapse by itself, but everything seems to point to a long wait. It is nonetheless true that Iranian society can give birth to surprises. Despite all the evils suffered under the Islamic Republic, Iranian consciousness of belonging to an ancient nation is stronger than ever. This allows them to believe in the future: the double curse, striking both religion's and society's progress toward modernity and democracy will, one day or another, eradicate the remains of heteronymous structuring and free Iran definitively from the grasp of Islam.

Bibliography

Abrahamian Ervand, *Khomeinism, Essays on the Islamic Republic*, Berkeley, University of California Press, 1993.

——, *Iran Between Two Revolutions*, Princeton, Princeton University Press, 1982.

——, *The Iranian Mojahedin*, New Haven, Yale University Press, 1989.

Adamiyat Fereydoon, *Fekre Azadi va Moqadameye nehzate mashrootiyat (Le concept de liberté et le commencement du mouvement constitutionnel en Iran)*, Téhéran, Sokhan, 1961.

Afary Janet, *The Iranian Constitutional Revolution, 1906–1911: Grassroots, Democracy, Social Democracy, and the Origins of Feminism*, New York, Columbia University Press, 1996.

Afrassiyabi Bahram & Dehqan Saeed, *Taleqani va tarikh*, Téhéran, Nilufar, 1981.

Alavi Bozorg, *Panjah-o seh nafar (Les cinquante-trois)*, Téhéran, Amir-Kabir, 1944.

Amir-Arjomand Saeed, *The Turban for the Crown, The Islamic Revolution in Iran*, New York, Oxford University Press,1988.

Arkoun Mohammed, *L'Islam: approche critique*, Paris, Jacques Grancher, 1992.

——, *L'Islam, hier, demain*, Paris, Buchet-Chastel, 1982.

——, *Penser Islam aujourd'hui*, Neuchâtel, Unesco/La Baconnière, 1977.

Arendt Hannah, *Du mensonge à la violence*, Paris, Calmann-Lévy, 1972.

Aron Raymond, *Démocratie et totalitarisme*, Paris, Gallimard, 1965.

——, *Les étapes de la pensée sociologique*, Paris, Gallimard, 1967.

——, *Paix et guerre entre les nations*, Paris, Calmann-Lévy, 1962.

Bayat Mangol, *Iran's First Revolution. Shi'ism and the Constitutional Revolution of 1905–1909*, New York, Oxford University Press, 1991.

Behrooz Maziar, *Rebel for the Cause: The Failure of the Left in Iran*, London, I. B. Tauris, 2000.

Benzine Rachid, *Les nouveaux penseurs de l'Islam*, Paris, Albin Michel, 2004.

Berdiaev Nicolas, *Le sens de la création: un essai de justification de l'homme*, Paris, Desclée, 1955.

Bergson Henrie, *L'Évolution créatrice*, Paris, Alcan, 1913.

Bloch Ernst, *Le principe espérance*, Paris, Gallimard, 1991.

Bourdieu Pierre, *La domination masculine*, Paris, Points Essais, 2002.

Bottéro Jean, *Naissance de Dieu*, Paris, Gallimard, 1992.

Boyle J. A., *The Cambridge History of Iran*, Cambridge, Cambridge University Press, 1968.

Broué Pierre, *Histoire de l'Internationale communiste, 1919–1943*, Paris, Fayard, 1997.

Churchill R. P., *The Anglo-Russian Convention of 1907*, Cedar Rapids, Iowa, The Torch Press, 1939.

Claudine Fernando, *The Communist Movement. From Comintern to Cominform*, 2 vols., London, Monthly Review Press, 1975.

Corbin Henry, *En Islam iranien: aspects spirituels et philosophiques*, 5 vols., Paris, Gallimard, 1971.

———, *La philosophie iranienne Islamique aux xviie et xviiie siècles*, Paris, Buchet-Chastel, 1981.

———, *L'Iran et la philosophie*, Paris, Fayard, 1990.

Dani A. H., Litvinsky B. A., *History of Civilizations of Central Asia*, 5 vols., Paris, Unesco Publishing, 1992.

Daniel Elton L., *The History of Iran*, New York, Greenwood Press, 2001.

Desroche Henri, *L'Homme et ses religions: sciences humaines et expériences religieuses*, Paris, Cerf, 1972.

———, *Sociologie de l'espérance*, Paris, Calmann-Lévy, 1973.

Digard J.P., Hourcade B., Richard Y., *L'Iran au xxe siècle, Entre nationalisme, Islam et mondialisation*, Paris, Fayard, 1996.

Dumont Fernand, *Les idéologies*, Paris, Presses Universitaires de France, 1974.

Durkheim Émile, *La science sociale et action*, Paris, Presses Universitaires de France, 1970.

———, *Les Formes élémentaire de la vie religieuse*, Paris, Presses Universitaires de France, 1960.

Ebadi Shirin, *Hoquq-e zan dar qavanin jomhouri eslami* (Les droits de la femme selon les lois de la République Islamique), Téhéran, Ganj-e Danesh, 2004.

Elias Norbert, *La civilisation des moeurs*, Paris, Calmann-Lévy, 1973.

———, *La dynamique de l'Occident*, Paris, Calmann-Lévy, 1975.

———, *La société de cour*, Paris, Flammarion, 1985.

———, *La société des individus*, Paris, Fayard, 1991.

Eshaq Eprim, *Cheh Bâyad Kard?* (Que faut-il faire?), Téhéran, Éditions de Toudeh, 1947.

Eskandari Iraj, *Khaterate siyasi* (Mémoires politiques), Téhéran, Babak Amir-Khosravi, 3 vols., 1986.

Freund Julien, *Études sur Max Weber*, Genève-Paris, Librairie Droze, 1990.

Furet François, *La Révolution en débat*, Paris, Gallimard, 1999.

———, *La Révolution française*, Paris, Hachette, 2001.

Gauchet Marcel, *La condition historique*, Gallimard, 2005.

———, *La religion dans la démocratie*, Paris, Gallimard, 2000.

———, *La révolution des pouvoirs*, Paris, Gallimard, 1995.

———, *L'avènement de la démocratie, tome III: À l'épreuve du totalitarisme (1914–1974)*, Paris, Gallimard, 2010.

Ghani Cyrus, *Iran and the Rise of Reza Shah*, London, I. B. Tauris, 2000.

———, *Iran and the West*, London, Routledge & Kegan, 1987.

Gilliot Claude (ed.), *Dictionnaire de l'Islam, religion et civilisation*, Paris, Albin Michel, 1997.

Girard René, *La violence et le sacré*, Paris, Hachette Littérature, 1998 (1972).

Honneth Axel, *La lutte pour la reconnaissance*, Paris, Cerf, 2000.

Jazani Bijan, *Capitalism and Revolution in Iran*, London, Zed, 1980.

———, *Pishahangan-e enqelab va rahbari* (*Les pionniers de la révolution et leadership*), Téhéran, Éditions des Fadaiyan du peuple, 1973.

Kadivar Mohsen, *Nazariyeh-hâyé dowlat dar féqhé shi'i* (*Les théories de l'État selon la shari'at*), Téhéran, Ney, 1997.

Kasravi Ahmad, *Târikh mashrouteh Iran* (*Histoire constitutionnelle de l'Iran*), Téhéran, Amir Kabir, 1940.

Katouzian Mohammad-Ali Homa, *Mossadeq and the Struggle For Power in Iran*, London, I. B. Tauris, 1990.

Kazemzadeh Firuz, *Russia and Britain in Persia, 1864–1914*, New Haven, Yale University Press, 1968.

Keshavarz Fereidun, *Man motaham mikonam* (Je condamne), Téhéran, Nehzat-e Azadi, 1997.

Khameh'i Anvar, *Panjah nafar va seh nafar* (Cinquante personnes et trios personnes), Téhéran, Diba, 1983.

Khan-Baba-Tehrani Mehdi, *Negahi az daroon beh jonbeshe chap iran* (Un regard interne sur la Gauche iranienne), Saarbrücken, Hamid Sholat, 1998.

Khomeyni Rouhollah, *Kashf al-Asrar* (La découverte des mystères), Bayrût, Mussassat al-wafa, (1943) 1983.

———, *Walâyat-e faqih*, Téhéran, Fondation Imam Khomeyni, 1989.

Kianuri Nur-al-Din, *Goft-o gu ba tarikh* (Dialogue avec l'histoire), Téhéran, Fondation Negareh, 1997.

Kitsikis Dimitri, *L'Empire ottoman*, Paris, Presses Universitaires de France, 1994.

Ladjevardi Habib (dir.), *Iranian Oral History Collection*, Cambridge, Harvard University Press, 1981–1996.

Lenczowski George, *Russia and the West in Iran* 1918–48, Ithaca, Cornell University Press, 1949.

Mahmudi Ali, *Irané demokrat* (L'Iran démocratique), Téhéran, Diba, 1945.

Majlesi *Allamah, Bihar al-Anwar*, 25 vols., Téhéran, Amir Kabir, 1943.

Marx Karl, *Œuvres philosophiques*, Paris, A. Costes, 1927.

———, *Œuvres politiques*, Paris, A. Costes, 1929.

Mason V. M. (ed.), *History of Civilizations of Central Asia*, 5 vols., Paris, Unesco, 1992.

Milani Abbas, *Eminent Persians: The Men and Women Who Made Modern Iran, 194–1979*, 2 vols., New York, Syracuse University Press, 2008.

———, *The Shah*, New York, Macmillan, 2011.

Miquel André, *D'arabie et d'Islam*, Paris, Odile Jacob, 1992.

———, *Les Arabes, du message à l'histoire*, Paris, Fayard, 1995.

———, *L'Orient d'une vie*, Paris, Payot, 1990.

Miquel André and Laurens Henry, *L'Islam et sa civilisation*, Paris, Armend-Colin, 1990.

Mohit-Tabatabaï Mohammad (ed.), *Majmué asare Mirza MalkomKhân* (Œuvre complète de Mirza MalkomKhân), Téhéran, Foruq, 1948.

Montazam Mir-Ali Asghar, *The Life and Times of Ayatollah Khomeini*, Londres, Anglo-European Publishing, 1994.

Motahhari Morteza, *Fundamentals of Islamic Thought*, Berkeley, Mizan Press, 1985.

Moussavi-Lari Mojtaba, *Mas'aleh emamat* (La question de l'imamat), Téhéran, Centre de la diffusion des connaissances Islamiques, 1994.

Nafisi Saeed, *Tarikh-e edjtémaï va siasi Iran dar doreye mo'aser* (Histoire politique et sociale de l'Iran contemporain), 2 vols., Téhéran, Ahoura, 1965.

Nahavandi Houshang, *The Last Shah of Iran—Fatal Countdown of a Great Patriot Betrayed by the Free World, a Great Country Whose Fault was Success*, Los Angeles, Aquilion, 2005.

Najmabadi Afsaneh, *Land Reform and Social Class Change in Iran*, Salt Lake City, University of Utah Press, 1987.

Namvar Rahim, *Yadnameh Sahidan* (Mémorial des martyrs), Éditions de Toudeh, Téhéran, 1954.

Nicholson Reynold A. (Traducteur, 1868–1945), *The Mathnawi of Jalâloddin Rûmi*, Cambridge, E. J. W. Gibb Memorial, 1971.

Nietzsche Friedrich, *Ecce homo*, Paris, Mille et une nuits, 1997.

Ovanessian Ardeshir, *Osule tashkilatiye hezb tudeh* (Principes Organisationnels du Parti Toudeh), Téhéran, Éditions de Toudeh, 1943.

Pirnia Hassan (ed.), *Tarikh-e Iran* (History of Persia), Téhéran, amir-Kabir, 2002.

Puyan Amir-Parviz, *Mobarezeyé mossalahaneh va raddé téorié baqâ* (La nécessité de la lutte armée et le rejet de la théorie de la survie), Téhéran, l'Organisation des Fadayian du peuple, 1971.

Rials Stéphane, *La Déclaration des droits de l'homme*, Paris, Hachette, 1989.

Rosanvallon Pierre, *La démocratie inachevée. Histoire de la souveraineté du peuple en France*, Paris, Gallimard, 1995.

Ruhani Hamid, *Nehzat-e Imam Khomeiny* (Le mouvement de l'Imam Khomeiny), Téhéran, Fondation Imam Khomeyni, 1994.

Saeedi Jafar, *Shakhsyat va andisheyé Shariati* (Pensée et personnalité d'Ali Shariati), Téhéran, Chapakhsh, 1987.

Saeedi-Sirdjani Ali-Akbar, *Tarikh bidari Iranian* (Histoire du réveil des Iraniens), 2 vols., Téhéran, Agah, 1967.

Sallmann Jean-Michel, *Le Grand Désenclavement du monde 1200–1600*, Paris, Payot, 2011.

Schnapper Dominique, *La communauté de citoyens*, Paris, Gallimard, 1994.

———, *La compréhension sociologique. Démarche de l'analyse typologique*, Paris, Presses Universitaires de France, 1999.

———, *La démocratie providentielle*, Paris, Gallimard, 2002.

———, *Qu'est-ce que la citoyenneté?*, Paris, Gallimard, 2000.

———, *Qu'est-ce que l'intégration*, Paris, Gallimard, 2007.

Shakeri Khosrow (ed.), *Asnad-e tarikhi-ye jonbesh-e kargari, social delokrasi va komonisti-ye Iran* (*Documents historique du mouvement communiste et des travailleurs socio-démocrates et en Iran*), 20 vols., Florence, Mazdak, 1974.

Shariati Ali, *L'oumma et l'immat*, Beyrouth, Albouraq, 2007.

———, *Madjmou'é asar* (Œuvre complète), 25 vols., Téhéran, Hosseyniyé Ershad, 1979.

Shirali Mahnaz, *La malediction du religieux, la défaite de la pensée démocratique en Iran*, Paris, François Bourin éditeur, 2012.

———, *Entre Islam et démocratie, parcours de jeunes Français d'aujourd'hui*, Paris, Armand-Colin, 2007.

———, *La jeunesse Iranienne: une génération en crise*, Presses Universitaires de France /Le Monde, 2001.

Shoaian Mostafa, *Pasokhhaye nasanjideh beh qadamhaye sanjideh* (Réponses peu judicieuses aux démarches judicieuses), Florence, Mazdak, 1976.

Soroush Abdulkarim, *Asnâfé dindâri dar eslâm* (Pluralisme en Islam), Téhéran, 2002.

———, *Reason, Freedom and Democracy in Islam*, Oxford, Oxford University Press, 2000.

Tabari Ehsan (ed.), *Tahlil az Ozaye hezb* (Examen des conditions du parti), Téhéran, Éditions du Toudeh, 1947.

Tabâtabâ'i *Allahmeh* Mohammad-Hosseyn, *Bidayat al-Hikmah* (Phénomènes de l'Islam métaphysique), London, Islamic College for Advanced Studies Press, 2003.

———, *Shi'ite Islam*, London, G. Allen and Unwin, 1975.

———, *Universalité de l'Islam*, Paris, Publications du Séminaire Islamique, 1991.

Touraine Alain, *Critique de la modernité*, Paris, Essais, 1992.

———, *Un nouveau paradigme*, Paris, Fayard, 2005.

Vojdani Mostafa, *Sargozashthay-e veejeh az zendegi emam Khomeyni* (Biographie de l'Imam Khomeyni), 3 vols., Téhéran, Fondation Imam Khomeyni, 1983.

Weber Max, *Économie et société*, 2 vols., 1921, Paris, Plon, 1971.

———, *Sociologie du droit*, Paris, Presses Universitaires de France, 2007.

———, *Sociologies des religions*, Paris, Gallimard, 1996.

Wolikow Serge, *L'Internationale communiste (1919–1943). Le Komintern ou le rêve déchu du Parti mondial de la Révolution*, Paris, Éditions de l'Atelier, 2010.

Zabih Sepehr, *The Communist Movement in Iran*, Berkeley, University of California Press, 1966.

———, *The Left in Contemporary Iran*, Stanford, Hoover Institution Press, 1986.

Zarinkoub Abdolhossein, *Ruzgaran tarikh-i Iran az aghz ta saqut saltnat Pahlvi* (Histoire de l'Iran, du premier empire perse jusqu'aux Pahlavis), Téhéran, Sukhan, 1999.

Index